Living with the Wall

Published in cooperation with the
Aspen Institute Berlin and the
International Institute for Comparative
Social Research, Science Center Berlin

LIVING WITH THE WALL   WEST BERLIN, 1961–1985

Edited by Richard L. Merritt
and Anna J. Merritt

Duke Press Policy Studies
Duke University Press

© 1985 Duke University Press
All rights reserved
Printed in the United States of America
on acid free paper
Library of Congress Cataloging in Publication Data
Main entry under title:
Living with the wall.
(Duke Press policy studies)
Bibliography: p.
Includes index.
   1. Berlin wall (1961-   )—Addresses, essays,
lectures.   2. Berlin (Germany)—Politics and government—
Addresses, essays, lectures.   3. Germany (West)—
Politics and government—Addresses, essays, lectures.
I. Merritt, Richard L.   II. Merritt, Anna J.
III. Series.
DD881.L58   1985   943.1'554   85-10234
ISBN 0-8223-0657-3

To Hanni, Helga, and Ina,
who have each stored
our Koffer in Berlin

Contents

Foreword / *Shepard Stone*   ix
Acknowledgments   xiii

Part 1   The Wall and Its Consequences

1 A Transformed Crisis: The Berlin Wall / *Richard L. Merritt*   3
2 The Wall and West Berlin's Development / *Klaus Schütz*   37
3 Puzzling about the Wall / *Richard L. Merritt*   42
   Discussion   53

Part 2   Quadripartite and Inter-German Agreements

Introduction   75
4 The Quadripartite Agreement on Berlin in the Context of Past and Future East–West Relations / *Jonathan Dean*   79
   Discussion   85
5 From the Wall to the Quadripartite Agreement: Some Underlying Trends / *Dieter Mahncke*   98
   Discussion   104

Part 3   Berlin in Its New International Context

6 Twenty Years of Berlin History / *Martin J. Hillenbrand*   119
7 The West Berlin Economy / *Wolfgang Watter*   136
   Discussion   139
8 Berlin between East and West: Lessons for a Confused World / *Jürgen Engert*   149

9 Interpersonal Transactions across the
   Wall / *Richard L. Merritt* 166
   Discussion 184

Part 4 Living with the Wall

10 Living with the Wall / *Richard L. Merritt* 191

   Notes 219
   Index 235
   Contributors 241

Foreword

Shepard Stone

It is now almost a quarter of a century since the Berlin wall was built. Its construction was a watershed in European and, indeed, international politics. It put a seal on Germany's postwar division, made it clear that the Soviet bloc was not prepared to stand by as the German Democratic Republic appeared to fall apart, and demonstrated the Western determination to maintain West Berlin as part of its world. Looked at in another way, however, the wall was one more event in a long series of situations in which East and West learned how to live with one another.

Ever since August 13, 1961, there have been many interpretations of what had happened and predictions of what was to come. The range of such analyses included: that the West would not tolerate the wall, that it would insist on its removal as a precondition to any negotiations aimed at stabilizing the political situation in central Europe; that the wall symbolized the moral collapse of communism and signaled its eventual political bankruptcy as well; that sealing off the borders of West Berlin would give the German Democratic Republic the breathing space it needed to develop its own sense of national or at least political identity, which in turn would lead to an easing of living conditions for its citizens; and finally, that the wall would undermine the political raison d'être of West Berlin and inevitably push the city to the periphery of West German life.

None of these dramatic predictions came true, though each has not been without significance. The West did insist on an amelioration of conditions before signing final agreements with the East; the harshness of Soviet control over eastern Europe has softened albeit not disappeared; life in the GDR has improved in some respects; and, although

West Berlin is not the crisis center it once was, such events as the Berlin elections of May 1981 and its reception of President Ronald W. Reagan thirteen months later indicate that the city's impact is felt throughout the Federal Republic and the West.

Yet the question remains: What difference has the wall made—to Berliners, to Germans, to the rest of the world? This and related problems led the Aspen Institute Berlin and Science Center Berlin, with financial support from the West Berlin Senate, to convene a conference in June 1981 to focus on changes in the city since the construction of the wall.

The participants included policy makers active in setting Allied and West German policy during the crisis of 1961, officials from West Berlin and the Federal Republic, and interested scholars. The first two days of the conference considered the impact of the wall on West Berlin itself. An initial question was, What actually happened? Memoirs, reports of interviews, and scholarly analyses that have appeared since 1961 have provided us with extensive information—information that frequently was not publicly available in the immediate aftermath of the crisis. And yet a number of questions remain: Do we know all we need to know to understand the implications of the wall itself and the role it played in the policies of the countries it affected? Policy makers and analysts sitting together at one table had opportunities not only for exchanging views and information but also for probing points on which there is insufficient information or conflicting interpretations.

A second question addressed in this part of the conference was the complicated Quadripartite Agreement of September 1971. Given the history of Four-power negotiations on Berlin, the completion of a useful agreement did not seem probable at the time. Moreover, in addition to the four principal Powers negotiating Berlin's new status, the participants in the overall process included the governments of East and West Germany as well as West Berlin. The two years preceding the agreement were in many ways a tense period; the two subsequent years were significant as German negotiators worked out the details implicit in the broad framework developed in the Four-power negotiations.

A third kind of question explored at the conference focused on the effect that the wall and the various agreements of the early 1970s had on West Berlin itself. How did the city's political life adjust to the new status quo? To what extent can we trace its economic problems to changes wrought by the wall and treaties? How has the city's cultural life changed in response to its new circumstances? And how have ordinary citizens reacted? Have they made significant efforts to keep up their contacts with friends and relatives in East Berlin and the GDR? Or has there been slippage as people adjusted to the new political realities? All these questions deal directly with the future viability of West Berlin.

This volume presents the papers (updated at the end of 1984) and remarks delivered at the conference, as well as an edited transcript of its give and take among policy makers and scholars. A second volume, *Berlin in the World,* edited by Ronald A. Francisco and Richard L. Merritt (Boulder, Colo.: Westview Press, 1985) contains the papers presented during the last two days of the conference, which dealt with Berlin in an international perspective. Together, the two volumes provide a comprehensive picture of what has been—and retains the potential for becoming once again—one of the world's most fascinating cities, Berlin.

Acknowledgments

In addition to the scholars and policy makers recorded in these pages, several others took part in the conference and have earned our thanks. These include Tim Garton Ash, correspondent for *The Times* and *Der Spiegel;* Peter Bender, correspondent for the Westdeutscher Rundfunk; Professor Nils Diederich, Free University of Berlin and member of the Bundestag; Paul-Henri Gaschignard, French minister in Berlin; Professor William Griffith, Massachusetts Institute of Technology; Edwina Moreton, foreign department of *The Economist;* Ulrich Schamoni, film director in West Berlin; Eberhard Schulz, Research Institute of the German Society for Foreign Affairs; Richard von Weizsäcker, about to be elected governing mayor of West Berlin at the time of the conference and now president of the Federal Republic of Germany; Gerhard Wettig, Federal Institute for Eastern and International Studies; Professor Lawrence L. Whetton, University of Southern California; and several observers. Many of these people contributed to the second two days of the conference, which focused on Berlin in an international perspective (and the papers from which are published in a companion volume, *Berlin in the World,* edited by Ronald A. Francisco and Richard L. Merritt [Boulder, Colo.: Westview Press, 1985]).

A number of people made this volume possible. These include, most notably, Shepard Stone and James A. Cooney of the Aspen Institute Berlin and Karl W. Deutsch of the International Institute for Comparative Social Research, Science Center Berlin. Dr. Peter Glotz, at that time West Berlin's senator for higher education and research, was generous in supporting the transport of policy makers and scholars from five countries to the idyllic setting on Schwanenwerder of the Aspen Institute Berlin. At the University of Illinois at Urbana-Champaign, Janie Carroll supervised the production process, and Susan Radzinski and Eileen Yoder produced the manuscript on their Apple II+. Ina Frieser of the Science Center Berlin helped us in myriad ways as we moved from the idea of a conference to the realization of this volume. To all these contributors we are grateful.

R.L.M. and A.J.M.
March 1985

Part 1 The Wall and Its Consequences

1 A Transformed Crisis: The Berlin Wall

Richard L. Merritt

Saturday night, August 12, 1961, was like any other summery Saturday night in Berlin. The day itself had been pleasant, neither too hot nor too sultry. West Berliners had already begun their weekend of relaxation. They visited their relatives and friends in West or East Berlin, watched television at home, or sat down to a beer at their neighborhood bar. Or they mingled with the plethora of tourists strolling down the brightly lit Kurfüstendamm on their way to see the latest movie or to drink a cup of coffee at one of the broad avenue's many sidewalk cafés. At the reception center in Marienfelde clerks were recording the arrival of the last of the day's 2,400 East German refugees. By 1:10 in the morning most of these Berliners had gone to bed. The movie houses had locked their doors. Waiters at sidewalk cafés had piled chairs upon tables and turned down the lights. The subways were closed, and all but a few of the buses had gone to their garages. There was little in the air to suggest the dramatic developments that would break upon the city only a few seconds later.

Precisely at 1:11 in the morning of Sunday, August 13, 1961, the East Berlin news agency flashed a bulletin to the world. "The governments of the participating states of the Warsaw Pact," the teletyped message began, "have sought for many years a peace settlement with Germany. . . ." And as the bulletin continued in its tendentious Soviet-bloc officialese, trucks loaded with armed men stopped on the boundary of the Soviet sector of the city. The men assumed battle positions. Other trucks brought men carrying pneumatic drills, shovels, crowbars, and other demolition equipment. Systematically they began to tear up asphalt and cobblestones along the line at which East Berlin becomes

West Berlin. Barricades of barbed wire, streetcar tracks planted vertically in the ground, wooden bars, and concrete slabs of varying sizes and shapes sprang up. The construction of the Berlin wall had begun.

The Continuing Berlin Problem

The physical barriers that rose in the gray hours of that Sunday morning merely capped a process of division underway since World War II. At Casablanca in January 1943, President Franklin D. Roosevelt, Prime Minister Winston Churchill, and Marshal Joseph Stalin united in demanding an unconditional surrender from Nazi Germany. Total capitulation, of course, implied devising some form of subsequent occupation, a task that occupied the Allies' attention until the end of the war itself. The London Protocol of September 12, 1944 (as subsequently amended), divided Germany into four zones of occupation *"and* a special Berlin area, which will be under joint occupation" by Great Britain, the Soviet Union, the United States, and France.[1] Berlin itself lay in the middle of the Soviet zone of occupation, 100 miles from the British zone and nearly twice as far from the American zone. For administrative purposes the Allies split the city into four sectors. These were to be administered jointly by an Inter-Allied Governing Authority, more frequently known by its Russian name, *Kommandatura.*

The principle of unified control, however, dissolved under the practical pressure of divided purpose. An early culminating point of the rampaging cold war came in June 1948, when, after the Western allies had introduced a currency reform for the areas under their control, the Soviet Union imposed a full-scale blockade on the three western sectors of Berlin. The Western response was to airlift needed supplies to these sectors. Barriers between the Soviet sector and the western sectors began to rigidify. And, before the Soviets lifted the Berlin blockade in May 1949, private organizations, municipal services, and government were split between East and West Berlin. The formal division of Germany followed. In September 1949 came the promulgation of the Federal Republic of Germany (FRG) for the three western zones of occupation, followed a month later by that of the German Democratic Republic (GDR) for the Soviet zone.

The decision-making apparatus that subsequently has grown up in West Berlin is one of shared authority. At the first level is the municipal government. Its basis is a popularly elected House of Representatives of 140 members (with approximately 60 additional seats held vacant for the eventual election of representatives from East Berlin). This body in turn elects the governing mayor and a cabinet or Senate consisting of the deputy mayor and as many as sixteen senators, who are simultaneously heads of executive departments. The governing mayor, in conjunction with his Senate, is responsible for setting and carrying out policy. The House of Representatives enacts legislation initiated either by the Senate or by individual representatives.

At the second level is the federal government in Bonn. Although prevented by Allied reservation from full-fledged membership in the Federal Republic, West Berlin acts in most respects as one of the *Länder*. The exceptions, however, are critical. First of all, Berliners do not participate in federal elections. The Berlin House of Representatives appoints the city's delegates to the Bundestag. Second, these representatives, although otherwise possessing full rights of Bundestag membership, may not vote in its deliberations. Third, legislation passed by the Bundestag is technically not valid in Berlin until the municipal government formally adopts it and publishes it in the official register of laws. For almost all items of legislation, however, this is a pro forma procedure that seldom requires a detailed reconsideration of the measures in question.

The exceptions result from action taken on a third level of authority: the Allied Kommandatura, in which the Soviet government no longer participates, still retains ultimate sovereignty in West Berlin. As far as Berlin is concerned, in a formal sense the Allied occupation begun in 1945 continues today. Kommandatura decisions reflect the process of mutual adjustment among the representatives of three sovereign countries. The fragmentation of authority, however, does not stop here. The American commander of the Berlin garrison, for instance, must coordinate policy with the American minister in Berlin, the U.S. Army commander in Europe, and the United States ambassador to the Federal Republic, which in turn makes both the Defense and State Departments interested partners in Kommandatura decision making. The governance of Berlin is thus a complicated system. Its shared authority and partially overlapping competences have upon occasion produced friction and even immobility; for the most part, however, it has worked.

The city's political division and the termination of the blockade did not resolve the "Berlin problem." Even if the West was willing to settle for a tenuous stability until the attainment of reunification, the East saw in a rather different light the existence of a West Berlin tied to the Western political system. The communists saw that the mere existence in its midst of a city as glittering, vibrant, and full of material wealth as West Berlin—the "showcase of democracy," as the cliché has it—posed a psychological barrier to East German efforts to solidify its population. Far more important is the fact that, as long as the intersectoral borders remained open, flight into West Berlin was a real possibility for those East Germans dissatisfied with the brand of socialism that their government was trying to implement. A small amount of emigration might have benefited the East German government by purifying the population of its least cooperative elements. But the number of those seizing the opportunity to flee was staggering.

In the twelve years between the founding of the GDR and August 1961, 2.7 million East Germans registered in refugee camps in the West, well over half of them in Berlin alone. They comprised East Germany's most productive elements: a quarter of them, aged between eighteen and twenty-five, stood at the beginning of their careers; another quarter were even younger; and, relative to their share of the entire East German population, the proportion of such highly trained persons as doctors and engineers—trained, it should be noted, at tremendous state expense—was particularly large among the refugees. Their departure may have left a "purer" population, but it was also a population significantly poorer in manpower resources.[2]

As West Berlin continued to blossom, the GDR government under Walter Ulbricht and the Soviet government under Nikita Khrushchev, each for its own reasons, began seeking ways to minimize the impact of the conspicuous prosperity of West Berlin. Above all, the East Germans wanted international recognition of their sovereign status—something denied them by most countries of the world, with the notable exception of other socialist states. To the East Germans the continued existence of West Berlin was an open wound. The glaring contrasts between West Berlin and East Germany redounded to their own distress; moreover, Western insistence upon continued occupation rights merely made apparent the Soviet presence and the subordinate status of the German Democratic Republic. They continued to covet the prize that the Anglo-American airlift had denied them in 1948–49: West Berlin. The Soviets for their part wanted a legitimation of the political boundaries arising out of World War II and its aftermath.

Khrushchev reopened the question of Berlin in November 1958 with his proposal to turn *West* Berlin into a demilitarized "free city." Independent of both East and West Germany, it could be under the supervision of the *four* Powers and even the United Nations. Routes of access would rest upon arrangements made between West Berlin and East Germany. Implicit in the proposal was an ultimatum: Western failure to take steps toward such a settlement within six months would force the Soviet Union to negotiate a peace treaty with the GDR, thereby unilaterally terminating Western rights stemming from occupation agreements. That the free-city idea would give the Soviet Union a voice in decisions on West Berlin without any reciprocal privileges for the West in East Berlin (besides leaving the city at the not-so-tender mercy of the East German government) led the West to reject it. Informally, however, both through its compromise proposals and its behavior on such issues as high-altitude flights in the Berlin air corridors, the West signaled its intention to avoid a rigid stand that could lead to a serious confrontation with the Soviet Union. But discussions came to naught. The breakdown of the Paris summit conference of May 1960 brought with it a temporary postponement of this discussion, resumed only after John F. Kennedy's accession to the presidency in January 1961.

". . . to Build a Wall"

What ensued in the months following Kennedy's inauguration stemmed primarily from initiatives undertaken in East Berlin.[3] Informed that the Soviet Union intended to postpone the conclusion of a peace treaty and apprised of the continuing flow of refugees—almost 200,000 in 1960 (76 percent of them through West Berlin), a rate that continued into the first two months of 1961—Walter Ulbricht began to press for action. His proposal for reinforced border controls and even a fence of barbed wire to halt the crippling mass flights met the solid opposition of a special Warsaw Pact Council meeting in late March. Not only did the East European leaders foresee the negative psychological effects upon the international communist movement that such a fence through the heart of Berlin would have, they also felt that such action would surely lead to open conflict with the West. Khrushchev for his part wanted to retain a flexible situation for use in his forthcoming talks with the newly elected president.

The Vienna meeting of June 3–4, 1961, between Kennedy and Khrushchev merely altered the tone, not the content, of the East–West dialogue on Berlin. Neither statesman carried new proposals into the conference. Khrushchev in effect restated his ultimatum of 1958, setting as the time limit December 1961. Kennedy reaffirmed his government's position, expressed in its most explicit form at a NATO meeting in Oslo during the previous month: the three essentials of (1) continued Allied presence in Berlin; (2) unrestricted use of access routes to and from the island city; and (3) freedom for West Berliners to choose their own form of government.[4] In the heated exchange that followed, Khrushchev interpreted the American position as a challenge that the Soviet Union would have to accept even if it meant war. The stage was set for a Berlin showdown of gigantic, thermonuclear proportions.

How to avoid, but at the same time be prepared for, such a confrontation became the chief concern of both statesmen. In Washington, Kennedy stepped up his contingency planning.[5] Most of it, significantly enough, proceeded from the premise that a separate peace treaty between the Soviet Union and the GDR would lead to a new blockade of West Berlin. (Consciously or unconsciously, Ulbricht himself had fanned this particular flame: in his press conference of June 15 he had hinted that, after signing the peace treaty, his government might have to close West Berlin's Tempelhof Airport in the interests of "air safety.") The idea currently under discussion in the East—a barbed-wire fence to halt the nationwide refugee flow—received little serious attention. Ultimately, on July 25, in a nationwide television address, the president reiterated his firm intention to protect the "three essentials" as well as his willingness to consider all reasonable proposals about the future of the city. To give force to his words, Kennedy also announced increases in the military budget and manpower level, designed primarily to beef up the Seventh Army in Germany. "We cannot and will not," he concluded, "permit the Communists to drive us out of Berlin, either gradually or by force."[6]

In Moscow, meanwhile, Khrushchev played a waiting game. To be sure, he moved fresh troops to Poland in the middle of June and ordered Soviet military units to secure railway bridges, electrical plants, and other strategic points in East Germany. But these moves were oriented toward suppressing possible uprisings in the GDR, not toward conventional or nuclear conflict with the United States. Indeed, Khrushchev seemed confident that the West would sooner or later accept the idea of a separate peace treaty. When the president's address shattered these hopes, however, Khrushchev decided to play a different game altogether, one more in keeping with the rules proposed by his East German colleague.[7]

For, in East Berlin, Walter Ulbricht had been far from idle. The reticence of his Warsaw Pact allies about coming to his aid, no less than the apparent willingness of the Soviet leader to postpone a final resolution of the Berlin problem in the interests of reducing international tension, led him to view the unabated refugee flow in a new light. In June, to the Soviet ambassador, he lamented the powerlessness of his government to halt it. The ambassador's suggested remedy—strengthened controls—he dutifully passed along, simultaneously letting it be known that he was not particularly interested in its application. A more significant step came in his press conference of June 15. When a West German journalist asked whether his conception of a "free city" meant the creation of a national border between East and West Berlin, Ulbricht reinterpreted the question to mean that some West Germans wished him to mobilize his construction workers to erect a wall. His workers had better things to do, he responded. "No one," he said, "intends to build a wall."[8] To East Germans long accustomed to reading between the lines, the meaning of Ulbricht's response was clear. The refugee flow rose accordingly. In July the rate was almost double that of the previous eighteen months: an average of 1,000 citizens fled the GDR daily, 3,859 on the last Saturday and Sunday of the month alone! Thus Ulbricht made the situation of the German Democratic Republic one that his friends in Eastern Europe could no longer ignore. On July 23 he demanded that the Soviet bloc use "all means" possible to stop the refugee flow.[9]

It was this predicament, together with Kennedy's unrelenting attitude, that led Khrushchev to accede to the idea of building a wall. This time, at a meeting of the Warsaw Pact Council called for August 3, Ulbricht could meet the objections of the previous March. For one thing, the situation in the GDR was steadily and visibly deteriorating, the danger of an uprising growing. For another, America seemed to have announced its unwillingness to take counteraction against measures in East Berlin alone. Kennedy had limited his "three essentials" to *West* Berlin (and indeed in practically every other way indicated that American responsibility did not extend to *East* Berlin), and, as recently as July 30, Senator William J. Fulbright, chairman of the Senate Foreign Relations Committee, had stated in a television interview: "I don't understand why the East Germans don't close their border because I think they have a right to close it."[10] Khrushchev's support for Ulbricht's proposal began the extensive debate that followed. On the next day, August 4, the Warsaw Pact Council unanimously agreed to measures sealing the boundaries of West Berlin.

The shrewd tactician of East Berlin, Walter Ulbricht, had won hands down. What remained was to prepare the operation. Khrushchev recalled from retirement Marshal Ivan Konev, widely known for his World War II tactics for conquering cities, and placed him in charge of the Red Army in the GDR. The twenty Soviet divisions in East Germany, as well as troops from neighboring Warsaw Pact members, were placed in a state of readiness—readiness to quell riots and subdue domestic turmoil and, if need be, to repel attacks from the West. Ulbricht returned to East Berlin to update plans existing since 1958 for closing the borders of West Berlin. The decision to build the barriers through Berlin was not optimal from his point of view. It permitted him to stop the refugee flow once and for all, which in turn would force East Germans to make their peace with the GDR's communist government, and it would speed up his efforts to integrate East Berlin into the German Democratic Republic, a process that he had begun a year earlier.[11] Even so, Ulbricht would doubtless have preferred a solution giving him greater control over West Berlin itself. It nonetheless gave him opportunities that he could exploit later. And it demonstrated conclusively how a smaller ally can utilize to its own advantage the unwillingness of the nuclear giants to face a showdown.[12]

The Tactical Crisis

After a few anxious hours, the immediate implications of the feverish East German activities on August 13 seemed clear to observers in the West. The Warsaw Pact Council's decision, announced at 1:11 a.m. and repeated frequently throughout the day, fooled few. To be sure, it spoke of "revanchists" and "militarization" in West Germany; of the Western powers, who were "stepping up their military preparations, fanning up war hysteria, and . . . threatening to use armed force"; and of the Western powers' use of West Berlin for "subversion, recruiting spies, and inciting hostile elements to organize sabotage and to provoke disturbances in the GDR." But, in establishing "reliable safeguards and effective control . . . around the whole territory of West Berlin," the Warsaw Pact Council said that it planned no interference with the "existing order of traffic and control on access routes." A subsequent decision of the GDR Council of Ministers, reached on August 12, but not proclaimed until the early hours of the following morning, announced that until such time as West Berlin is turned into a "demilitarized, neutral, free city," citizens of the GDR could enter that part of the city only with special permission. Meanwhile, "visiting the capital of the German Democratic Republic (Democratic Berlin) is possible for peaceful citizens of West Berlin by presentation of their West Berlin identity cards." The Ministry of the Interior reduced from eighty-one to thirteen the number of control points at which West Berliners could cross over into the East. And the Ministry of Transportation announced changes in elevated railway and subway travel that might inconvenience, but certainly not hinder, them from entering the Soviet sector.[13] In short, the entire gamut of activity pointed to restrictions on East Berliners, not on West Berliners. It had the earmarks of a sudden crackdown on the flow of refugees. The thought that Ulbricht would build a modern Chinese wall about the 100-mile perimeter of West Berlin was, after all, preposterous.

Widespread agreement in the West on the immediate implications of the East German action did not mean, however, agreement on what counteraction was to be taken. Each of the major participants in the fragmented political decision-making structure of West Berlin—the Western allies, the Federal Republic, and the West Berlin authorities—viewed the incipient wall from a different perspective. These varying perspectives governed in turn their assessment of its long-term meaning. And it was these perspectives that lay at the root of the real Berlin crisis that was yet to come.

The Western Allies

The most significant decision made by the Western allies on August 13 was to take no action. Underlying this decision was a simple explanation: they had expected much worse. In an atmosphere laden with the possibility of nuclear conflict, President Kennedy had drawn a line around West Berlin and Western rights in that city, earnestly hoping that the East would not cross it. Signs from Moscow and East Berlin were clouded. True, the Soviets had signaled their intention to end the refugee flights and had taken pains to assure the Allies that any action would not impinge upon Western occupation rights.[14] But what did these assurances mean in practice? In Heidelberg the U.S. Army Commander in Europe, General Bruce C. Clarke, and his staff followed closely reports of Soviet troop movements in the area around West Berlin during the night of August 12-13, fearing that a new blockade of the city was imminent. When they realized that these troops were moving into defensive rather than offensive positions, their sighs of relief were almost audible. Ulbricht's real activity was indeed brutal, besides breaching legal rights that had long since ceased to exist in fact; it may have seemed to be a first step in a new Soviet offensive aimed at resolving the Berlin question once and for all. Whatever steps the East Germans had taken, however, they did not breach Kennedy's line. There was no reason to initiate countersteps that could catapult the world into war.[15]

It turned out that the East German action had its positive side, too. For one thing, it dramatically demonstrated the bankruptcy of the GDR's political system. This fact would prove to be of great propagandistic value. More important, the closure of the Berlin border resolved one of the West's most serious dilemmas: how to achieve a relaxation of tension in the Berlin area without actually taking steps in the West to halt the flow of refugees. By cutting the Gordian knot of the refugee problem, the East Germans also enabled the Soviet Union to postpone the conclusion of a separate peace treaty, in effect putting on ice the nagging question of Berlin's future.

The relief that the Allies felt because the feared contingency had not materialized expressed itself in their rather casual approach to the events that did in fact take place. To be sure, the Berlin commandants gave Police Chief Erich Duensing authorization to mobilize 3,000 policemen for emergency duty on the border; they even alerted the 11,000 men comprising their own Berlin forces. But not until ten o'clock that morning did the Kommandatura actually meet to discuss the situation and possible countermeasures. In response to Lord Mayor Willy Brandt's plea for action, for sending to the border military patrols that would demonstrate Allied responsibility for Berlin's security and calm any feelings of uneasiness arising among West Berliners, the Kommandatura made it clear that in the circumstances it had no authority to undertake any action without prior approval from higher up.

Nor was there a greater sense of urgency higher up the Allied line of decision making. In the American case, for instance, communications continued to flow through normal channels. Major General Albert Watson II, American Commandant in Berlin since May, reported both to General Clarke in Heidelberg and to Ambassador Walter C. Dowling in Bonn. (Later in the day Dowling was seen watching a baseball game, calmly processing the reports that he was receiving from Berlin and elsewhere and sending them on to Washington.[16]) Official Washington learned of the border activity in Berlin late Saturday night EDT.[17] But not until noon of the following day (5:00 p.m. in Berlin–almost sixteen hours after the announcement of the Warsaw Pact Council's decision) did Secretary of State Dean Rusk telephone Kennedy in Hyannis Port, where the President was spending the weekend with his family.[18] They quickly agreed that the East German action did not seem to impinge upon Allied rights in West Berlin. While Kennedy then went sailing, Rusk gave a short statement to the press. After noting that the East German actions were contrary to Four-power agreements, he said, "Available information indicates that the measures taken thus far are aimed at residents of East Berlin and East Germany and not at the Allied position in West Berlin or access thereto." The West, he concluded, would protest these measures most vigorously.[19] And then he, too, took advantage of the warm summer day by going to a baseball game. The level of activity was not higher in France or Great Britain. President de Gaulle, spending the weekend at his estate in Colombey-les-deux-Eglises, did not return to Paris, nor did vacationing Premier Michel Debré, Foreign Minister Maurice Couve de Murville, or Minister of the Armies Pierre Messmer. No official source commented on the events in Berlin. British Foreign Secretary Lord Home was also away from his office, visiting his home in Scotland, and Prime Minister Harold Macmillan was preparing to hunt grouse in Yorkshire on the following day. The only official word from London came from a spokesman in the Foreign Office. He said merely that Britain was consulting with its allies on the East German actions and that the restrictions on intersectoral movement were "contrary to the Four-power status of Berlin and therefore illegal."[20]

The Federal Republic

The events of August 13 hit West Germany at a time of partisan politics, for parliamentary elections were scheduled for the seventeenth of the following month. The Christian Democratic Union (CDU) and its Bavarian ally, the Christian Social Union (CSU), again offered Konrad Adenauer as its candidate for chancellor. Adenauer, eighty-five years old at the time, had had a remarkable political career. Long known as Cologne's mayor, he had refused to play along with the Nazi regime, preferring instead to suffer various forms of harassment and to tend his rose garden. After the war he played a key role in building first his party and then his nation. As chancellor since 1949, he had worked strenuously to tie West Germany permanently to the Western alliance system.

Adenauer's opponent was Willy Brandt, West Berlin's governing mayor. A former underground fighter against Nazism who had worked his way up in the Social Democratic party (SPD), Brandt, now 47, was taking on the "old fox" himself. News of Ulbricht's action nonetheless led Brandt to remove himself from active campaigning and, subsequently, to appeal for the adjournment of political activity during this time of national crisis; the election was scheduled to take place anyway.

The task of federal officials was less clear-cut than that facing Brandt. At approximately 4:00 a.m. began several hours of telephoning among leaders of the CDU/CSU coalition: Federal Minister for All-German Affairs Ernst Lemmer and Deputy Mayor Franz Amrehn in Berlin; State Secretary Hans Globke, Bundestag Majority Leader Heinrich Krone, and Lemmer's Deputy, State Secretary Thedieck, in Bonn; Chancellor Adenauer at his home in the Bonn suburb of Rhöndorf; and, ultimately, Foreign Minister Heinrich von Brentano, campaigning at the time in southern Germany. (Later in the day, significantly enough, it was his confidants Globke and Krone whom Adenauer received, not von Brentano and Lemmer, the two ministers who, according to the organization table of the FRG, should have been responsible for this particular type of problem.)

The outcome of this round robin was a pair of basic decisions. The first was to place responsibility for responding to the East German measures squarely upon Allied shoulders. CDU circles credit Adenauer with being the first major German politician to realize that the West, and particularly Kennedy, would view these measures in a context much larger than just Berlin.[21] Adenauer was aware that not only would the West make no response itself, but it would also prevent the federal and municipal governments from undertaking steps that could increase the danger of war. Hence, initiatives on Adenauer's part would be as damaging to West Germany's relations with the West as they would be useless for the hapless East Germans affected by the border closure. The second decision followed from the first: the federal government would minimize the issue of the border closure to avoid popular unrest.

Behind this second decision—eminently sound given the circumstances—partisan politics reared its ugly head. Any public attention focused on Berlin would inevitably place opposition candidate Willy Brandt in the public spotlight. This could not be avoided in Berlin itself, but then West Berliners would not vote in the federal elections. Keeping to a minimum the West German attention focused on Brandt was politically expedient since the West Germans would go to the polls in five weeks. So the Adenauer campaign went on unabated. The chancellor did not go to Berlin, eighty minutes away by airplane. Nor did he address the nation by television to discuss the day's events.[22] Indeed, on the very next day he launched his most vicious personal attack against Willy Brandt. And, during the following week, he would even suggest that Ulbricht had built his wall for the electoral benefit of the

Social Democrats. For the West Berliners, mystified by the passivity of the Allies, the behavior of the federal chancellor and his government was outrageous.

West Berlin

Shortly after 4:00 a.m., Brandt, aboard his campaign train in West Germany, was given a telegram from Senate Director Heinrich Albertz.[23] An hour later he got off the train at Hanover and flew to Berlin. However simple it may have been for Brandt to decide to return to Berlin, the problem facing him there was immense.

As a representative of the West Berliners, Brandt now had to anticipate their reaction to the border closure and to guide them through the crisis. As the leader of the city in which the Allies of World War II still held the ultimate reins of power, he had to move the Kommandatura to action. But, as the agent of the Kommandatura, Brandt was responsible for maintaining law and order in West Berlin. As the leader of a government that still claimed to represent 1.1 million East Berliners, Brandt had a responsibility to them, too. How could he demonstrate his solidarity with them without fomenting riots that the East German and Soviet armies would crush with force? For Brandt and his associates, none of whom had had a full night's sleep, it promised to be a long day.

The first steps had been arranged by telephone with Albertz. An official car met his plane on the runway to take him to City Hall for a special meeting of the Senate. A stopoff at Potsdam Square gave the governing mayor his first glimpse of the actual state of affairs at the border and a chance to gauge the mood of his fellow West Berliners. "When will the Americans come," one man is said to have asked Brandt, "and end this nightmare?"[24] The Senate meeting itself took place in an atmosphere of controlled excitement. In addition to calling an afternoon meeting of the House of Representatives, the Senate worked out a common position to present to the Allies.

From City Hall, Brandt, Albertz, and Amrehn went to the Kommandatura meeting. The commandants and their advisers had been talking for more than an hour before the Berliners' scheduled appearance. British Minister Geoffrey McDermott recalls that the governing mayor was "grave but statesmanlike" and that he "never demanded any rash action from the protecting powers nor reproached us for lack of firmness."[25] Other participants, however, told pressmen that Brandt was considerably more agitated. "You must do something," he is reported to have said excitedly; and, when the Western representatives did not respond, "Last night you let Ulbricht kick you in the pants!"[26] In the subsequent, considerably calmer discussion, Brandt proposed strong protests in Moscow and other Warsaw Pact capitals as well as Allied patrols along the West Berlin border. As he subsequently told the press: "I let the three Allied commandants know in no uncertain terms that we expect from our Western friends, as an answer to the communist provocation, energetic steps that will be effective."[27]

The rest of the day was spent in consultation and preparation for the extraordinary session of the House of Representatives at 6:30 that afternoon. The House not being in session, only somewhat more than half of the 133 representatives were present. The rest were on vacation in West Germany or abroad. In addition, some borough mayors and other officials attended, as did the three Western commandants, who, according to press reports, were greeted tumultuously. The main item of business was Brandt's carefully balanced speech, surveying the situation, admonishing the Allies to take "energetic steps," and repeating Rusk's statement promising a "sharp step" on the part of the West.[28] "It cannot be my task to anticipate the decisions of the governments responsible for our security," Brandt went on to say. "But surely I convey the feeling of this House and speak in the name of the entire Berlin population when I express the opinion that it will not let the matter rest with protests alone." Sustained applause interrupted him at this point.

Brandt then turned to the task facing West Germans. He had contacted the federal government, the governing mayor of Berlin and Social Democratic candidate for the chancellorship said, and expected that the Bundestag would meet on the following Wednesday (three days after the fait accompli!). To West Germans he appealed for solidarity with the people in the Soviet zone. Of West Berliners he expected an orderly alertness, a demonstration of "soberness in the face of the anger that unites us." "Thoughtless actions will not help our city," he added, "nor our countrymen who have been cut off from us." In his final words Brandt implored East Germans not to give way to bitterness and doubt. In short, there was little hope that he could hold out to either East or West Berliners. Nor could he ask much of anyone. Having searched his own soul, inquiring what should be done now, Brandt could only respond, in effect, "Sit tight." But, then, why should he expect that anyone, most particularly the West Berliners, would do anything else?

West Berliners

Berliners have long prided themselves on their political acumen and militance and on their resistance to both Nazism in the early 1930s and communism in the late 1940s. Moreover, they had demonstrated their willingness to act collectively. On a cold and drizzly August day in 1948, 50,000 of them assembled after only a few hours' notice to hear Governing Mayor Ernst Reuter warn the communists that he would not sit by idly if they tried to take over the city's government. Two weeks later, after communist-led gangs had forced city councillors from the western sectors to leave the city hall, over a third of a million persons gathered at the Square of the Republic to protest. Afterward, some demonstrators stormed the nearby Brandenburg Gate, a few feet inside the Soviet sector. A handful of youths climbed to its top to haul down the red flag that had hung there since Berlin's capture by Soviet troops in April 1945. Apparently having lost their nerve, some Red Army guards fired into the crowd. One dead and several wounded were the toll before Soviet and British officers succeeded in restoring order. A repetition of the event almost occurred in November 1956, after a protest demonstration held in front of West Berlin's city hall to express solidarity with the rebellious Hungarians. A cry went out, "To the Brandenburg Gate!" and thousands of demonstrators surged into the streets, their way lit by torches. The way to the Brandenburg Gate was long enough—two and a half miles to the northeast—that the up-and-coming Social Democratic president of the House of Representatives, Willy Brandt, was able to dissuade them with impassioned speeches (and water throwers). Meanwhile, armed East German border guards waited nervously at the Brandenburg Gate. Thus, in one sense the anger and frustration expressed by West Berliners on August 13 were cause for concern.

Yet in another sense the concern over this very real threat was exaggerated. An officially sanctioned, emotion-laden demonstration might well have touched off a popular explosion. But it was the possibility of crowd mismanagement or the inability to control a mob egged on by a few hotheads that alarmed those who had witnessed the convulsions of 1948 and 1956. And it was this possibility of uncontrolled mob violence that led Brandt, against the wishes of some of his associates, to rule out a protest meeting on August 13. There was little danger, however, that a mob would organize itself spontaneously to take drastic steps. This could only happen if some incident incited the crowds forming along the border. To prevent this was the function of the police.

Two factors enhanced the likelihood of such an incident. The first was what has come to be called the "Berlin mentality," entailing both an extreme sensitivity to real or imagined threats from the East as well as a double standard for evaluating behavior. In the months following the construction of the wall, for instance, some students participated actively in helping East Germans to flee. Although they frequently acted outside of, and even contrary to, the law, the public and press reaction was praise. And when the president of the Free University of Berlin tried to put an end to the use of dormitory rooms for storing illegal munitions, he received for his efforts sharp criticism and little else. (The students subsequently learned that demonstrations and resolutions could be tolerated only so long as they were directed against the East and not against institutions and the way of life in the West.) Similarly, few people condoned the willful destruction of property, but youthful rowdies had discovered that ripping up seats or breaking windows in the Eastern-controlled elevated railway that runs through West Berlin did not encounter stiff social opprobrium. In such a "friend–enemy" climate, it was quite possible that West Berliners would applaud any assault on the new barrier imposed by the communists.

The second factor that enhanced the likelihood of a border incident consisted in the messages communicated to the population by political leaders and news commentators. Stripped of their finery, they were three in number: (1) there is excitement at the border; (2) what the East is doing there is illegal and outrageous; and (3) the West Berlin police are at the border to prevent trouble caused by West Berliners. Such a set of messages not only invited sensation seekers and the curious to go to the border (despite specific requests that they remain away from the area) but also gave them a forewarning that there would be trouble to watch. Prophecies of trouble tend to be self-fulfilling. And this was particularly so on August 13, when leaders and population alike were at once furious at the East and frustrated at their own powerlessness in the face of the situation confronting them.

Given these circumstances, it is remarkable that West Berliners did not rush in large numbers to the border and that the incidents that did occur were minor and brought quickly under control. In fact, the largest estimate of the largest crowd was 10,000—out of a population of two and a quarter million—standing at 8:00 p.m. in Hindenburg Square in front of the Brandenburg Gate.[29] Most of these people, however, had merely gone to see what was going on; a few joined in occasional chants or shouts at those on the other side of the boundary, and still fewer appeared anxious to take action. Of those who did anything more than watch, most were young men who appeared to be acting from motives that had little to do with politics. At some points in the evening an almost festive atmosphere reigned!

What accounts for this relatively mild reaction? For one thing, as suggested earlier, anomic outbreaks of mass violence are the exception and not the rule in West Berlin. The police could handle individuals intent upon creating an incident or carried away by their exasperation, and the only persons in a position to organize upon such short notice the type of mass demonstration that could get out of hand expressly ruled out such a gathering. For another thing, by 1961 West Berliners had become accustomed to pressure from the East. The most recent wave of pressure had commenced with Khrushchev's ultimatum in November 1958 and had continued with greater or lesser intensity since then. For some, the events of August 13 were merely another manifestation of the long-standing Soviet intent to throttle West Berlin. Third, few West Berliners were really surprised that the East Germans had acted. For days, and even weeks, the crisis had been coming to a head. Any reader of a West Berlin newspaper knew that the GDR would have to take steps to stop the refugee flow.[30] That the GDR actually moved on August 13 and, particularly, the form its measures took nonetheless caught West Berliners off their guard since East German secrecy about specific plans had been all but complete. Finally, West Berliners found out early that the border closure would not seriously restrict their access to East Berlin. That this would change before too many days was not at all clear on August 13.

The consequence was that most West Berliners on this first day of the crisis behaved as they usually do on warm, sultry, and hazy Sundays in August. They doubtless listened to the radio more than usual; they unquestionably talked more about the political situation than they normally did; and some even went to the border to see for themselves what was happening. Despite an underlying apprehension that the situation might be more serious than it seemed, the general expectation was that it would cause most of them only minor—and in all likelihood temporary—inconveniences. But there were no masses surging upon the Brandenburg Gate. There were no mobs at the city hall howling for action.

The Developing Political Crisis

Before the last West Berliners had turned homewards from Hindenburg Square shortly after midnight, activity had picked up on the other side of the Atlantic. Increasingly impressed with the urgency of the situation, the president and his associates decided to call General Lucius D. Clay, the hero of the Berlin blockade, out of retirement and send him to Berlin as a token of support. An informal attempt by one of Kennedy's friends to communicate this intention to Brandt failed, however, since Press Secretary Egon Bahr, to whom the message had been relayed, did not pass it on to the governing mayor.[31] The result was that when Germans and Berliners woke up on Monday morning the situation seemed much as it was when they had gone to bed.

Bonn drops the ball

If subsequent initiatives had been left in the hands of the Bonn government, there the matter would have lain for a good, long while. Responsible members of all three major parties continued to give out statements condemning the East and declaring their solidarity with Berliners on both sides of the barbed wire. Bundestag President Eugen Gerstenmaier (CDU), Social Democratic party chairman Erich Ollenhauer, and Free Democratic party chairman Erich Mende even flew to Berlin. Early Monday morning Foreign Minister von Brentano received (at his own request) the American, British, and French ambassadors to the Federal Republic. Later that afternoon he and Chancellor Adenauer sat before television cameras, filming a dialogue to be presented in the evening to the nation. On Tuesday and Wednesday mornings came Cabinet meetings, followed by a special session of the Bundestag on Friday. The point is not that Bonn officials were idle or insincere. Far from it. Rather, the many messages that flooded the airwaves and press added little to what had already been said on Sunday. And, in all their activity, they not only accomplished precious little, but they also let opportunities for constructive action slip by.

Adenauer's activity during the course of the week was designed to put the Berlin crisis into the broader perspective of foreign policy. On the one hand, aware that the West did not intend to restore the status quo of August 12, he evidently saw no reason to risk damaging his good relations with the Allies either by demanding Western initiatives or by taking precipitous action himself.[32] On the other hand, if the new situation in Berlin was not to be changed, did it make sense to heighten the existing strain between the Soviet Union and Germany? And would fulminous—but ultimately hollow—threats make West Germany's bargaining position on other issues more credible? Avoiding any such deterioration of relations was so important that Adenauer met with Soviet Ambassador Andrei Smirnov on Wednesday morning. The two men exchanged assurances that neither country would do anything that could either damage their mutual relations or exacerbate the international situation.

However understandable his concern with foreign policy, it was his emphasis on domestic politics that aroused Adenauer's critics. In trying to keep the level of tension low, he underestimated the impact of the East German action on the West German and, particularly, the West Berlin populace. Over nationwide television on Monday the chancellor prefaced his expectation that the Federal Republic would cooperate with its NATO allies in working out an appropriate response with the comment, "There is no reason to panic." "I think you are completely right," responded Foreign Minister von Brentano, who went on to characterize the current crisis as merely a part of a larger war of nerves.[33] This apparently casual position, together with Adenauer's failure to visit Berlin personally during these critical days, was seen as inspired by partisan motives, an unwillingness to permit more publicity to be given to a situation in which his political opponent was hero of the day. The chancellor himself did little to dispel such charges. His references on Monday and then again on Wednesday to Brandt's illegitimate birth, as well as his subsequent charge that Ulbricht's action had been designed to assist the SPD at the polls, embarrassed some of the most prominent CDU leaders, a few of whom sought to distance themselves from Adenauer's remarks, and brought cries of outrage from opposition and press alike. Some even viewed with suspicion his gentlemen's agreement with Smirnov. The unrest that the Berlin crisis had brought in its wake consituted a challenge to the basis of Adenauer's current campaign for the chancellorship: the stability that he had brought to the Federal Republic during his twelve years of rule. Had Adenauer now sold the Berliners down the river in exchange for an assurance that the Soviet Union would upset no more applecarts before the election?

Monday: A city in abeyance

Meanwhile, in West Berlin, Mayor Brandt and his associates initially followed through the course that they had begun on Sunday. Early Monday morning the Senate met to consider what should be done. On several points they were agreed. First, there should be no public demonstrations, at least for the time being.[34] Second, the Senate should petition the commandants to review East Berlin's jurisdiction over the elevated railway in West Berlin, the right of the communist Socialist Unity party (SED) to exist in West Berlin, and the financial privileges accruing to West Berliners working in East Berlin. Third, the Senate would discontinue support to groups participating in events sponsored by the East. Finally, it would seek a reversal of Allied regulations prohibiting West Germans from moving to West Berlin.[35]

While the Senate was still deciding what countermeasures to take, some West Berliners had already begun to act out their political frustrations. Two thousand workers from the AEG Turbine Factory in Moabit began marching to the City Hall, some three miles to the south. En route they tripled their numbers, confirming fears that an organized demonstration could easily have drawn hundreds of thousands. Soothing words from Mayor Brandt sent the men back to their workplaces. The promise of a fifteen-minute work stoppage at 2:00 p.m. to enable workers throughout the city to express their solidarity was by and large successful. Even so, another group of about 3,000 workers reached City Hall at 2:30 p.m. Another type of anomic behavior took the form of reprisals against the Socialist Unity party and its West Berlin representatives, who were seen by many to be agents of the East or even traitors: in some factories workers struck until management had fired their SED colleagues; printers shut down their printing plant rather than print the party organ, *Die Wahrheit* ("The Truth"); and SED offices in Moabit and Friedenau were vandalized by unknown persons.[36]

The most serious incident, however, took place before the Brandenburg Gate. Frequently during the course of the morning West Berlin policemen had to restrain those who had gathered—again, mostly young men—from throwing stones or pushing at the barricades. By the middle of the afternoon the situation was turning ugly. West Berliners chanting and the increasing likelihood of violence led the East Berlin People's Police to throw tear-gas bombs into the crowd and to seal off the Brandenburg Gate itself. Cognizant of the potential danger, the West put into action for the first time its auxiliary police force to maintain order. Eventually the crowds dispersed and relative quiet returned to the area. The net result was that the East reduced from thirteen to twelve the number of crossing points between West and East Berlin.

At about the same time that workers were gathering for a second time before the city hall, the People's Police were closing off the Brandenburg Gate, and Mayor Brandt was holding a hastily called information session for the diplomatic and consular corps accredited to the city, another conference was taking place in the residential suburb of Dahlem.[37] The host was Axel Caesar Springer, postwar Germany's most successful press magnate, whose newspapers (*B.Z., Berliner Mor-*

genpost, Bild Zeitung, and *Die Welt*) accounted for more than two-thirds of daily newspaper sales in West Berlin. The main guest, in addition to a few of Springer's Berlin editors, was Edward R. Murrow, known to millions of American television viewers as a top-notch political commentator, but in August 1961 on tour of the worldwide installations of the United States Information Agency, of which he was chief. As early as February of that year, Springer had tried to alert President Kennedy to the likelihood of an explosion in East Germany. Now that Ulbricht had closed the borders in an effort to control popular unrest in the GDR, Springer felt it imperative that the United States act. Not to tear down the barriers and not to insist upon the maintenance of legal rights would be to undermine the entire Western position in Berlin, and it could even increase the likelihood of war. Convinced, if not by the arguments themselves then by the force with which Springer and his editors presented them, Murrow returned to the headquarters of the United States Mission in Berlin to send a teletyped message to his friend in the White House. E. Allan Lightner, American Minister to Berlin, simultaneously sent his own message to the President. The gist of both messages was the same: the United States must act immediately to prevent panic by giving moral support to the Berliners.

The balance to be drawn at the end of Monday, August 14, 1961, was not a particularly happy one. East of the Brandenburg Gate, the authorities had taken two new ominous steps: not only had they severed telephone and telegraph communications between East and West Germany (those between the two halves of Berlin had been cut a decade earlier), but they had also begun to replace some of their rickety barriers with more durable walls of concrete block and mortar. West of the Brandenburg Gate, the authorities had proved able to control the situation. Throughout Berlin, however, people were waiting—waiting for the Bonn government to do something. The counsel of maintaining trust and calmness was beginning to wear thin.

A Tuesday of disenchantment

By Tuesday morning the demand for substantive measures was growing louder. West Berliners reaching for their morning newspapers found a united front. Headlines in the *Morgenpost* blurted out, "We Appeal to the World—Protest Marches—Conferences—Countermeasures." The editorialist for the *B.Z.* protested, "Enough of this Sluggishness!" Shortly before noon *Der Kurier* appeared on the newsstands, announcing in its headlines: "Berlin Is Waiting for Countermeasures," and reporting, somewhat sadly, that it was not yet decided when the Bundestag would meet. Still later in the day, the German Trade Union Association, in a public statement calling for action, felt constrained to note "with displeasure" that Chancellor Adenauer had still not found his way to Berlin.

In this climate of growing impatience, the Senate met again. Interior Senator Joachim Lipschitz could report that, since eight o'clock that morning, the entire police force was on full alert to prevent a repetition of Monday's incidents. (During Tuesday the West Berlin police would have their hands full. In Neukölln scuffling broke out when members of the East German People's Police jumped over the barriers to swing their clubs at some youthful protesters; they even dragged one of the youths back into East Berlin. Later, as tempers were flaring on both sides of the border in Neukölln, the East German police began lobbing tear-gas bombs and percussion caps into crowds of young West Berliners. It seemed likely that this would be the prelude to the closure of still more border crossings.) The Senators then drafted a letter to be sent to the Western commandants, embodying the proposals communicated informally to them on the previous day, and decided to call a protest demonstration for the following afternoon.

The Senate meeting ended abruptly, however, with the news of Adenauer's campaign speech on the previous night in Regensburg. Sickened by the personal nature of his opponent's attack on him, Brandt left the room. Was this the kind of solidarity that the Bonn government was going to give the Berlin leadership in its time of need? Political commentators later expressed understanding for Brandt's distress, while taking him to task for letting his personal emotions get in the way of his function as the political head of beleaguered West Berlin.

While City Hall was in an uproar over the chancellor's remarks and the governing mayor's reaction to them, the Allies were making their first tentative move. It was not a gesture likely to inspire confidence in the West's willingness to go to battle for the restoration of Berlin's Four-power status: a courier was delivering the Allies' protest to the Soviet commandant in the East Berlin borough of Karlshorst. That a messenger, rather than one of the commandants, delivered the note seemed to indicate either that few in the Western camp took it seriously or that they were deliberately trying to play down its importance. Moreover, its contents comprised nothing more than polite objections to the measures taken on August 13. In no sense did the note demand a return to the status quo before that day. Was this the countermeasure for which West Berliners had waited for more than two days? A Senate spokesman merely said, "It cannot be assumed that this is the last word."[38]

The prospects for Brandt looked grim. The population that had elected him governing mayor was clamoring for action, as was the press. The Allies, however, had made it abundantly—and publicly—clear that they had no intention of taking any steps that could exacerbate the situation, and Brandt had failed to receive the message that Kennedy intended to send Clay to Berlin. Not only was the federal government in Bonn dragging its feet, but its chief representative was attacking him where it hurt most. And from the border came word that the East had sharpened its controls: henceforward, any person driving a motorized vehicle into East Berlin would need a travel permit. (For a few hours, significantly enough, some border guards were interpreting their orders to mean that *all* persons needed such permits! This step would not take place formally for another week.) In short, it certainly appeared as though Berlin were being thrown to the wolves.

It was in this situation, shortly after the breakup of the Senate meeting, that Brandt received Murrow and Lightner. The best hope for Berlin, the two Americans said, was to make Kennedy sharply aware of the dangers engulfing the city. Brandt should write personally to the President. The governing mayor was inclined to agree. "Kennedy had told me that, whenever I thought it useful or important, I should contact him directly," Brandt later wrote, with reference to this event, "and now it was important."[39]

That very afternoon Brandt sat down to draft a letter to President Kennedy. Its first part painted a black picture indeed of the situation in Berlin and the effects of the Allies' failure to take immediate and forceful action. Brandt then proposed several concrete steps. First, of course, the Western powers should insist upon the restoration of Berlin's Four-power status, "but at the same time proclaim a Three-power status for West Berlin." The purpose of this, as Brandt would make clear in later statements, would be to facilitate the integration of West Berlin into the Federal Republic. Second, the West should bring the Berlin problem before the United Nations. At the very least it should charge the Soviet Union with a breach of the Declaration of Human Rights. Brandt warned against negotiating on the Berlin issue under pressure from the Soviet Union. Instead, the West should seize the political initiative. Finally, he noted that he would welcome a demonstrative strengthening of the American military garrison in Berlin.

After revising the draft, Brandt gave it to his secretary with the comment that he wanted to sleep on it.[40] On the following day he would give a copy to Lightner, who would teletype it to the White House.

Wednesday: The political crisis erupts

Tension rose markedly as Wednesday's demonstration approached. At once indicative of, and conducive to, further strain was the press, which was as outspoken as it was unanimous in expressing its disappointment at the Allied protest of Tuesday. Loudest were the bright red headlines in the Springer-owned *Bild Zeitung:* "The West Does NOTHING!" Even more disturbing, however, was the news confronting readers of *Der Kurier*. The article under the front-page headline, "Marshal Konev Had Informed the Western Powers in Advance," reported as fact a Soviet-inspired rumor that was floating around the city: at a reception in Potsdam on August 10, after his appointment as Chief of the Red Army in the GDR, Konev was said to have given the three Western commandants details of the pending action on the Berlin border.[41] This information, however inaccurate it turned out to be, certainly seemed plausible at the time. The languor of the Western powers no longer seemed mystifying. They had merely made a deal with the Russians at the expense of the Berliners!

Preparations for the demonstration went on amid a barrage of activity. From East Berlin came rumors that the authorities planned to seal the borders completely. From Bonn came word that Chancellor Adenauer would fly to the island city early in the following week. In Berlin itself the German Trade Union Association called for a boycott of the elevated railway.[42] The Commander of the U.S. Army in Europe, General Bruce C. Clarke, arrived in Berlin to gather firsthand impressions of the situation. Meanwhile, in the city hall, Willy Brandt was chewing at the end of his pencil, trying to work out a speech for the rally.[43] The governing mayor was well aware of the possibility of incidents that could have incalculable consequences: "One word too many, but also one word too few, could serve as a spark."[44] As a precaution, the police had strengthened their garrisons both along the border (particularly at the Brandenburg Gate) and near the headquarters of the United States Mission in Dahlem. Reserve units and water throwers stood ready for action, if necessary. But what could Brandt tell his Berliners? At the time he left his office to address the assembled masses not even his closest associates were certain of what he would say.

The quarter million Berliners gathered before the city hall appeared impatient. Some of them carried placards or banners: "Paper Protests Don't Stop Tanks!"; "Doesn't the West Know What to Do?"; "We Demand Countermeasures!"; "Where are the Americans?"; "Betrayed by the West?"; "Kennedy Is Selling Us Out!"; "Munich, 1938—Berlin, 1961!" The first speaker of the afternoon, Deputy Mayor Franz Amrehn, did little to reduce the emotional content of the atmosphere. "The East bloc has thrown down the gauntlet to the West," he declaimed. Protests were no longer sufficient. "The barbed wire must come down," he concluded. And then, turning what should be done into what would be done, Amrehn added, "The barbed wire will come down." The Berliners thundered their approval.[45]

Given all these circumstances, the governing mayor's address from the steps of the city hall on that cold and stormy summer afternoon stands as a remarkable document of clarity and reasonableness. Brandt recapitulated at the outset much of what he had been saying since Sunday: that the border closure was a "flagrant injustice," that "paper protests" were not enough, that his appeals for soberness rested upon a desire to prevent additional hardships and bloodshed, and that the nation stood on the brink of a crucial test. He then discussed the many proposals for action that he and the Senate had suggested during the course of the week.

The most significant part of Brandt's address came near the end. On the one hand he expressed an understanding for the Allied position: the West had upheld its guarantees for *West* Berlin—the familiar three essentials enunciated in the previous May—and would continue to do so; and in fact the East German border closure had not struck at the vitals of West Berlin's existence. But, on the other hand, Brandt had a warning for the West: "This city wishes peace, but it will not capitulate. . . . Never has peace been saved through weakness. There is a point at which one must recognize that he will fall back not one step more. This point has been reached."

After comparing the Berlin situation to that of the Rhineland in the mid-1930s, Brandt went on to say that, this time, there must be no new Munich. "We are not afraid," he said, by way of preface to the only real hope that he could give to Berliners that afternoon: "Today, in all candor, I expressed our opinion in a letter to the President of the United States, John Kennedy. Berlin expects more than words. Berlin expects political action." The applause and cheers that echoed across the square told Brandt that this had been what his audience wanted to hear. The governing mayor of West Berlin had publicly put the president of the United States into a position in which he had to do something.

Brandt ended his address with the words "unity and justice and freedom," the motto of the Federal Republic. After the band played the national anthem and the assembled Berliners sang its third verse, which begins with the phrase "unity and justice and freedom," the rich tones of the Freedom Bell pealed out from the tower of City Hall over the square in which the West Berliners stood. Perhaps it was the tolling of the Freedom Bell, a gift from the American people in 1950; perhaps it was the hope held out by Brandt's words and the response that would now surely come from Kennedy. At any rate, the people quietly turned around and returned in the directions from which they had come. The demonstration had passed without incident.

The Transformation of the Berlin Crisis

The Berlin crisis of August 1961 began as a tactical exercise within the framework of the cold war. The West, long since having given up its claim to the practical (albeit not to the theoretical) exercise of control in East Berlin and expecting much worse than what came in the early hours of August 13, reacted only mildly. In its view, since the steps by the East left the West's strategic position basically unchanged, they should, by themselves, be no cause for rash reactions that could force a confrontation between nuclear giants.

What this line of reasoning overlooked was the West Berliners and their leadership. First of all, that the commitment of the Kennedy administration did not extend to the whole of Berlin was not sufficiently spelled out. The United States had been about as specific in public as it could be. Indeed, Brandt's closest adviser feared that Kennedy's statement of the three essentials in May 1961 amounted "almost to an invitation for the Soviets to do what they wanted with East Berlin."[46] What the West had failed to do was to inform the Berlin leadership about the actual extent of its commitment. And it also did nothing to destroy popular illusions, nurtured by the press, that viewed claimed rights and enforceable rights as one and the same thing. Neither leadership nor population in West Berlin was prepared for the Western reaction to potential steps on the part of the East. Second, Allied leaders underestimated the effect that the events of August 13 had upon the morale of the West Berliners, with their somewhat exaggerated sense of importance brought on by so many years at the front of the cold war.

Adenauer's virtual dismissal of the West Berliner's problems even verged on callousness.

However understandable from the West's point of view—that is, from the point of view of the grand strategy of international politics—this behavior revealed a remarkable lack of insight into the psychology of the beleaguered West Berliners. Traditionally, and not entirely in a jocular vein, Berliners have been chided for believing their city to be the hub of the universe. They had come to view any local crisis as one of much larger dimensions. More important, in their fight for the city's freedom during the previous fifteen years they had in fact suffered much. For this they had garnered Western and especially American guarantees of support as well as praise for their steadfastness. But now, when West Berliners were engulfed by what they perceived to be a critical situation, those who had promised backing seemed to have forgotten all about the city. Indeed, rumors were current that the Western allies had even known in advance about and shut their eyes to the border closure. The snail-like speed with which the West responded to this closure, no less than the sterility of the note that was ultimately sent to the Soviet commandant in East Berlin, did not soften the blow to West Berliners' morale.

By concentrating upon the worldwide aspects of the tactical crisis and ignoring the local situation, the Allies also gave maneuvering room to Ulbricht. This, too, affected morale in the western half of the city. The border closure of August 13 turned out to be only a first step in the renewed effort to isolate West Berlin. By August 15, the wooden and barbed-wire barriers were beginning to give way to the construction of a concrete wall, a wall that ultimately would assume formidable proportions; by the same day East Berlin authorities were requiring permits for motorized vehicles entering their sector; by August 18 police and army units were walling up houses along the border and relocating their inhabitants elsewhere; and by August 22 the GDR was announcing its intention to require entry permits of all West Berliners crossing into East Berlin. When Western authorities refused to allow the GDR to set up offices for this purpose within West Berlin, the communists simply stopped allowing West Berliners into the eastern sector altogether.[47]

It is difficult to say whether all these steps were planned in advance, to be carried through according to a timetable in any event, or whether the plans as well as the timetable were contingent upon Allied reactions to each initial measure. Elements of both were doubtless present. That the Allies failed to respond immediately and effectively nonetheless seems to have encouraged East Berlin authorities. Very soon jubilant communists were boasting of the success of their "protective wall" and taunting the frustrated West Berliners. On the evening of Brandt's address before the city hall, East Germany's foremost television commentator, Karl-Eduard von Schnitzler, asked his viewing audience rhetorically, "Have you heard that Brandt called the Allies for help?" His answer dripped with sarcasm: "Yes, I heard it, but the Allies didn't."[48]

All these circumstances were conducive to a situation out of which a crisis of confidence in the Allies might have sprung. Nationalistic elements in postwar West German society—among the most respectable and articulate of which was the Springer press—might even have welcomed such a development, since it would have generated support for their argument that the Federal Republic dare not rely too heavily upon its allies but must pursue its own course in world politics. Moreover, the changing climate of opinion in Berlin from Sunday to Wednesday seemed to presage just such a crisis of confidence.

Without a specific focus and with no effective outlet, the anger felt on the first day or two turned into frustration. Although 52 percent of a sample of West Berliners interviewed in the spring of 1962 thought that the Americans could have removed the barriers along the border, at the time no responsible person spoke in public of such a possibility. Indeed, the editorialist of the Springer-owned *B.Z.* even wrote that this could not be accomplished without the use of force, "and the West will not and cannot use force against whatever Ulbricht does in his sphere of power."[49] Simply to protest against the East was fruitless since arguments and protests, however well-reasoned, could have no effect upon those in East Berlin who had initiated the measures of August 13. And, for the few West Berliners who tried to take direct action, there was the West Berlin police to hold them in check.

The West's failure to take immediate and effective steps to support the West Berliners provided them with a substitute target for their anger. This is not to say that they forgot their hostility toward East Berlin, but only that their expression of hostility toward the Allies was more purposeful. Against the liberal democracies of the West popular demonstrations frequently have some effect. By the middle of the week the press was sharply critical: on Tuesday an independent tabloid was accusing the West of having sold Berlin down the river; on Wednesday all newspapers, particularly those controlled by Springer, were outspoken in their dissatisfaction with the West's policies. Placards visible at

Wednesday's demonstration clearly indicated that some elements of the public were more interested in expressing their anger and resentment toward the Allies than in condemning Ulbricht and his regime. Even Mayor Brandt's address was less concerned with injustices perpetrated by the communists than with Western inactivity.

In short, by Wednesday afternoon the process of transferring hostility was well under way. This process, if continued unabated, would doubtless have led to a major crisis of confidence on the part of West Berliners vis-à-vis the Allies who were supposed to defend them. Since the security of the city rested upon Allied guarantees, a lack of faith in the willingness of these Allies to make good their guarantees could have had incalculable consequences: investors would have found the financial situation precarious at best; young people seeking careers would have been less inclined to take West Berlin seriously; and judging from available public opinion data, a mass flight of citizens from the city would have ensued.

What prevented this from occurring was Brandt's realization of the course of events and his timely, if also politically risky, efforts to change them. As early as Sunday afternoon, after the discussion with the Kommandatura, Brandt and his closest associates saw that, if the indecision of the Allies were to continue, the danger of popular disaffection would grow. An armed effort to tear down the barriers along the border was out of the question. The governing mayor did not propose it, and the commandants would have dismissed the idea if he had done so. In the view of the city's political leadership, immediate and symbolic gestures of support were needed: border controls to demonstrate vividly continuing Allied responsibility for the protection of West Berlin, strong and immediate protests to Moscow and other Warsaw Pact capitals. His attempts to move the Kommandatura to action, however, had been unsuccessful. It was not that his proposals had fallen on deaf ears. It was simply that, without instructions from above, the commandants could not take any action whatever.[50] The question facing Brandt on Sunday afternoon was, then, how to force the Allies to do something.

Brandt decided upon a calculated risk. Through his public comments to the press and before the House of Representatives on Sunday evening, he would call attention to the need for the Allies to act. The danger of such public pressuring was that it could encourage among the West Berliners not only an awareness that the Allies had in fact done little or nothing but also an anxiety that nothing would be done in the future. In short, it was possible that his open comments to the Allies would create the very crisis of confidence that he wanted to avoid. And, unfortunately, as the Allies continued to debate in private while revealing virtually nothing to the public, the immediate effect was to sharpen tension within West Berlin. Before long the hounds of popular sentiment and the press were at the gate, yapping that something be done.

Encouraged by Murrow and Lightner, Brandt finally took an even greater risk and appealed personally to President Kennedy. His letter aroused criticism on both sides of the Atlantic. In Bonn, governmental officials were irritated that Brandt had not consulted them before sending it off. Adenauer thought that his political opponent had displayed a "monstrous arrogance and lack of instinct" in clubbing Kennedy "with a mallet."[51] The Foreign Office expressed indignation that it had had to ask for information about the letter (although a copy of it was under way to von Brentano). And CDU politicians, still engaged in the electoral campaign, saw in the letter an attempt by Brandt to capitalize on his special relationship with Kennedy and the unfortunate situation of his city. In Washington, Kennedy's initial reaction was rage. Not only did the letter put him on the spot in his touchy relations with the Soviet Union, but it also seemed to be little more than an attempt on Brandt's part to enlist for partisan political purposes the prestige of the United States and the president himself. As late as the following day Press Secretary Pierre Salinger, in response to a reporter's question, said coolly that it was not yet certain when or even whether the president would respond, and that the letter itself had been sent on to the State Department.[52] Subsequent consideration, however, together with telegrams from Murrow and the United States Mission in Berlin, led Kennedy to write a three-page response on White House stationery.[53]

Brandt's letter was, in effect, an attempt at political extortion. As such, it entailed risks for both sender and recipient. By writing it in the first place and then by announcing at a public demonstration that he had sent it, Brandt put the president in an exposed position. Kennedy had no real choice but to do something. If he did not, the crisis of confidence in the credibility of the United States would surely break out—and not just in West Berlin. But Brandt's head, too, was on the chopping block. What if Kennedy did not respond? Then Brandt might well have been just another discredited leader who had gambled and lost. Still worse, the ensuing crisis in West Berlin might have had very grave consequences. Even if Kennedy did respond with action, there was no guarantee that he would do so willingly. If he remained angered by the governing mayor's presumptuousness, there was a good possibility that cooperation between Allies and West Berlin officials would deteriorate rapidly. Among the lesser consequences of this would have been the end of Brandt's own political career, but it might also have led to an Allied willingness to make adjustments with the Soviet Union that could have destroyed the city's future. Kennedy responded positively, however, thereby taking Brandt off the tenterhooks.[54]

Brandt incurred still another risk, albeit of more theoretical than practical import. Since drafting the West German constitution in 1949, Berlin and FRG leaders had sought the full integration of the city–state into the federal system. Allied refusal in principle notwithstanding, Bonn agencies were permitted to play an important role in the city's life and to represent it as far as the outside world is concerned. Brandt had bypassed Bonn totally in his direct appeal to Kennedy. The reason for this was perfectly clear: all efforts to enlist Adenauer's assistance in the early part of the week having proved unsuccessful, it seemed likely that the Chancellor would balk at the idea of a letter to the President. Indeed, Adenauer's sour reaction when he read the letter merely convinced the Berlin leader that he had been right in ignoring Adenauer in the first place. By doing so, however, he had implicitly denied the responsibility of the federal government in general and the Foreign Office in particular as agents for Berlin. This in turn lent credence to the Eastern bloc's claim that West Berlin is a separate political entity distinct from both the German Democratic Republic and the Federal Republic of Germany.

The Political Crisis Abates

Kennedy's response to the political crisis did not end with his decision to answer Brandt's letter. He sent Vice-President Lyndon B. Johnson, accompanied by General Clay, to Berlin to deliver the response to Brandt personally.[55] His military advisers also persuaded him to send a contingent of 1,500 soldiers to strengthen the Berlin garrison.

Initial signs of the West's decision to act came on Thursday. In the early hours of the morning British soldiers erected barbed-wire barriers around the Soviet war memorial in Tiergarten. The Red Army had created this small enclave of Soviet authority in the British sector, about a hundred yards west of the Brandenburg Gate, in the first weeks after Berlin's capitulation, before the arrival of American and British troops. But now, since the East had drawn a barbed-wire line around West Berlin, so, too, the British had isolated this statue of a Red soldier (termed by Berliners the "unknown looter") and its small staff of Soviet guards—ostensibly to protect them from the wrath of the West Berliners. America made its presence felt all day long through helicopter flights along the border. Later in the day the Allies delivered their protest notes to Moscow. "At Last the Right Language!" read the headlines in the following day's *Bild Zeitung,* although the tone and wording of these messages and those sent on Tuesday to the Soviet commandant in East Berlin did not differ significantly. Still another sign of solidarity came from West Germany, where the German Sport Federation announced that it had canceled all athletic contests to be held with East German teams. Friday brought West Berliners the news that the United States planned to strengthen its military forces in Germany, that Ambassador Dowling had visited the sectoral boundary (as had British Ambassador Sir Christopher Steel on the previous day), and that all three political parties had declared their solidarity with Berlin in speeches before the special session of the Bundestag.[56] All these steps notwithstanding, the West had still not undertaken the dramatic steps that Brandt felt were necessary to end the incipient crisis of confidence. News of these steps would not reach Berlin until late that night.

Most Berliners probably did not hear of the full extent of Kennedy's response to Brandt's appeal until they picked up their Saturday morning newspapers. There they learned that Johnson and Clay would arrive in West Berlin (via Bonn) that very afternoon and that reinforcements for the Berlin garrison were expected on the following day. The stopover in the Federal Republic's capital was arranged at the last moment. Learning of the special deputation to Berlin, Chancellor Adenauer had asked whether he might accompany the vice president. Advice from Lightner that Brandt would view Adenauer's appearance at that point as inopportune led the president to veto the proposal. Rather than have it seem as though he were ostentatiously ignoring the chancellor—an act that could be interpreted as Kennedy's mixing into German electoral politics just as much as if he had permitted Adenauer to share with Johnson the spotlight in Berlin—Kennedy agreed to a stopover in Bonn for "consultation" with the West German chief of state.[57]

The welcome awaiting him in Berlin overwhelmed Vice-President Johnson. As many as half a million Berliners lined the streets to cheer as he drove from the airport to Potsdam Square and then on to City Hall. An estimated third of a million stood before the city hall to hear him proclaim America's continuing support for the island city. The high point of his speech, written by Kennedy's White House advisers, came when Johnson said: "To the survival and to the creative future of this city we Americans have pledged, in effect, what our ancestors pledged in forming the United States: our lives, our fortunes, and our sacred honor."[58] After a tremendous ovation, Clay, too, said a few words to "his" Berliners: "Thanks to your courage, with the support of my own countrymen and the support of all freedom-loving people, what we started together twelve years ago we will finish together and Berlin will still be free." As the Freedom Bell again rang out over the city, it seemed to be echoing what the governing mayor had said in introducing Johnson. "On Wednesday we stood here and called out to the world for our brothers in the East," Brandt's husky voice had roared out jubilantly. "The dispatch of American troops and this visit are the answer!"

The rest of the weekend continued in the same vein of triumphal jubilation. Saturday evening Johnson turned over President Kennedy's letter to Brandt. Ambassador Charles E. Bohlen (who, as confidant of the president and special assistant to the secretary of state, had accompanied Johnson and Clay to Berlin) later told the governing mayor that, in the future, he should not hesitate to telephone the president should an emergency arise, but that he should avoid sending letters which could easily be misinterpreted.[59] In the early afternoon of Sunday, August 20, the First Battle Group of the Eighteenth Infantry, a 1,500-man contingent under the leadership of Colonel Grover S. Johns, arrived in West Berlin. The welcome awaiting these American soldiers as they paraded through the center of the city was, if anything, even stormier than that which Johnson had received. Colonel Johns told reporters that it was "the most exciting and impressive reception I've seen in my life, with the possible exception of the liberation of France."[60] Throughout the course of Sunday, in his many chats with Brandt, in his statements to the press, in his greeting to Colonel Johns at the border, and in his talks with refugees at the Marienfelde reception center, Johnson seized upon every opportunity to express his government's and his own solidarity with Germans on both sides of the newly built wall.

By this time the incipient crisis of confidence among West Berliners had been nipped in the bud. Kennedy's response had changed the objective situation of their city little, if indeed at all. Even as Johnson's plane was leaving the runways of Tegel Airport on Monday morning, East German workers were moving equipment into position, preparing for another day of wall building. Nor had the Allies acceded to the bulk of Brandt's proposals (to control the elevated railway, for instance, or to stop the activity of the SED or East German journalists). Brandt was among the first to realize the impracticability or outright undesirability of other proposals, such as the termination of voluntary contacts between East and West Germans.

Brandt's gamble had nonetheless paid off. Even if Kennedy's response had not changed the objective situation, it had undoubtedly been sufficient to satisfy the West Berliners' need for moral support. Ironically, had the president chosen to act earlier, less dramatic measures would doubtless have had the same effect without at the same time running the risk of a clash with the Soviet Union.

Kennedy's gesture did not, however, end the continuing Berlin crisis. In a sense he had had to overreact to the stimulus of the East German border closure of August 13. The very success of the Johnson mission—the vice-president's personal commitment to West Berlin's cause and his subsequent willingness to support a tougher policy, no less than the enthusiastic response of the West Berliners themselves—swayed the administration toward a "harder" line on the Berlin question. In late August, when Adenauer appealed to Kennedy to take renewed steps, the president agreed to send General Clay back to Berlin (but not until after election day) as his permanent personal representative.

Upon his arrival, Clay immediately initiated a policy aimed at restoring the city's Four-power status by forcing the Soviet Union to recognize its own responsibility for East Berlin as well as the rights of the three Western allies in Berlin as a whole.[61] Despite limited successes, this policy sharply increased tension within Berlin. Indeed, at one point, on October 27, Soviet and American tanks faced each other at Checkpoint Charlie, separated by a distance of only a few yards. The administration, not at all anxious to force a showdown in Berlin, began to withdraw support from Clay. Finally, in April 1962, without power and all but isolated from policy making in Berlin, the General resigned his post to return to private life.

In subsequent years the continuing Berlin crisis cooked on a low flame. The city learned to live with the wall. Few, either in the East or the West, appeared ready to take initiatives to change the new status quo. And, with conflicts raging in Southeast Asia, the Middle East, and Africa south of the Sahara, who was going to pay much attention to past or potential conflicts in Berlin? Even the occasional attempts by desperate people to breach the wall lost their newsworthiness. Not until September 3, 1971—a decade after the wall was built—were the former wartime Allies able to agree upon a provisional solution for the Berlin problem. It was not one that tore down the wall. Instead, the Quadripartite Agreement of 1971 provided a basis for later agreements that would make the wall more permeable for West Berliners and reduce the likelihood of conflict in and around Berlin.

2 The Wall and West Berlin's Development

Klaus Schütz

There can be little doubt that August 13, 1961, was an important date for Europe—decisive for what we used to call the "German question" and a turning point for Berlin itself. The construction of the wall changed the internal operation of the city and its living structures. More importantly, it altered what we then termed the city's raison d'être and its prospects for the future. We did not know all this when we saw the wall being built. Looking back, however, I think we felt that this was a critical juncture, that something more significant was occurring than the usual East–West "incident" of which there had been so many over the course of the years.

Those of us working with Willy Brandt's campaign for the chancellorship had been worried that the GDR government was about to undertake something, but we did not think about the possibility of a wall. We were primarily concerned with the huge numbers of refugees entering West Berlin from the East—in the last days before the wall well over a thousand per day. Although we anticipated restrictions of movement in the GDR aimed at halting the refugee flow, we had in mind special permits that might be required of people leaving certain districts of the GDR so as to make it more difficult for them to go to West Berlin.

As it turned out, the wall affected West Berlin in two important respects. The first was that, from one day to the next, the three western sectors were cut off from the eastern sector and their natural environs. The individual citizen was separated from relatives and friends in the East; and for many years there would be a separation of families, not only in Berlin but also between Berlin and the GDR. Second, the wall put an end to those plans and hopes, those illusions and dreams, whatever we may call them, that the reunification of Germany, which many thought was right around the corner, would restore Berlin to its former role as capital and center of the country. Reunification in peace and freedom may still be a political goal, since it is part of the Basic Law of the Federal Republic of Germany, but since August 13 it is no longer a realistic prospect for Germans in the two parts of Germany. The idea that Berlin would be, in the foreseeable future, once again the center of an undivided Germany became, at a stroke, devoid of any political reality.

It must be said that family separations and changed perspectives were not in the forefront of our thinking in the first days and months following the building of the wall. The main problem troubling us was, quite simply, security. The question we asked was very clear and straightforward: was this the beginning of a new assault against West Berlin, something akin to the blockade of 1948 or Khrushchev's ultimatum of 1958? We know now, but did not in those days, that the wall did not change the basic elements of West Berlin's security. There were, of course, military alerts, and there were military preparations. But in retrospect we see that it was not a new blockade or some other assault in a new disguise.

Although the wall changed many fundamental aspects of West Berlin's situation, it did not alter the status of its security. The basic position of the three Western powers was clear even before 1961, and President Kennedy's enunciation of his three "essentials" made this position even firmer: the West would guarantee access to the western sectors of the city, their security, and their viability. These Western guarantees covered all of West Berlin, but not one square foot more. They stopped at the wall. Even so, what was in the center of our thinking in those days was the fact that West Berlin was under Western protection, its security guaranteed by Western power and all that that implied.

But what did it mean to guarantee the *viability* of the city? I must confess that even today I do not know in any precise sense what this guarantee means. Whatever it is, however, it covers many dimensions of West Berlin's life, and it is a dynamic process rather than static institution. Viability in this sense is not only industrialization, although without industry and commerce there can be no viability. It is not only culture and science, although they are important, too. It is not only welfare, housing, and schools. In short, everything impinges on the task of guaranteeing the city's viability, for it includes a good quality of life for its citizens as well as a certain vitality in the development of the city itself. Such a guarantee means to ensure that life in Berlin will be as good and as stable as that in any other part of our society, that West Berlin will continue to exist for all its citizens and those who would like to go to the city.

Just as security was mainly the domain of the three Western allies, so the question of viability needed a German answer. Germans in West Berlin and the Federal Republic had to tackle three kinds of problems: morale, divided families and contacts across the wall, and economic and social stability. These problems are, of course, interlinked. Thus the morale of the population depends directly on the city's internal stability, perceptions of its interests, vitality of its cultural life, and, indeed, all its other institutions. It is also tied directly and reciprocally to the humanitarian aspects of a divided city. Such interlinking notwithstanding, each of the three kinds of problems required its own particular response.

The building of the wall, a profound shock to the *morale* of West Berliners,[1] raised some burning questions. If it was true that the wall was a symbol of the defeat of the Western powers, would there be other and possibly greater defeats in the future? If the Western powers had nothing more at their disposal than mere protest, would they be able and willing to defend West Berlin in another period of trial and tribulation? The immediate answer to such questions was, as I saw it, the decision by President Kennedy to send Vice-President Johnson and General Clay to West Berlin, along with a military brigade transferred from the Federal Republic, as well as, ultimately, his decision to visit the city himself in June 1963, when he made his famous "Ich bin ein Berliner" speech.

Such symbolic steps indicate that the answer to the crisis of morale in West Berlin had to be more or less a psychological one. Shortly after the wall went up, Governing Mayor Brandt wrote to Kennedy demanding "action, not words,"[2] but the fact is that the crisis, being psychological in nature, required a psychological response. Indeed, what kind of action was possible? I know of no one who had a realistic answer to this question. What Germans actually initiated was a series of proposals and measures aimed at boosting West Berliners' morale: Adenauer's idea of what came popularly to be called a "jitters premium," that is, the payment of 100 marks to each individual West Berliner; economic and social improvements to keep people in the city and, more generally, to keep them happy. No one should underestimate this aspect of our response to the wall, since without it low morale would have led to the flight of West Berliners from the city.[3] The problem of morale had to be dealt with, and on all possible levels.

The humanitarian aspect of Berlin's division was not very apparent to us in the first days after the wall went up. We from West Berlin could still go over to East Berlin, to visit members of the Social Democratic organizations in the eastern boroughs, for instance.[4] Even after West Berliners were denied access to the East we felt that, somehow, and probably in the very near future, we would find appropriate formulas and make the necessary arrangements for dealing with divided families and other humanitarian matters. In fact the history of West Berlin's efforts to make such arrangements was long and exasperating. One recalls the bright spots, the Christmas and Easter passes of the early 1960s, but there were long periods when we had neither passes nor other opportunities to keep up our contacts with relatives and friends in the East. We were, in short, not very successful in this regard. But, then, in retrospect it seems unlikely that we could have been more so, since any final resolution of the wide range of humanitarian issues needed agreement among the four Powers, agreement which did not come until 1971.

Here is not the place to go into detail on efforts to strengthen the economic, social, and cultural vitality of West Berlin. Suffice it to say that, taking into account some mistaken initiatives, the most important of these are still to be seen in operation. What was decisive in this respect is not this or that particular proposal, law, or administrative decision. The decisive factor was integrating West Berlin with the economic, social, and cultural system of the Federal Republic. All this cost money, of course, but money alone was not sufficient to bring long-term stability to the city and guarantee its viability.

More important for West Berlin were convincing answers to three basic questions. First, since the city's future relied on the fact that its security was guaranteed by the Western allies, could we find additional ways to underline this commitment and even get the Soviet Union publicly to accept it? Second, since the city's future development relied to a great extent on freedom of access, could we find new ways to shore up the Western commitment to maintaining that access and secure public acceptance of this arrangement by the Soviet Union? Third, since the city's existence was for all practical purposes geared almost entirely to the economic, social, and legal system of the Federal Republic, could we establish de facto links conferred permanently by the Western powers with the explicit consent of the Soviet Union?

With the full support of the Western alliance and significant contributions from all the governments concerned, and especially with the Four-power agreements on Berlin and the subsequent inter-German arrangements, we were able to answer these questions positively. West Berlin, especially in contrast to other areas of the world which have been and continue to be areas of crisis, managed quite well in establishing the cooperative base to overcome a difficult and very intricate crisis. The Western powers, governments in Bonn and West Berlin, and, of course, the citizens of the city have reason enough to be proud of this outstanding achievement.

3 Puzzling about the Wall

Richard L. Merritt

Despite a plethora of published and unpublished analyses of the causes and consequences of the wall in Berlin, a number of puzzles remain to challenge historians, political scientists, and policy makers alike. Some of these puzzles may be solved when we have full access to the documents of the time and memoirs written by participants. Others, however, will doubtless continue to intrigue future generations of analysts.

Before discussing some of the puzzles that I personally find most interesting, it may be useful to note some questions I shall not be asking. The first is, which party was in the right? This question certainly has relevance from a legal or moral perspective. Moreover, it is fraught with implications for the development of international law and the international communist movement. But whether or not the GDR, with approval of the Soviet Union and other Warsaw Pact nations, "should" have built the wall is a question that pales in the face of the fact that it did so. Time and again, such as when it suppressed uprisings in East Germany in 1953, Hungary and Poland in 1956, and Czechoslovakia in 1968, or marched into Afghanistan in 1979, the Soviet Union has taken drastic steps that flew in the face of traditional notions of international law when it has seen its own vital interests at stake.

Another such question is what motivated Walter Ulbricht and the GDR he controlled to build the wall in the first place? The failure of his regime to meet the needs of its citizens is well known. The need somehow to stop the flow of refugees and lessen West Berlin's sirenic role vis-à-vis the GDR and its people made Ulbricht ready for drastic action. Then, too, one might postulate (as I shall discuss later from another perspective) that Ulbricht was anxious to take a leading role in formulating foreign policy goals for the entire Warsaw Pact.

Still another question with which I shall not deal is the extent to which the West knew that the GDR intended to build a wall through the heart of Berlin. The most thorough study published to date of this aspect of the wall crisis indicates that American intelligence had an inkling of what was to come but no hard data to support the theory of a wall as opposed to other theories of what the East intended to do; also, that German intelligence did not have the full story either and, what is more, failed to make effective use of the intelligence it possessed.[1] The use of intelligence in foreign policy making, however fascinating, is a topic that would carry us too far afield here.

This paper instead will focus on the intentions of Soviet and Western leaders and the consequences of some colossal breakdowns in communications among the Western allies. It will raise puzzles, sometimes in a provocative manner, rather than providing definitive solutions to them.

Why Did Khrushchev Want the Wall?

A pair of assumptions underlies the question of why Khrushchev wanted the wall. The first is that 1961 saw Nikita Khrushchev actually in command of the Soviet foreign policy-making apparatus. We know in retrospect that he operated in many regards on the basis of a very tenuous coalition within the Soviet decision-making establishment.[2] The reverses he suffered—in such critical areas as agriculture (Virgin Lands Project) and foreign policy (U–2 crisis of May 1960 and the Cuban missile crisis two and a half years later)—were severe blows to his degree of control, and by 1964 he had suffered enough such reverses that his coalition would collapse while he was on vacation.

In the first half of 1961, however, Khrushchev appears to have been fully in command of Soviet policy making. For one thing, the Soviet Union was doing fairly well in economic and even in international political terms. This was symbolized perhaps most dramatically by the successful ventures into outer space of Yuri A. Gagarin (April 12, 1961) and Gherman S. Titov (August 6–7, 1961). For another thing, American foreign policy appeared to be in a state of disarray. The dismal failure of the episode at the Bay of Pigs (April 17–18, 1961) had made the new American president, young and inexperienced as he admittedly was, appear to be particularly vulnerable. Similarly, the well-known difficulties of the relationship between President John F. Kennedy and Chancellor Konrad Adenauer made inauspicious the prospects for their effective cooperation in any united policy on Berlin and Germany. When Kennedy met with Khrushchev in early June in Vienna, the president faced a man who glowed with confidence.

A second assumption is that Khrushchev's personal approval was required for the GDR to seal off West Berlin's boundaries. Intelligence reports reaching the West indicate that Ulbricht raised the issue at a meeting of the Warsaw Treaty Organization (WTO) on March 28-29, 1961, but was unsuccessful in eliciting support from the Soviet Union or any other country for the drastic measures he was proposing. By the end of July, however, Khrushchev was prepared to call a special meeting of the WTO, held on August 3-5, in Moscow, to sanction the construction of barbed-wire barricades and limited access by GDR citizens to West Berlin. It seems safe to say, in the light of the other WTO members' reluctance to test the West, that Khrushchev's intervention made the crucial difference in the outcome of the latter meeting.

The question is, what made Khrushchev (with, no doubt, the approval of the rest of the Soviet leadership coalition) change his mind? The literature on the Berlin crisis of 1961 provides a stock answer to this question. One part of it is that, ever since November 1958, when he issued his famous ultimatum on Berlin, Khrushchev had intended to take steps to end the threat that West Berlin's existence posed for the GDR. Apparent agreement on basic terms on the part of Secretary of State John Foster Dulles evidently gave him a short-lived hope that the United States would be reasonable on this issue.[3] Later developments nonetheless revealed that the administration of President Dwight D. Eisenhower had no intention of making significant concessions, and talks with Kennedy in Vienna did not indicate that the new administration would be any more prepared to give ground. Only firm action, in this view of Soviet behavior, would resolve the situation.

A second part of the standard interpretation is that the greatly increased flow of refugees from the GDR provided the Soviet Union with the occasion if not the basic grounds for such firm action. The fact that East German authorities deliberately undertook measures to dramatize the continuing crisis caused by this exodus was not seriously questioned. The result was that, by July 1961, an average of 1,000 people fled daily from the GDR—an obviously intolerable situation for the GDR and, Khrushchev argued at the WTO meeting in early August, the socialist world as a whole. Immediate action was required to close off the route used most heavily by refugees, namely, that into West Berlin.

A third part focuses on the risk of such a step. Western intelligence reports indicate that most WTO members considered the risk of sealing off West Berlin too great to take: they thought that it would surely elicit Western countermeasures and possibly even war. Khrushchev could argue, however, that Western leaders had sent clear signals indicating that they would make no such response, provided that Western rights in *West* Berlin remained untouched. "We assumed that the West didn't want to start a war and our assumption turned out to be correct," Khrushchev is supposed to have written in his memoirs; "Starting war over Berlin would have been stupid."[4]

The argument that Khrushchev, after shrewdly guessing Western intentions, seized upon the opportunity provided by drastically increased numbers of refugees to accomplish a long-standing goal is logical and conforms with at least some available facts. It nonetheless raises a number of questions about the Soviet leader's intentions.

Perhaps the most important of these concerns the relationship between the Soviet Union and the GDR. If we accept the proposition that the refugee issue was the occasion for a response, then we must ask what role Khrushchev played in tolerating GDR actions designed to turn the issue into one of major proportions. At the WTO meeting in March 1961 Khrushchev is reported to have told Ulbricht to use internal mechanisms to end such flows of people. In fact Ulbricht did the opposite. Given the extent to which the Soviet Union had penetrated East German political life and the nature of its intelligence network throughout Eastern Europe, can it be that Khrushchev did not know what the East Germans were doing or that he was duped by Ulbricht? But to argue that he did know is to say either that Khrushchev was Ulbricht's accomplice in creating a major problem that required a drastic solution or else that the Soviet Union was powerless to control the course of politics in the GDR. None of these arguments is very plausible.

No less implausible is the proposition that Khrushchev needed the occasion provided by the intensified refugee flow to set in motion his plans for changing the status quo in Berlin. On the one hand, pressure on the East German government might have reduced its citizens' incentives to take flight or increased the controls aimed at deterring it. On the other hand, Khrushchev might have taken any of a series of other unilateral steps—for example, implementing the practice, evidently acceptable to Secretary of State Dulles, of having GDR officials serving as "agents" of the Soviet occupiers, integrating East Berlin fully into the political system of the GDR, perhaps even negotiating a firm declaration, if not an actual treaty, stating that the status of war was replaced by that of peace between the Soviet Union and the GDR. Any attempt by Soviet leaders to design a scale of options would unquestionably have come up with something other than the wall.

Even more difficult to accept is the argument that the refugee problem and the Berlin wall as its only solution were necessary to achieve Khrushchev's goal of stabilizing the German situation. However frequently one may refer to it as a "wall of peace" or "modern state boundary," the wall was and remains a spectacularly visible demonstration of a failure of policy. It said to the world that the GDR was insufficiently attractive to retain its own citizens and that the Soviet Union could exert control insufficient to keep GDR policy makers in line. Moreover, even if Khrushchev was correct in assuming that the West would not go to war over Berlin, he erred greatly in his thinking if he believed that the wall would lead to a demilitarized West Berlin. The result was rather that the United States strengthened its garrison and public resolve to defend the city—besides, of course, creating a situation in which misunderstandings that could lead inadvertently to war (such as the confrontation of Soviet and American tanks at Checkpoint Charlie on October 27–28, 1961) would be more probable. These points must also have been evident to Soviet leaders, including those who were already concerned about Khrushchev's adventurism.

We may, of course, never find out for sure what Khrushchev had in mind when he consented to the construction of the Berlin wall. The standard interpretation, however, ignores some major factors that cry out for explanation and further research. Was Khrushchev merely inattentive to events in the GDR? Or were hardliners in the Red Army or other branches of the Soviet government not providing him with information that could have prevented a fait accompli? Or was his fantasy so poverty-stricken that he could think of nothing other than the rather clumsy policy decision to build a wall?

What Was President Kennedy Trying to Achieve in his Berlin Policy?

The untimely deaths of President John F. Kennedy and his brother Robert robbed subsequent political analysts of key sources on the thinking of the Kennedy administration with respect to the Berlin problem. We are reasonably sure of some things that Kennedy did *not* want. He did not want, for instance, an unthinking continuation of the status quo, which he saw as one in which the 85-year-old West German chancellor determined what American policy on Germany and Berlin would be. Nor, after the fiasco at the Bay of Pigs, did he intend to suffer a similar blow to American prestige in Berlin. What is less clear is what he actually hoped to accomplish.

The standard interpretation of American policy under Kennedy is that the President was prepared to write off the Soviet sector of Berlin in exchange for a defusing of the situation that could help move the superpowers toward some measure of arms limitation. Thus his pronouncements from the very outset substituted the term "West Berlin" where the Eisenhower administration had said simply "Berlin." Nowhere, in this view, was the intentional nature of this symbolic step clearer than in Kennedy's televised address of July 25, 1961. In it he stressed what had by then come to be called the "three essentials": (1) continued Allied military presence in Berlin; (2) unrestricted use of access routes to and from the island city; and (3) freedom for West Berliners to choose their own form of government.

This view of Kennedy's behavior has led to widely varying interpretations. The President's supporters thought that it touched just the right note of firmness together with a willingness to discuss issues. Others have seen in it Kennedy's betrayal of Berlin and America's staunchest ally in Europe, the Adenauer government. From this perspective, the United States should have insisted on Four-power control over the whole of Berlin, as well as continued to push for German reunification on Western terms. Still others, sometimes projecting their own predispositions onto Kennedy,[5] find that the president realistically assessed the strategic situation and acted accordingly. Publicists in the socialist world as well as revisionists in the United States saw Kennedy's actions as aggressive, a "macho" effort to recoup the image of strength lost at the Bay of Pigs, a failure to be sufficiently forthcoming in accommodating Soviet interests in stabilizing the status quo in Central Europe.[6] One also finds the suggestion by some American policy makers and former policy makers that Kennedy simply did not understand the implications of his insistence on guaranteeing only Western presence in and access to a free West Berlin.[7]

In short, the response to a fairly common view of what Kennedy did has been strongly colored by the predispositions of the analysts and how well his behavior matched what the analysts thought *should* have been done. Not all these interpretations are incompatible with each other, to be sure, but together they point to a central intellectual puzzle in the entire Berlin crisis: what was the reality which these varying interpretations sought to reflect? Or, phrased more directly, what did President Kennedy want in Berlin?

The evidence points in two directions. First, Kennedy was seeking to negotiate tacitly with the Soviet Union in a manner not dissimilar to what Charles E. Osgood has called "graduated reciprocal initiatives in tension–reduction" (GRIT). In a stalemate, de-escalation of tension requires one side to take the first step. This can be a positive step toward reducing tension, of course, such as explicitly accepting a condition imposed by one's antagonist, or it can be a refusal to respond negatively to a tension-increasing action taken by the antagonist. (The latter process is akin to the Christian metaphor of "turning the other cheek"— but in doing so the cheek-turner need not abandon weapons that can be used if the antagonist does not respond in kind.) In the case of Berlin, Kennedy was offering a unilateral concession. He was legitimating the Soviet Union's claim to be able to do what it wished in *East* Berlin, in exchange for a Soviet willingness not to push further on *West* Berlin and, possibly, preparedness to enter into arms control negotiations.[8]

Second, Kennedy did not fully appreciate the implications of his actions. At one level, it is not clear that the Soviet Union understood the nature of Kennedy's initiative. Khrushchev's initial response was to see it as a sign that the United States would swallow whatever the Soviet Union should choose to do in the Berlin area. Else would he have been so bold at the WTO meeting in early August 1961 as to endorse such a drastic and self-destructive measure as a wall around West Berlin? It can be (and has been) argued that Khrushchev eventually understood the strategy of GRIT,[9] but its short-term effect was to bolster the Soviet leader's belief that the United States would shy away from any confrontation over Berlin. Perhaps Kennedy was prepared for such a Soviet response, but there is little evidence to suggest that he was.

At another level, Kennedy seriously misjudged the secondary effects of his "message" to the Soviet Union. This was clear on August 13, 1961, the day on which the GDR sealed off the borders of West Berlin. The failure of the United States and its allies to respond vigorously to this measure, at least in a symbolic fashion, produced a crisis of confidence among West Berliners, and confusion in the Federal Republic. (Chancellor Adenauer's comments and behavior at this time did little to ease the tension-filled situation.) Once he was aware of all this, to be sure, Kennedy responded, but the response contained strong elements of overreaction that at least temporarily reduced his control over the events and resulted in more serious crises later.

The sequence of events and policy decisions on Kennedy's part raises some basic questions about his behavior: Did the president fundamentally understand the Berlin situation? Why was he slow in responding to the wall that the East Germans began to build on August 13? Why did he permit General Lucius D. Clay a virtually free hand in September and October 1961 to set American policy in Berlin?

Did Kennedy understand the Berlin situation?
Officials at the State Department have complained that President Kennedy sought to man the "Berlin desk" himself.[10] There were certainly reasons why he should have wanted to follow events and policies in Berlin very closely. The most obvious is that West Berlin was a bone in the Soviet throat. Since Khrushchev's ultimatum of November 1958 the issue of the city's future had been simmering on the back burner, from time to time threatening to explode. Any future dealings with the Soviet Union would have to pass through the bottleneck of Soviet interest in this issue. Then, too, the special role of Germany and Berlin in John Foster Dulles's foreign policy—the part played by his sister, Eleanor Lansing Dulles, in formulating this policy, and the virtual veto right over aspects of American foreign policy which Kennedy felt Dulles had given to Chancellor Adenauer—seemed to make control over policy on this nexus of issues the key to any new foreign policy conceptualization.

The need to pay attention to other matters may nonetheless not have given Kennedy much time to think through the problems associated with Berlin. On a global scale, in the conflict between the superpowers, Berlin may have been a pawn, to be dealt with much as princes of the seventeenth century traded lands and peoples according to the fortunes of war. Alternatively, it was possible to view it as a tender spot in the Western alliance system, one on which the Soviet Union could bring pressure to bear whenever it wished, and hence a spot to be hardened or otherwise made less vulnerable to the caprices of the Kremlin. Or else it could be seen as the symbol of that which tied the United States to decisions made in Bonn.

But, whatever the metaphor used in viewing the Berlin problem, and this seems to be the point Kennedy neglected, the city was an entity unto itself and an important link tying West Europe to the United States. The maintenance of the Allied position in Berlin, in pragmatic if not juridical terms, rested on the morale of the Berliners. Any solution envisioned for the Berlin problems had to take them into account. By the same token, it is the current presence of the United States troops in

West Berlin that gives the ultimate concrete reality to the North Atlantic Treaty Organization and ensures that West Germany will continue to support American security policy. Recent efforts to reduce sharply or even end the American military commitment in West Europe have foundered on several grounds, one of the most important of which is the need to continue the occupation of Berlin. A loss of morale leading to a mass exodus of West Berliners from their city would seriously damage the very basis of the American role in West European security.

It may well be that President Kennedy understood all this in the summer months of 1961. His increasing focus on Berlin as a counter in Soviet–American relations, however, and his failure to take account of the psychological needs of West Berlin's two and a quarter million residents belied such an understanding. Especially problematic in the latter regard was what was widely viewed as callousness in his initial response to news that the East Germans were erecting barriers between the Soviet and Western sectors of the city. After ascertaining that his "three essentials" had not been challenged, Kennedy was content to have a routine note of protest sent to the Soviets before returning to his pleasures of a Sunday afternoon in Hyannis Port. It may well be true, as Walt W. Rostow, Kennedy's deputy special assistant for national security affairs, wrote in 1979, that the president "had thought through the Wall and decided on his policy before the event,"[11] but this is difficult to believe.

Why was Kennedy slow in responding to the wall?

Whatever President Kennedy decided on that Sunday, August 13, it was not communicated effectively to Mayor Brandt until the following Thursday.[12] Nor did the British and French governments do much more than issue protests and silence questioners by saying that they were consulting with their allies. In the meantime, a serious crisis of morale had emerged among West Berliners. On Sunday they watched in disbelief while the barriers were erected and the Allies did nothing; the outrage that spread on Monday as the Allies continued to do nothing was turning by Tuesday into bitterness and the belief that the West had no intention of coming to the assistance of West Berlin. Finally, on Wednesday, facing pressures that were reaching the exploding point, Brandt wrote directly to Kennedy: "Berlin expects more than words," he exhorted; "Berlin expects political action."

After calming down somewhat over the tone of the letter, President Kennedy evidently realized that there had indeed been a breakdown of communications with Brandt's government and that the emerging crisis of confidence needed his serious attention. He responded quickly with the news that both Vice-President Lyndon B. Johnson and General Lucius D. Clay, his personal envoys, would arrive in West Berlin by Saturday, August 19.

These visits, together with a strengthening of the U.S. garrison in West Berlin, may well have assuaged the bruised feelings of the West Berliners.[13] Kennedy's quick if belated action had nipped the incipient crisis of morale in the bud. The remarkable thing, however, is that he had been insufficiently attentive to developments in Berlin to be aware that the crisis was brewing until he received Brandt's letter. This lapsus reinforces the impression that Kennedy did not fully appreciate the nature of Berlin's situation.

Why did Kennedy permit General Clay a free hand?

Worse was yet to come. The very success of the Johnson-Clay mission—the vice-president's personal commitment to West Berlin's cause and his subsequent willingness to support a tougher policy, no less than the enthusiastic response of the West Berliners toward Clay's presence and remarks—swayed the Kennedy administration toward a harder line on the Berlin question. In late August, when Adenauer appealed to Kennedy to take renewed steps, the president agreed to send General Clay back to Berlin as his permanent personal representative.

Upon his arrival on September 19, Clay immediately initiated a policy aimed at restoring the city's Four-power status by forcing the Soviet Union to recognize its own responsibility for East Berlin as well as the rights of the three Western allies in Berlin as a whole. Despite limited successes, this policy sharply increased tension within Berlin. Clay's demonstrative helicopter flights to the exclave of Steinstücken emphasized the fact that it belonged to the West Berlin borough of Zehlendorf but incurred risks with global consequences. At one point, on October 27–28, Soviet and American tanks faced each other at Checkpoint Charlie, separated by a distance of only a few yards. The Kennedy administration, not at all anxious to force a showdown in Berlin, began to withdraw support from Clay. Finally, in April 1962, without power and all but isolated from American policy making in Berlin, General Clay resigned his post to return to private life.

What started out as an effort to repair a breakdown in communications thus created its own dynamic that threatened to destroy what President Kennedy had originally set out to accomplish and much more besides. A tacit concession, which Khrushchev took advantage of, became a serious threat to world peace. Instead of opening the way to talks aimed at limiting arms, the support given to Clay by Kennedy had the superpowers at each other's throats.

We do not yet have a satisfactory explanation of this reversal in American policy. Most writing on the topic, proceeding on the basis of predispositions outlined above, judge the president's behavior in accordance with these selfsame predispositions. Did the thunderous response in Berlin and the United States to the cold-war rhetoric of Johnson and Clay give the president pause to rethink his own attitude toward laying the groundwork for future Soviet–American negotiations on major issues? Had he become persuaded by the "old German hands" in the State Department and elsewhere? Or was Kennedy the "realist" unable to pass up the opportunity that the worldwide outrage against the wall provided to push the Soviet Union further into a corner, to seek a better position of strength from which to deal with Khrushchev? Or did he more simply lose control over Clay's actions?

There are still other questions we might ask ourselves today, two dozen years after the wall went up. Some are of a basic historical nature. Why, for instance, did the wall crisis abate without a resolution of the issues it raised? The tension that built up in the days and weeks after August 13, 1961, persisted into the next year, as numerous East Germans risked and a few lost their lives trying to get out of the GDR, as the wall took on awesomely massive proportions and was enhanced by mine fields and attack dogs, as Western students ignored legality in seeking to help East Germans to escape through tunnels and by means of other subterfuges, as MIG fighter planes skimmed the rooftops in downtown West Berlin. It took a full decade before the four Powers could resolve some of the problems made more pointed by the wall. Other questions are of a more speculative nature: What would have happened had Western troops torn down the barriers erected by the GDR on that Sunday morning in August 1961? What would have happened had a nervous shot been fired at one of the tanks posted at Checkpoint Charlie? Would there have been a different outcome to the Berlin crisis had General Clay not been there in the early autumn of 1961? Would a demilitarized "free city" of West Berlin have been a viable political and economic unit?

These questions, however interesting, must nevertheless take a back seat if we would understand the dynamics of superpower negotiation as they emerged during the Berlin crisis of 1961 and if we would prevent future incidents of this sort (and, in terms of the global struggle between the superpowers, the wall crisis was only an incident, not a major turning point) from being magnified into armed confrontations.

Discussion

SHEPARD STONE: Before we start the general discussion, would you, Francis Mac Ginnis, like to say anything about the British point of view in those days?

FRANCIS MAC GINNIS: I would make two points. The first concerns the immediacy of the problem posed by the wall. In retrospect it may indeed be true that Western governments were too slow to react publicly. But, and this is my second point, there was very little they could have done about the wall. There was an underlying assumption in some of the contributions this morning that the Allied writ ran throughout Greater Berlin. But that was never in fact the case. From 1945 onward the Western allies were never in a position to exercise military or executive power in the eastern sector, although perhaps it was not until the uprising of 1953 that this fact became completely clear. Building the wall did not really change anything in that respect.

I wonder too whether it is fair to charge President Kennedy with overreacting subsequently. One must never lose sight of the fact that in Berlin East–West relations do ultimately come down to a test of willpower. If necessary the West has to be prepared to face an eye-to-eye confrontation. To suggest that pre-August Kennedy viewed Berlin as just another counter on the international checkerboard is to ignore this fundamental fact. I doubt whether that is fair. Although British ministers may not have understood all the various legal intricacies, what they certainly did understand was the nature of the Western commitment and its fundamental importance, not only to two and a quarter million West Berliners and to the German people, but also to the North Atlantic alliance itself.

DAVID KLEIN: Although the case of General Clay may suggest that Kennedy was overly attentive to the views of the military,[14] he remained firmly in control of American policy regarding Berlin. While some of his advisers, most notably those around Arthur Schlesinger, felt that the inactivity of the past administration had made the crisis sharper, this view ultimately did not prevail; as Richard Neustadt has pointed out, the president had learned what many of his advisers did not, namely, that action is not always necessary, and sometimes it is very important to decide not to act.

Kennedy's purpose was to establish a dialogue with the Soviet Union to preserve the peace.[15] But there were also immediate crises and challenges which taxed the Western alliance and to which there were no easy answers. Berlin was one of these within the broader framework of East–West confrontations. There was a certain realization of the nature of the problem and concern about the possibility of error, since those who run governments are, after all, human. But the alternatives in the situation were not either sacrificing the morale of two and a quarter million West Berliners or taking the world to a nuclear war. There was a substantial middle ground.

MARTIN HILLENBRAND: An answer to the question of why Khrushchev did not do much at the beginning of 1961 lies in the fact that it was the breaking-in period for the Kennedy administration. Khrushchev had in effect written off Eisenhower at the failed summit of May 1960 in Geneva because of the U-2 incident and evidently decided then to have a moratorium on the Berlin question until the new administration took over. The Bay of Pigs incident perhaps misled him into thinking that Kennedy was going to be somewhat of a patsy. Then, too, the way in which Khrushchev roughed up Kennedy at the Vienna meeting both verbally and by means of threats was significant in the eyes of both the President and some of his entourage, both the hardliners among them and those who emphasized the necessity for negotiations.

As a result of Kennedy's confrontation in Vienna with Khrushchev, the United States government went through a tremendous exercise that led to presidential decisions in early summer to build up the military, call up the reserves, and engage its North Atlantic Treaty allies in discussions, first at the Four-power ministerial level, and then for NATO as a whole. All this produced, prior to the wall, a psychology in the West epitomized in an influential memorandum prepared by Dean Acheson on June 29, which called for a tough Western stance to defend its vital interests in West Berlin: continued Allied presence, access to the city, and the security and viability of the city.

The wall itself, in the view of both Kennedy and those of us in the State Department who were dealing with the question, was an illegal monstrosity and yet, given the real drain of top-flight East Germans in what was popularly called a *Torschlusspanik,* the kind of action that seemed inevitable in one form or another.[16] The question of whether or not, or the extent to which, Western intelligence failed to predict the

East's behavior is intriguing, but the fact is that the precise form this behavior took was not generally predicted. That it turned out to be a wall keeping East Germans from fleeing, however, produced a mixed reaction in Washington. First came a sense of relief that it was nothing more than a wall. Once an appreciation of the wall's effect on Berlin had come home, a feeling emerged that something had to be done.

It is quite clear that the appointment of Clay was not one that was particularly sponsored by the Department of State at that point. It was a decision taken pretty much in the White House—and, judging from the several statements which he made, it was a decision the president learned to regret. Clay was a much more powerful and potent personality, independent in his thinking and in his conduct, than anyone had thought he would be. The decision to send him to Berlin showed, perhaps, a certain lack of prior experience with the man.

Once Clay was in Berlin and had taken various initiatives, the White House was faced with a problem, and so was the State Department. Clay, who had become a symbolic figure, could not be withdrawn arbitrarily and summarily from Berlin, for that would have had a bad effect on morale in Berlin and negative political consequences in the United States. The policy adopted was progressively to restrict his authority, to hem in his ability to maneuver in Berlin, to the point where he finally got fed up and quit. This is not to deny that the things he did while in Berlin were a necessary stimulant to Berlin morale. Despite the various conflicting currents, which were very complicated, his net impact on Berlin morale was a positive one. Even the confrontation of Soviet and American tanks at Checkpoint Charlie, especially given the motives involved and hesitancies on both sides, did not have the global implications attributed to it by Professor Merritt.

DAVID KLEIN: I do not think that the Clay mission was thought through. He in fact had no place in the organization scheme when he got to Berlin. After Clay's helicopter trip to Steinstücken, however, and still more after the confrontation of the tanks at the sectoral boundary, the problem was: how do we pull this guy back without having a great political flap in the United States? After the Bay of Pigs fiasco, the recall of General Clay could have meant another MacArthur affair in the United States. Although this was a problem, Kennedy was not careless in dealing with it.[17]

DIETER MAHNCKE: What exactly was it that troubled Kennedy about the Clay mission? I mean, if Kennedy indicated that he was unhappy with Clay, what exactly was he unhappy about?

MARTIN HILLENBRAND: Not too long after Clay had arrived in Berlin, Kennedy decided that he had been mistaken in sending him, and the instructions going to Clay became increasingly restrictive. Clay, meanwhile, was acting increasingly independently of the U.S. Army Commander in Europe, General Bruce C. Clarke, as well as the U.S. commandant in Berlin, Major General Albert Watson II; the American ambassador to the Federal Republic, Walter Dowling, was anxious to reassert his own authority. The critical juncture came with the confrontation at Checkpoint Charlie. And, while it is true that lines of authority in Berlin were not completely clear at that time, it was pretty much Clay who sent the American tanks to the border crossing. Khrushchev sent a message saying that he was alarmed. As it turned out, however, no one in the State Department was informed about what was happening in Berlin.

DAVID KLEIN: It was General Lauris Norstad, the NATO commander, whose equipment Clay was using and who ultimately put the bee on Clay.

DIETER MAHNCKE: Policy analysts tend to overestimate the extent to which central policy makers are able to exert control over detailed points, that is, over the execution of the details of policy. What is important for an effective policy is to delegate authority to the "right" people, those who can muster authority and are able to use their leeway effectively. Clay was sent to Berlin to do a job: to raise morale. And this he did very successfully. Of course, every effort at raising morale involved risk, although it was obviously considered manageable, at least by Clay himself. It seems somewhat easy now to quibble after the fact about whether Kennedy would have preferred this or that in the detailed execution of the mission. If indeed there were things that Clay did that later on were judged to have been carried out poorly, what were they? We need to be precise here. To what extent, for example, were personal jealousies on the part of other American authorities involved?

ROGER MORGAN: When speculating about Soviet motives and asking why Khrushchev took the steps he did, Richard Merritt said that apparent agreement on basic terms on the part of Secretary of State John Foster Dulles had given him hope that the United States would be reasonable. It is doubtful that Khrushchev put that much credence in the sentiments Dulles expressed, for they were denied very soon after they were made. The two sets of remarks nonetheless raise some general issues that merit further attention. The first was Dulles's immediate reaction to Khrushchev's ultimatum in November 1958, when he said that perhaps one should think about an international agreement on access to West Berlin. This same idea came up again in negotiations during spring 1962 and in the kinds of plans Secretary of State Dean Rusk and Foreign Minister Anatoly Dobrynin were considering at the time. The second was the remark by Dulles to the effect that German reunification did not have to come through a free election, that we could also think about a confederation of the two German states. This remark certainly produced a bad impression in Bonn and probably in Berlin as well.[18] But, to return to my original point, we do not have much evidence that Khrushchev himself was much impressed by either assertion, especially since both were subsequently set aside by the Americans.

HANS OTTO BRÄUTIGAM: I was a student in West Germany at the time the wall went up, but I remember vividly the pictures which appeared on television. This was the view that most of the German public had of the wall. They saw it as a further escalation of tension between East and West, a process which had been going on for some time, and as an assault on West Berlin's security, at the weakest point of the dividing line between East and West. It hit at the morale of all Germans, especially, of course, the Berliners. However we interpret the significance of the wall today, we should not lose sight of this central fact.

From the vantage point of over twenty years later we can also see that the wall was a turning point in Soviet policy toward the West as a whole. It was a decision to consolidate East Germany and to forgo for the time being any further expansion into Western Europe. It was perhaps also a decision against further pursuit of the ideas that had appeared in the famous Soviet note of March 1952 which proposed Germany's reunification under certain conditions. In this viewpoint—and possibly some people shared it in 1961—the building of the wall could be seen as a decision against further attempts to gain control over West Berlin.

Back in 1961, however, we, as Germans, certainly did not feel that way. Thus, while I would not disagree with Ambassador Schütz's argument that the wall was an important step affecting the German question in that it drew a very strong line that would separate a people for a long time to come, I would argue that the wall was also a monument to a very artificial situation in the middle of Europe. It, too, is a part of our everyday reality. In concentrating here on the events of August 1961, we should not leave aside their meaning and consequences for the world today or their impact on its peoples.

SHEPARD STONE: The wall also stripped away much of the propaganda and rhetoric as to what the West and the Federal Republic would do and led to the chain of events that culminated a decade later in the Quadripartite Agreement. Herr Gradl, you were there.

JOHANN BAPTIST GRADL: It is a bit difficult for someone who was in Berlin during the entire period to talk about all of this. The city's leaders were faced with a very serious situation. It was a complete surprise to the people. I was awakened during the night and, very early in the morning, went to a few spots along the border near Klein-Machnow. Few people were out, but what heartrending scenes there were! People from the western sectors hurried to the crossing points where they had previously met with friends and relatives in the eastern sector. Standing between them, however, were some kind of soldiers, not always in uniforms one could identify, so the people just stood there, waiting.

It is also difficult for a German, even today, to criticize the behavior of our Allied protectors, and I am not here to make accusations. But it is true that we asked ourselves then: Is that all? Does the West have to accept this? I understood completely what Willy Brandt meant when he wrote that the Berliners wanted "action, not words." We were also aware of the fact that, on the eastern side of the barriers, people were behaving very carefully. I personally saw no Soviet soldiers there, on Potsdam Square, but only the troops of the People's Police. Naturally we questioned whether or not this was an indication that the authorities in the East were not quite sure about what they were doing.

No one in the West had known exactly what was planned. We had all heard rumors circulating that the East intended to close the borders to Berlin, but they always emphasized the whole of Berlin and did not even hint that a border would be put right through the middle of the city. We heard such reports from visitors, in the Christian Democratic Union's Eastern Bureau, and even over the radio. That something was afoot was no secret. What came was nonetheless a total surprise. Berliners were especially shocked that their Four-power city could be thus divided and its residents separated from one another.

The man on the street had expected more from the Allies. As I stood that morning near Potsdam Square, I heard a man say, "It's about time that the Allies did something." Another man responded, "They'll just make another protest!" These people thought that something had to be done. The troops on the eastern side were unarmed, it occurred to me, so it would not even be necessary to use weapons: "Why don't we," I asked myself, "simply send over bulldozers to knock down the fenceposts holding the barbed wire?" The general sentiment was that something like this should not be permitted in the Four-power city—at least not with our acquiescence. In those first days of uncertainty about what was happening and doubt springing up from the behavior of our Allies, such arguments were heard all over Berlin.

Only one thing was clear: we should not lose our courage. From their behavior we knew that the Soviets, although intent on carrying through their plans to build a wall, still respected the power of our Allies. That these Allies intended to continue protecting us gave us encouragement.

A final word: I would warn against considering the wall as a stabilizing factor in European politics. It has endured for twenty years, to be sure, and may even have influenced the current international situation, but in the long run it is destabilizing.

MICHAEL SODARO: I should like to pursue a bit further the question of Soviet intentions, especially the question of why Khrushchev changed his mind between March and August 1961 regarding a wall in Berlin. One reason, ironically, may be similar to the considerations that impelled President Kennedy to send Johnson and Clay to Berlin: like Kennedy, Khrushchev had to address a crisis of confidence, of low morale, in his German ally. After all, ever since 1958 he had been promising to secure legitimacy for the GDR, if not through a pact with the West, then through a separate treaty between the Soviet Union and East Germany. By summer 1961 neither had been signed. Ulbricht was in a position to exert enormous pressure on Khrushchev, who was out on a limb, and may even have felt he could encourage emigration from the GDR as a means to force Khrushchev's hand.

A second consideration was that the Soviets and, presumably, the East Germans saw the United States and especially Kennedy in a weak position after the Bay of Pigs incident and the Vienna meeting. Their feeling that the time was ripe to do something forceful in Berlin may have been strengthened by Senator Fulbright's remarks on July 30 in a televised interview in the United States, when he said that the Soviet Union and the East Germans had the power and the right to close the border. It is doubtful that Ulbricht got the idea of building a wall from Fulbright, but the fact that the chairman of the Senate Foreign Relations

Committee would make such a statement was a clear sign that powerful figures in the United States were prepared to accept such a solution.

Third, although I would agree that Khrushchev was pretty much in control of Soviet foreign policy during this period, his domestic difficulties cannot be ignored. Groups within the military and other sectors of the Soviet political system had compelled him to scuttle the summit conference in mid-1960, and, I would suggest, were trying a year later to force Khrushchev to bite the bullet on the Berlin question once and for all.

The decision to build a wall was, of course, a "solution" from the Soviet point of view. It was not, however, a victory for Ulbricht, who did not get his separate treaty—and we may recall that, after Khrushchev's fall in 1964, Ulbricht had some nasty things to say about him, especially that Khrushchev had not dealt with him squarely. But did the Soviets in fact have any alternatives to this solution? One might have been to dump Ulbricht, but that would have been very difficult. Another might have been to come up with an agreement satisfactory to Ulbricht and the West, but it was precisely this that Khrushchev had been unable to do since 1958. It is difficult to escape the conclusion that, when he agreed to support building the wall, Khrushchev was acting out of weakness both in domestic and foreign policy terms.

RENATA FRITSCH-BOURNAZEL: If we view Khrushchev's position from a cybernetic perspective, we might ask what signals the West had given him during the period we are considering. Signals are important in crisis situations, as we saw, for example, before the Korean war, when Dean Acheson outlined an American defense perimeter that did not include South Korea. In the Berlin situation we saw, in addition to Fulbright's comments, those of Dulles on appropriate modes of German reunification and especially Kennedy's televised speech in which he clearly enunciated the three "essentials" applying to West Berlin. Even Ulbricht may have been sending a signal to the West or his own population when he stated on June 15 that no one had intended to build a wall. Signals may, of course, be misinterpreted, but they cannot be ignored.

Moving to a different point, we might question the extent to which the Soviets linked the situation in Berlin to their desire to change the status quo in the Caribbean by planting missiles in Cuba. Constructing the wall may well have been the starting point in a Soviet strategy to change the world's balance of power by putting pressure on the United States.

Finally, I think we should not ignore the destabilizing effect that West

Berlin had and continues to have on the GDR by its mere existence. We saw this in 1980 again, when two well-known Soviet journalists wrote a series of articles about the GDR, in which they pointed to the destabilizing effect of visitors from the West and even Western television programs. (One article in the series was entitled, "The Enemy Comes to the Hearth Every Evening.") Eventually the East German communist party chief, Erich Honecker, spoke out on television against the insidious impact of too much interaction with Westerners, and the government raised drastically the financial outlay West Berliners and West Germans had to make to visit the GDR. If visits and television programs are seen even now as a threat, it is not difficult to imagine the destabilizing effect of the open border up through August 1961. Quite possibly in March of that year Khrushchev did not realize, as he did some months later, that through the steady flow of refugees and other problems the GDR was once again becoming the weakest link in the chain of socialist countries.

CLAUS DUISBERG: It struck me while listening to Klaus Schütz's presentation that all the elements he listed as consequences of the wall find parallels in the East. To be sure, the wall, by stopping the drain of people, helped the GDR to consolidate itself and become economically viable, but it had other effects as well. One was on the morale of the East Germans. The Western response to the wall made it clear to Germans on both sides of the border that Western guarantees were limited to the three western sectors of Berlin, that the boundary between the two sides of the city was definite, and that there would be no attempt on the part of the West (perhaps also not by the East) to change the new status quo. The option that East Germans had previously had—life in a different system through emigration—ceased to exist for all practical purposes. They would now have to adjust their thinking to living permanently in the GDR. That started the process of consolidation in East Germany.

Although the GDR still is hardly a consolidated state, it is considerably more consolidated now than it was before the wall was built. Its internal stability continues to hinge to a large extent on the existence of the wall. The stability that has been established nonetheless made possible the agreements of 1971 and subsequently provided for more contacts between East and West Germans.

KLAUS SCHÜTZ: I want to return to the role of General Clay, this time from the perspective of the West Berlin government. As far as I can recall, we never had the impression that Clay went beyond the general mandate that President Kennedy or his administration had given him. When, in his first speech after arriving in the city, he spoke of freedom for Berlin, I doubt that anyone really thought he was referring to East Berlin. When he took tanks to Checkpoint Charlie, we did not really think that he intended to go one step further, to take some kind of action in East Berlin itself. General Clay fulfilled his mission here, I think, because he was a very stabilizing factor.

Second, it bears repeating that the city was, to all intents and purposes, divided before August 1961. There was movement across the sectoral boundaries, but in administrative terms there were two separate units. The wall did not change this latter fact, nor did it change the status of the four Powers. For one thing, even after the wall the Western allies continued to send patrols into East Berlin, the commandants visited the theater there, and so forth. For another, since there was never a Western commitment to East Berlin, it would not be realistic to expect that the West could have done much for morale there. In short, what Clay and the others did was in the framework of what was there before the wall.

Third, in response to Hans Otto Bräutigam, I would say that the wall was decisive for what was then called the "German question" because it forced us to rethink the situation and begin planning for what was a new one. Although perhaps little of practical importance changed, the building of the wall meant that there was no more room for dreams and illusions. It meant an end to plans and policies based on the assumption that Germany would be reunified in the foreseeable future. Moreover, though we may want to discuss what we mean by "permanent," the endurance of the new status quo for the last two decades suggests the kind of permanence that made possible the *Ostpolitik* of the 1970s and the series of agreements that facilitated contracts between East and West in Germany.

DAVID KLEIN: I would agree with Klaus Schütz that the wall was a relief to everyone—including the West Germans, although it is very hard for a West German politician to say that in public. It provided stability on both sides of the frontier. (Indeed, I discovered in subsequent war games that the American military took satisfaction in the fact that, given the consolidation created after 1961, a problem on the frontier seemed much less likely to develop into a more serious conflict.) Without the stabilizing influence of the wall, including its role as a visible symbol of division, we would not have obtained the Four-power agreement.

RONALD FRANCISCO: If the wall ever comes down, it will be taken down by the same governments that put it up. But to understand the probability of this occurring requires that we know why they built the wall in the first place. What did the Soviets and the GDR hope to accomplish? One way to answer such a question is to look at what they did after they built the wall.

After the wall the GDR changed its policy toward its own population in significant respects. It was, of course, unpleasant for many, such as those East Berliners who continued to adhere to the Social Democratic party (but even many of them managed to get into the West). In the agricultural sector, however, with many of the more recalcitrant farmers having already left and with the rest having no place to go, a full-scale policy of collectivization could be implemented—and a rather successful one at that. This crash program, carried out in the first half year after August 1961, contributed substantially to the consolidation that several participants have mentioned.

To pick up on a theme introduced by Michael Sodaro, I would say that, far from the Soviets' timing of the wall suggesting an emergency, it could hardly have come at a better time from their point of view. In addition to American frustration in the wake of the Bay of Pigs incident, Soviet leaders could note their enhanced prestige due to Soviet accomplishments in outer space, success in bringing the Cossacks into line, and a rapidly improving situation as far as food was concerned. In fact, at the time the Soviet Union was supplying 96 percent of East Germany's foreign grain needs. In short, it was a good time to do something. And, we know from other incidents, when they can choose a time to do something, the Soviets will do it at a time when they do not need resources from the West. When they want to invade Czechoslovakia, they will do it when they do not need Western credits; when they want to invade Afghanistan, they will do it when they have just bought 20 million metric tons of grain and can hold out for a while.

Once the wall was built, the Soviet Union and East Germany undertook policies that turned out to help consolidate the country. What is more, the policies were rather more gentle than most people had anticipated. They provided more resources than expected to ease the burdens of collectivization, raised industrial wages, and were more responsive to the needs of consumers. They were, in short, on the road they needed to travel before they could take down the wall.

SHEPARD STONE: That the wall is becoming simply another fact of life was shown once again recently when Erich Honecker visited Japan, where he received a tremendous reception. At a press conference a Japanese reporter asked him about the wall. Honecker replied, "Oh, you know, every day it gets easier and easier for both sides, for us East Germans and the West Germans, to come and go across the wall." And that was the end of the story. No one asked him any other questions on the topic. His assertion that the wall is now a very pleasant place where both East and West can cross was simply accepted.

FRANCIS MAC GINNIS: The question of whether or not the West could have prevented the construction of the wall or torn it down subsequently is one that is very often raised in Berlin. I once asked the British commandant at the time, Major General Rohan Delacombe, the same question. His answer was very simple. "Of course I could have, and so could the Americans and the French," he said; "but then they would have built it a hundred yards back and, you know, how far did I want to send my tanks in?" This remark illustrates the fact that the West really had no control over what the Russians did in their own sector of Berlin. It had been decided at the time of the uprising in 1953 and, still more directly, in the Hungarian crisis of 1956 that the line drawn across Europe in 1945 was not going to be infringed upon.

In Berlin the West had to draw a sharp distinction between the troops merely holding on to what they had and venturing beyond that, venturing into the eastern sector to tear down the wall and open the closed streets. The position of the West in Berlin was and is simply too exposed to risk starting a military intervention in the eastern sector (or giving the Russians a precedent for intervention in the western sectors). The real task was political, and that meant, as Klaus Schütz pointed out, maintaining the security and viability of the western sectors as well as the morale of their people. In these respects, we and West Berlin did not come out too badly.

SHEPARD STONE: But, we must still ask whether or not there were other alternatives. A government need not respond to a threat or other initiative at the place it occurred, but can look around to see where counterpressure can be applied elsewhere. Were we too excited to think of such things as the trade embargoes and Olympic boycotts the United States applied after the Soviet invasion of Afghanistan? In short, were there any real alternatives to merely pushing back the wall?

KLAUS SCHÜTZ: In this respect I should note that, so far, we have spoken about the actions of the Soviets, the East German government, and West Berlin, but we have not asked what Bonn did. The only thing that happened there was that Chancellor Adenauer sought out the Soviet ambassador to tell him that he did not believe the West would go to war. While we in Berlin were angry, Bonn remained quiet. I do not think that Paris, London, or Washington gave much thought to alternatives either.

MARTIN HILLENBRAND: It is fair to say that no one in Washington, and I believe that the same was true of London and Paris, seriously contemplated or advocated military action in response to the wall.

SHEPARD STONE: Was there any action other than military that conceivably could have affected the situation?

MARTIN HILLENBRAND: The wall has to be seen as one episode in a much larger process of planning, a process of planning that had begun at the outset of the Kennedy administration, produced the basic decisions made prior to the wall, and continued after the wall crisis had receded toward the background of world events. So far as I am aware, there was no serious consideration given to countermeasures to be taken specifically because of the wall.[19]

JOHANN BAPTIST GRADL: I am familiar with Adenauer's comment. We have, I think, seen few situations in which responsible leaders—and not only in the Federal Republic—were so helpless as on the first Sunday and Monday of the wall crisis. I recall that Prime Minister Harold MacMillan made a rather similar comment and then went off to Yorkshire to hunt grouse. My impression is that the Western leaders struck an agreement at the very outset to avoid anything that could turn the situation into an armed conflict. When members of his own party asked Chancellor Adenauer why he did not go immediately to Berlin, he responded: "What shall I say there? If I say what the people want to hear, then I simply do not know how they will react, what they will do." As Dietrich Spangenberg, one of Brandt's closest advisers at the time, said recently at a conference, "We in City Hall had organized a demonstration, but we were terrified that someone would say the wrong thing, something that would cause the mass of people to explode." Subsequently, when Adenauer wanted to go to Berlin, people simply stared at him. He was not permitted to go to Berlin with Johnson. Later, of course, he did do so.

UWE SCHLICHT: I should like to ask David Klein what he meant when he said that the construction of the wall brought stability to both sides, to the German Democratic Republic and, on the other side, West Berlin and the Federal Republic. That it helped stabilize the GDR is clear to me, but what about the West? Does destroying the dream or desire for reunification provide stability?

DAVID KLEIN: I suspect that the dream of reunification remains. What the wall does is to reduce the kinds of incidents that could create unrest and other problems. The wall solidified what was the physical reality and, by destroying any expectation that the division of Germany would soon end, provided a kind of stability that was not possible before. It does not get in the way of any long-term dream of reunification.

HANS OTTO BRÄUTIGAM: While the wall may have provided a certain external stability, particularly for the GDR, it and what followed can hardly be termed a success story for East Germany. Even today the wall is necessary for the GDR's very existence. It is precisely the need for this particular kind of support that reveals the artificiality of the state itself. It underlines the fact that, although the Federal Republic has not made this a tenet of its foreign policy, the German question remains unsettled, simply because problems cannot be settled in this way. This demonstration of the very provisional state of affairs in Germany is, I think, a source of constant dissatisfaction for a certain segment of the GDR's population—and in a much more acute sense than we on our side can feel this dissatisfaction.

JOHN KORNBLUM: To ask whether or not the West had alternatives to allowing the wall to be built may be futile. In the years after 1945 both the East and the West had to deal with the division of an old and traditionally very powerful continent into two, rather shaky spheres of influence—less stable, perhaps, in the East than in the West—both of which needed to be solidified. In the West, for example, we developed the North Atlantic Treaty Organization and an approach to the German question that ensured the Federal Republic's adherence to the Western alliance. Accordingly, in August 1961 both sides were thinking more about how to maintain stability and consolidate what they had than about going off into new adventures. The West did not even consider the alternative that, ten years later, seemed quite plausible to some: trying to bring the GDR into a manageable situation, as opposed to refusing to recognize or have any dealings with that country.

The question of whether or not the wall is stabilizing or "permanent" also must be answered in terms of this long-term historical process of dealing with Europe's division. The process is a continuing one, not to be fixed permanently by an event in August 1961 or September 1971 or whenever, and it will go on as long as there are two blocs of countries with opposing philosophies and two superpowers with opposing interests. In this sense one could certainly agree that the wall generated a degree of stability, in that it forced upon us the need for medium-term management of a very difficult situation. This was more stability than we had before. But, at the same time, it is a dynamic stability, not one that fixes the Berlin situation for all times.

DAVID KLEIN: Historically speaking, the East sought to consolidate its gains after the war, and so did the West. With the building of the wall, however, there came another kind of thinking: how one builds on the division that exists and, in effect, secures general recognition of that existence. The Kennedy administration clearly recognized this point. In his speech in June 1963 at the American University, Kennedy made it clear that the American goal was to negotiate with the Soviet Union and preserve the peace; in a later speech at the Free University of Berlin he added that the reunification of Germany was not right around the corner, that we would have to live for a long time with Germany's division.[20] The Federal Republic demonstrated its recognition of that point when it initiated its *Ostpolitik*.

JAMES COONEY: The three basic conditions for West Berlin's stability cited by Klaus Schütz—access, linkages with the FRG, and a Western commitment to the city's security—presume the existence of the wall. This raises the question of when one accepted the wall as a fait accompli, that is, gave up trying to bring the wall down and moved ahead toward new types of commitments. I should like to ask Ambassador Schütz three questions on this point. Was there at the time a debate within the West Berlin government on this transition in perspectives? Were there factions in West Berlin pushing in both directions? And what connections to Bonn did West Berlin have in trying to argue its case there?

KLAUS SCHÜTZ: We really did not consider such questions in the first days. We were primarily concerned with security and morale. Even later, when such questions arose, there were no strong differences among the parties (in part because at that time there was a coalition government in West Berlin of Social Democrats and Christian Democrats).

HELGA HAFTENDORN: One must distinguish between short-term and long-term stability in considering the effects of the wall. In the short run, as far as the Federal Republic was concerned, it had a destabilizing effect. It probably contributed to the CDU's poor showing in the subsequent election and to the credibility gap that arose over the foreign policy course of the next half dozen years. It also revealed basic flaws in the FRG's policy on Germany, which rested on the assumption that the GDR could not be maintained as a Soviet pawn in the face of the West's policy of strength. It thus led to an extensive debate in the FRG as we rethought our policy toward the East and especially the GDR. One recalls the many books by Peter Bender and others, Egon Bahr's policy of "change through approaching one another," the memorandum of the Evangelical Church in Germany (EKD), and Gerhard Schroeder's "policy of small steps" in dealing with the East European countries. Accordingly, although I would agree that the wall provided for long-term stability on both sides, its short- and medium-term effects shook the foundations of the FRG's Eastern policy and led to an extensive, and fruitful, debate on the future of that policy.

RICHARD MERRITT: Ambassador Schütz, given the importance of the morale factor in the first days after the wall went up, what was the West Berlin government doing about the fact that Kennedy was not responding meaningfully to the developments? What did the government in West Berlin know about what Kennedy was going to do?

KLAUS SCHÜTZ: In August 1961 we were engaged in a bitter electoral campaign in the FRG in which strong words were being exchanged (such as Adenauer's claim that the election of the SPD would mean the "end of Germany"). So, while we had to deal with problems of morale in West Berlin, we also were concerned with voting morale in other parts of Germany. Governing Mayor Brandt, as the SPD's candidate for the chancellorship, had to give up campaigning for at least ten days to attend to the situation in West Berlin.

When we resumed the campaign, we realized that a new strategy was needed. For instance, we had to take a step that was unusual in those days: renting airplanes to meet with voters in the various parts of the country. The West Berliners on the campaign trail had to be in the city for five or six hours every day to keep up local morale and then fly off to try to pick up some votes somewhere else. In Washington, perhaps, or in Moscow people were thinking calmly about the situation, trying to figure out what to do next. We were not able to do this. We were underway all the time.

In the absence of any reaction from Bonn we had to hammer with all means possible on the administration in Washington. This meant, as

Shepard Stone knows very well, using private as well as official channels. Incidentally, we were delighted when we heard that Kennedy was sending Clay to Berlin, because he was exactly the man we wanted to have in a situation such as the one that confronted us.[21] Everything boiled down to one simple task: to get as much support as possible from the leading power, that is, from Kennedy and the United States.

SHEPARD STONE: What role did the wall play in the outcome of the election?

KLAUS SCHÜTZ: I do not know whether or not it changed any votes. It did place additional burdens on Brandt and change the nature of the electoral campaign.

JOHANN BAPTIST GRADL: Proceeding from Klaus Schütz's description of the situation, that is, an electoral struggle during the middle of which a wall was built in Berlin, one might ask how appropriate it was that the governing mayor of the city was the leading candidate of one political party. At a time when West Berlin and its governing mayor needed the support of all parties, was not Brandt's continued candidacy endangering the city as a whole?

RICHARD MERRITT: Several nagging questions still remain. For instance, what was the relationship between Ulbricht and Khrushchev? Was Ulbricht in fact trying to tip Khrushchev's hand by creating, possibly with the cooperation of the Soviet military, a fait accompli?

SHEPARD STONE: Do you really believe that Ulbricht could have done anything without talking to Khrushchev first?

RICHARD MERRITT: It strikes me as being quite possible. Khrushchev was very busy that year. He had the space flights of both Gagarin in April 1961 and Titov on August 6. He had the continuing battle with his own military. The latter, we have learned, was not always playing fair with Khrushchev. There were factions in the military that would have been pleased to see Khrushchev knocked down (and ultimately these factions won out). It is quite conceivable that Ulbricht and the East German military were painting a picture of circumstances in the GDR that was less than accurate and, speculating a bit further, that some Soviet generals were for their own reasons receptive to the GDR's message. I strongly suspect that Khrushchev simply did not have complete and accurate information about what was actually taking place and what its consequences would be.[22]

Similarly, I am still not certain why it took the administration in

Washington four days to respond in any other than a token fashion to an emergency in Berlin. As Dieter Mahncke has pointed out, in any government there are many slips in policy, but we are speaking here of a major gap.

I would be interested to learn from Ambassador Schütz or others whether or not anything would have prevented the crisis of confidence that emerged. Suppose, for example, that President Kennedy had gone on television that very Sunday afternoon with a very strong statement worded carefully to condemn the actions of the East without arousing West Berliners to storm the wall and throw bricks at the East Germans. Such a step would surely have been more effective than the innocuous communiqué issued anonymously and routinely by the State Department. From my worm's eye view as a student then living in West Berlin, I can report that, when on August 13 I saw the armored personnel carriers and water cannons at the incipient wall, I wanted the president of the United States to do something. I did not want him or anyone else marching in to start World War III, to be sure. But a strong symbolic statement by the president would have gone great lengths toward preventing the crisis of confidence and the need, therefore, to rely as much on the Clay mission as President Kennedy did.

MARTIN HILLENBRAND: Whether the Soviets designed it or not, the fact that August 13 coincided with the vacation season had a lot to do with the delays.[23] As far as Washington was concerned, for example, the president was in Hyannis Port, and I, the deputy director of the Berlin Task Force, was on an island off the coast of Georgia. The operations room of the State Department was manned at that point by a very junior officer. When our ambassador in Bonn, who was attending a ball game, learned that something was happening in Berlin, he did not bother to leave the game. Not until much later that day, and then only in a very fragmentary way, did the American embassy actually report what was happening, with the result that, by the time the bureaucracy got reassembled in Washington, it was already Tuesday. Such delays, however understandable, may not be justifiable, but that is the way governments tend to operate at the height of the vacation season. One does not need to look for plots or collusion among governments to explain these delays.

SHEPARD STONE: What does this say about the State Department's intelligence capabilities?

MARTIN HILLENBRAND: There is no doubt that there was a certain failure of intelligence. How extensive it was is a much-disputed point. I have looked into some ex post facto claims that prior intelligence had predicted that the wall would be built on August 13 and find that they are simply not valid. Everyone was speculating that the East Germans would have to do something to stanch the hemorrhaging of their population. The prevailing theories as to what they would do bore little on the actual construction of the wall at the sectoral boundary. They focused rather on controls expected to be imposed between East Berlin and the German Democratic Republic proper, or other possibilities. What actually happened was an intelligence surprise, unanticipated so far as I am aware by any of the governments involved. I think that when the documentation, including that of the CIA, becomes fully available, it will bear out this view.

SHEPARD STONE: Francis Mac Ginnis, what about British intelligence?

FRANCIS MAC GINNIS: When I asked Major General Delacombe this question, he said, "Well, for some time it had looked as if *something* were going to have to be done to stanch the hemorrhage, and one of the possibilities was the wall."

RICHARD MERRITT: Delacombe's political counterpart in Berlin at the time, Geoffrey McDermott, later wrote, "Looking back with hindsight it is now clear that our intelligence was not too good."[24]

DIETER MAHNCKE: Had intelligence been better at the time, would the Allies have considered preventive action?

SHEPARD STONE: Klaus Schütz, would you like to put in the last word?

KLAUS SCHÜTZ: Looking back over the past twenty years, and taking into account the fact that Europe was divided before and after the wall, can we not say that life in West Berlin today is safer than before August 13, 1961? Did we not get simply a new guarantee, co-signed by the Soviet Union, that the city would be able to maintain its ties to the Federal Republic, have a clearer set of access rights, enjoy more security, and have a greater opportunity for contacts with the people of the GDR? Taking into account the fact that we could not alter the division of Europe into communist and noncommunist spheres, should we not view West Berlin as a success story?

Part 2 Quadripartite and Inter-German Agreements

Introduction

When Willy Brandt became chancellor after the federal election of September 1969, he initiated a far-reaching détente policy that, among other things, earned him a Nobel Peace Prize. Even as foreign minister in the Grand Coalition of 1966–69 he had tried to push toward relaxation of tension in Central Europe. One of his first moves in early 1967 was to take up diplomatic relations with Rumania, and a year later the FRG had resumed its interrupted ties with Yugoslavia. His push came to an abrupt halt, however. The Grand Coalition's senior partner, the CDU/CSU, continued to favor a policy of strength vis-à-vis the East. Walter Ulbricht, fearing the GDR's isolation by the Federal Republic's démarche, soon began rounding up bilateral pacts with other Warsaw Pact states by which they agreed not to enter into diplomatic relations with the FRG until the latter should recognize de jure the German Democratic Republic. The final blow came in August 1968, when the Red Army moved into Czechoslovakia to snuff out the short-lived "Prague spring" of liberalization. Even so, Foreign Minister Brandt had made a significant start at a new West German foreign policy.

As chancellor, Brandt sought to balance four delicate aspects of foreign policy. He negotiated separately but simultaneously with the Soviet Union, Poland, and the GDR, meanwhile encouraging the four Powers to negotiate on the status of Berlin. By early 1970 he had initiated the first direct contacts on a formal level that the Federal Republic had ever had with the GDR. Later in the year he signed treaties in Moscow and Warsaw that, in effect, recognized the territorial status quo resulting from World War II. But he also made clear that further progress toward détente, including ratification of the two treaties, would rest upon steps toward a satisfactory resolution of the Berlin problem. Four-power talks on Berlin, however, begun in March 1970, continued to drag on.

A year and a half of the periodic meetings finally produced on September 3, 1971, the Quadripartite Agreement on Berlin.[1] The document sought essentially to stabilize the status quo. Its preamble stressed that the protocol did not affect the wartime and postwar agreements and decisions of the four Powers, nor did it prejudice the legal positions that they had taken, and in Part 1 the four governments agreed that they "will mutually respect their individual and joint rights and responsibilities, which remain unchanged." Part 2 and its related annexes contained the heart of the mutual adjustments. The Soviet Union agreed to the principle of unimpeded access to and from West Berlin and specified adjustments to be worked out in detail by "the competent German authorities." It also promised ways to ease West Berliners' access to East Berlin and the GDR for periodic visits. Except in cases of serious illness or death, West Berliners had not been permitted to enter East Berlin since 1966, and East Germany since 1961, when the wall went up.

The Western powers, for their part, made quite clear what the relationship between West Berlin and the FRG was to be. First, they were retaining their own occupation rights in West Berlin. The city was not to be a constituent part of the Federal Republic. Those portions of the Basic Law or federal statutes that contradicted this principle would continue to be suspended, but otherwise the ties between the two areas would be maintained. Second, officers or state bodies of the Federal Republic, such as the chancellor or Bundestag committees, "will not perform in the Western Sectors of Berlin constitutional or official acts" that contradict the principle of constitutional separation. This did not preclude them from making an appearance in the city. Third, a permanent liaison agency would represent the FRG in West Berlin. Finally, and again in accordance with the principle of occupation, the Federal Republic would continue to represent West Berlin internationally.

Brandt's government accepted the agreement as "a solid basis for a satisfactory Berlin settlement." For purely practical reasons, however, it did not express overwhelming enthusiasm. The conservative opposition was already angry enough that Brandt's Eastern treaties had relegated to the dustbin of history Bonn's maximum demands of the previous twenty years (and perhaps a bit envious of Brandt's successes and the honors accorded him!). Some, including West Germany's largest newspaper chain, owned by Axel Caesar Springer, mounted an active campaign against the accords and their subsequent implementation jointly by the FRG and GDR. The agreement's implicit recognition of the continued division of Germany and the legitimacy of the German Democratic Republic was intolerable to them. West German acceptance of its conditions, according to this argument, would be at best unwise, if not unconstitutional and downright treasonable. The four Powers had not resolved the territorial and other issues left over from World War II, the critics said, but had merely agreed not to disagree about them any longer.

Fragmentary evidence suggests that GDR officials were not overjoyed either. The protocol had failed to make good the long-standing claim that West Berlin was on GDR soil, it failed to turn the western sectors into a "free city," and it even imposed limitations on East Germany's sovereignty by specifying what the conditions of travel through GDR territory and access to East Berlin would be. When spokesmen of the Chinese People's Republic accused the Soviet Union of having betrayed East Germany's vital interests, this claim found a favorable echo in East Berlin.

Both Germanies nonetheless sat down to work out details. Even this, of course, sanctioned as it was by the Quadripartite Agreement, gave force to the FRG's claim to be responsible for the fate of West Berlin. On December 17, 1971, State Secretary Egon Bahr, one of the architects of Brandt's Eastern policy, and GDR State Secretary Michael Kohl signed an inter-German agreement on "Transit Traffic of Civilian Persons and Goods between the Federal Republic of Germany and Berlin (West)." Less than a week later, representatives of East and West Berlin signed an agreement regulating visits to the East and making some minor border adjustments. But the serious work of implementing such arrangements had to await the West German ratification of the Moscow and Warsaw treaties.

The battle to secure the ratification of the Eastern treaties proved unexpectedly bitter. Brandt's opposition in the Bundestag mounted a strenuous campaign against them that at one point threatened to topple the government. But the firmness of the Brandt government in pursuing ratification, the generally favorable climate of opinion in the Federal Republic toward the treaties, subtle pressure exerted by the Western allies, and some timely verbal concessions by the Soviet Union and shows of good faith by the GDR (such as permitting West Berliners to visit East Berlin during the Easter and Whitsuntide holidays despite the absence of formally recognized agreements, and agreeing on May 12 to a treaty with the FRG on traffic questions) won the day. The opposition finally agreed to abstain from voting on the treaties rather than cast votes that might have returned Europe to the darkness and uncertainty of the cold war. On May 17, 1972, the Bundestag ratified the Moscow and Warsaw treaties, and six days later, President Gustav Heinemann signed them. The way was clear for the foreign ministers of France, Great Britain, the Soviet Union, and the United States to sign, on June 3, 1972, the Berlin accords of the previous September.

Even more progress toward inter-German détente was made in late 1972. On November 8, the FRG and GDR initialed a Basic Treaty defining their future relationships. The treaty itself does not mention Berlin. Both parties issued identical statements, however, extending to West Berlin any FRG–GDR cooperation in traffic, science, technology, health, culture, environmental protection, and other fields. The statements add: "The Permanent Mission of the Federal Republic of Germany in the German Democratic Republic shall, in conformity with the Quadripartite Agreement of September 3, 1971, represent the interests of Berlin (West)." In elections less than two weeks later, West Germans gave a solid majority to the coalition that, under Chancellor Willy Brandt, had broken the East–West impasse in Germany. Correctly or not, the new Brandt government interpreted the electoral victory as a vote of confidence in its policy of détente and a mandate to work toward easing inter-German tensions.[2]

The Berlin accords of 1971–72 promised to end the danger to international peace posed by the Berlin problem. But another dimension of the problem continued to exist: the tangled tie between the Federal Republic and West Berlin. West Berliners are still not FRG citizens and cannot vote in federal elections. And yet the federal parliament continues to enact legislation directly affecting their lives. The procedure for making federal law applicable in West Berlin is still indirect and subject to Allied veto. The Federal Republic still has to coordinate its overall Berlin policy with the tripartite Kommandatura. This gives the United States in particular a continued degree of leverage over West Germany that the latter may increasingly resent, especially should the two countries begin to differ more seriously on monetary issues, trade, and the FRG's relations with the East bloc states. West Berlin continues to be a financial drain on the Federal Republic's resources. All these aspects continue to limit West Germany's freedom of action both at home and abroad, and may well turn the Berlin problem into one of the country's major domestic political issues.

4 The Quadripartite Agreement on Berlin in the Context of Past and Future East–West Relations

Jonathan Dean

The 1971 Quadripartite Agreement on Berlin resulted from a general conclusion in both East and West that the situation in and around Germany that had emerged during the years since the end of the Second World War would probably continue in its main outlines for many years to come, but that this situation should be made more endurable and less risky for all those involved. "Those involved," where Berlin was concerned, were the Berlin Senate, the people of Berlin, the governments of the four signatory Powers, and the Federal Republic, as well as the GDR. In fact, a significant aspect of the Quadripartite Agreement—and of the access agreement connected with it—was that it associated the two German states in differing ways in the responsibility for maintaining Berlin. Henceforth, Berlin was formally, as well as in practice, a focus for the interaction of all six governments, the four signatory Powers, the FRG, and the GDR—both in good times and in bad. Since Berlin is located right in the middle of what continues to be the world's largest military confrontation, efforts to defuse and to stabilize the Berlin situation were in the general interest.

From the Western viewpoint, these objectives had to be pursued in the Berlin talks in a way that would not negatively prejudice the provisional nature of the situation in Central Europe, for example, by formally accepting the division of Germany. They also had to leave room for the future growth and development of Berlin. The experience of the past decade would appear to show that both criteria were met. The Quadripartite Agreement has already paid off by giving the West—and the East, too, for that matter—and the Berliners over ten years free of serious Berlin crises. I shall treat later the question of whether this outcome rests on the Quadripartite Agreement itself or on the general line of Soviet policy during this period.

Background to the Berlin Talks:
The World in 1968

Let's go back for a moment to the international situation at the beginning of the Berlin talks. In August 1968 European and American opinion was deeply shocked by the Soviet invasion of Czechoslovakia in circumstances which have many worrisome similarities with those of Poland today. The international standing and prestige of the Soviet Union were severely damaged as a consequence of that invasion. Soon thereafter, the Soviet Union began strenuous attempts to reestablish its relationship with the countries of the Western alliance, pressing, among other things, for holding a Conference on Security and Cooperation in Europe (CSCE). In a separate and even earlier development, Willy Brandt had begun to press for a Four-power review of the Berlin situation shortly after he became foreign minister of the Federal Republic. These two developments became connected in the discussion that led to the Berlin talks.

Foreign Minister Brandt, against the background of his own experience as mayor of Berlin, knew of many practical improvements that could be made in Berlin's situation, and he believed that the Soviets could be brought to accept at least some of them. But his efforts to promote a Four-power review of the Berlin situation initially encountered considerable skepticism from the three Western governments that had responsibility for Berlin and for Germany as a whole. There was a strong feeling among many political leaders and senior officials in these countries that the mechanism for handling the Berlin situation that had grown up over the years between East and West was so complicated and so intricate that it was wiser to leave it alone. They considered that, among other things, there was a risk that, if negotiations were held with the Soviet Union on the Berlin question, the Soviet Union might seek to revise even those aspects of the Berlin mechanism that were then working fairly well. The net result might, therefore, be a worsening of the Berlin situation, rather than an improvement.

My own view at the time, and that of many Americans concerned with European issues, was that the Soviet Union should not be permitted to act as though it had done nothing wrong when it moved 80,000 soldiers into a friendly, sovereign country and that it should make a concrete and explicit demonstration that its renewed declarations of peaceful intentions toward the members of the Western alliance had some substance. In this sense, we thought that it would be useful to discuss the Berlin issue with the Soviets and that it might be possible to gain something concrete out of such a discussion. A most important fact in the decision to proceed was the inauguration of a new American administration, which was soon to pursue the SALT negotiations with the Soviets.

The East–West Talks

Later, as the Federal German negotiations with the Soviet Union and then with Poland progressed to specific agreements, it became evident that Soviet leaders understood from statements of leaders in the Federal Republic, and also in other Western countries, that these agreements would not receive parliamentary acceptance and ratification by the Federal German Bundestag unless an acceptable agreement over Berlin was reached.

This deliberate connection of the Berlin issue with other issues was the main source of Western political leverage during the Berlin negotiations and a primary reason for their successful outcome. In essence, the members of the Western alliance were successful in agreeing among themselves that the Soviet Union should undertake a specific, constructive action—conclusion of an acceptable Berlin agreement—in order to demonstrate that there was a real point in entering on a broader range of East–West relations. Along with the positive motivation of the Soviets themselves, this agreement among members of the Western coalition as to what specific action they wanted from the Soviets at a given juncture was a second major ingredient of success in the Berlin talks. It also contains a general lesson for the future. In this sense the Berlin agreement, together with the release of ethnic Germans from the Soviet Union and Poland, was the short-term price paid by the Soviet Union for its policy of détente. The long-term cost, of course, was the acceleration of the forces of change within the societies of Eastern Europe and the Soviet Union.

As the Berlin talks began, the primary joint interests of France, the

United Kingdom, and the United States, as well as of the Federal Republic (which in a practical, if not formal sense was an active participant), were to defuse the Berlin situation and make it less dangerous, while maintaining the Four-power status of the city; to achieve improvements for the Berliners in all parts of the city and for their friends and relatives in the GDR; and to improve the economic situation of the western sectors. It was also to preserve the relationship that had grown up between the Federal Republic and the western sectors and to give this relationship an opportunity to grow and develop in the future. The main motive of the Soviet Union, within the framework of the Berlin negotiations—I have already described its broader motivation as we understand it—also appears to have been to defuse the situation in and around Berlin, while maintaining the Four-power status and, in addition, to support the efforts of the GDR to gain international status.

Procedures and Issues

The mechanism of the Berlin negotiation was complicated and, if one looks only at superficial appearances, very difficult to operate. On the Western side, the negotiators from France, the United Kingdom, and the United States, as well as their Federal German colleagues at all levels, were responsible to their national governments and received individual instructions from them. On the basis of these sometimes divergent instructions, they had to coordinate and agree among themselves on each word said to the East. In addition, in order to receive and to retain the support of their remaining allies, the negotiators had to report periodically to the NATO Council on the course of the negotiations and seek the Council's endorsement of their conduct of the talks.

This apparatus may seem unwieldy and ineffective. In actuality, it worked quite smoothly. National instructions were coordinated through the still existing mechanism, the Bonn Group, composed of representatives of the Federal Republic, France, the United Kingdom, and the United States. The interests of the Berlin Senate were taken into account, both in Bonn and through the Allied missions in Berlin. In fact, as I look back on those days from the MBFR negotiations in which I later participated, where nineteen countries from NATO and the Warsaw Pact are engaged, and where the NATO mechanism plays an even more active role, the Berlin negotiations appear very simple in comparison.

The detailed discussions in the Berlin talks between the East and West took place, of course, between representatives of France, the

United Kingdom, and the United States and representatives of the Soviet Union. But our full records of these discussions were made available to our Federal German colleagues and were discussed in detail with them, as were the positions that the Allied negotiators intended to take with the Soviets.

The techniques of negotiation were traditional ones: general discussion for a time; presentation by each side of draft texts, which conflicted to a large extent; efforts to extract common language from the two drafts and to develop this further—we used a blackboard for these purposes, and it proved a very flexible instrument; the elaboration of a common text with brackets and footnotes; and, finally, agreement on a draft text for initialing. While the negotiations were going on, they appeared to be lengthy, and many Western officials became from time to time pessimistic about the outcome. This was especially the case when the Soviets presented their draft agreement in March 1971. Many people in the Western capitals and in Berlin considered this standard recital of the Eastern position to be a sign that the negotiations would lead to no result. But, for me, the issue was never in much doubt, because it seemed evident that so many Soviet interests were dependent on reaching an agreement over Berlin. And compared to the eleven-year duration thus far of the Vienna talks on force reduction, the Berlin talks moved like an express train.

The subject matter of the Berlin negotiations and of the ensuing agreement can be divided into three themes which clearly show the main problem areas that had emerged over the years with regard to Berlin: (1) access for civilian personnel and goods between the western sectors and the Federal Republic; (2) access by Berliners in East and West to the other side; (3) the relationship between the Federal Republic and western sectors of Berlin, including the representation abroad by the Federal Republic of the interests of West Berliners. The latter question, because it has international significance, was perhaps the most difficult to resolve.

The Berlin Agreement

I believe that all participants did in fact gain something from the negotiations. Within the confines of the Berlin agreement itself, the GDR came perhaps least far toward its original objectives of international acceptance and of establishing the western sectors as a special international entity. After all, in the agreement, the Soviet Union, and not the

GDR, assumed ultimate responsibility for civilian access between Berlin and the Federal Republic. The Quadripartite status of Berlin and of Germany as a whole was left intact. The Soviet Union accepted not only the existing relationship between the Federal Republic and the western sectors, but the fact that this relationship would grow and be developed. In particular, the acceptance by the Soviet Union of the right of the Federal Republic to represent the interests of West Berliners abroad put a stop to the East German notion that West Berlin should be regarded as an independent international entity. And the agreement also put to rest General Secretary Khrushchev's threat in 1958 of a Soviet peace treaty with the GDR which would annul Quadripartite agreements over Berlin and over Germany as a whole.

How Well Has It Worked?

Most people would agree that the results of the subsequent years have been good in terms of the Western objectives established at the outset of the talks, which I have described above. There has been perhaps one change in Berlin: a diminution in the feeling of risk and danger and common enterprise which people here had at an earlier time. But to consider this change to be a one-sided loss for the West seems to be to take a limited view of the situation. The real point is that the Berlin agreement has formed a barrier to the use of Berlin as a hostage, insulating the western sectors to some extent against shocks from adverse developments in the general international environment. Several such adverse developments have taken place in recent years.

As I mentioned earlier, it can be argued that there would have been no major Berlin crises in the past fourteen years even without the Berlin agreement, that what has actually protected Berlin against such crises has been the Soviet Union's own détente policy toward the West, and that Berlin crises will recur if and when that policy changes. Perhaps so. Yet this is a hypothetical argument, difficult to prove or disprove. And, surely, it is the case that, if difficult times do return, the fact that a Quadripartite agreement was reached could have many benefits: the mere existence of a Berlin agreement will be an additional barrier, if not an insurmountable one, to repetition of past difficulties. Even in adverse circumstances, by establishing clear standards of contractual behavior, the agreement will be a source of strength to Western leaders, who will have to make clear to public opinion what is going on, and what the issues are, and who is at fault. But perhaps the most important point to make here is that the Berlin agreement contains a more precise set of rules for the interaction among the six governments concerned than was previously the case. This fact by itself will act to decrease the risk of miscalculation or misperception even in adverse circumstances. These advantages would not exist if the Berlin agreement had not been concluded.

These are the aspects of the Berlin agreement that protect against bad times and negative trends in the external environment. But the point I have been making about the Quadripartite Agreement providing a set of ground rules for the interaction of the six governments concerned is also valid for good times. At this point in time, we are very far from the end of Berlin's development as a city. The Berlin agreement contains the potential for further constructive development of Berlin itself, while the continued existence of a safer Berlin will contribute to keeping open in a constructive way the possibility of a further peaceful evolution in Central and Eastern Europe.

Discussion

SHEPARD STONE: Thank you, Ambassador Dean. In addition to a more general interest in détente, what were the long-range goals of Soviet policy toward Berlin?

JONATHAN DEAN: When I look back at the decade after the beginning of the Berlin talks, a decade during which I was negotiating uninterruptedly with the Soviets, I do not see any remarkable conclusions to be drawn as to specific, long-term Soviet aims in Berlin. I do not regard the Soviet Union as a country with a fixed political battle plan and both the capabilities and persistence required to achieve such goals. I regard it as a powerful country with somewhat confused leadership that does not see a clear way out of its numerous day-to-day problems.

As far as the immediate future is concerned, I think that the Soviets will be willing enough to leave matters as they stand in Berlin for quite some time to come. Their point of decision will come in a few years, perhaps, when they have assessed the policy of the Western governments, particularly the new administration in the United States, and will depend in part on whether they see those governments as striking out on a definite new line to which they must respond in a specific way, or whether they think they can continue their own Western policy vis-à-vis these governments, albeit possibly in a different rhetoric. During that period Soviet leadership will doubtless continue to attempt to show itself as conciliatory on European issues, including Berlin.

RICHARD MERRITT: In late 1969 and early 1970 there seemed to be a concentrated assault on the part of the Nixon administration against the efforts of the new Brandt government to achieve some sort of accommodation with the East. I recall a number of op-ed columns in the *New York Times* by such men as George Ball saying, in effect, "Hold on a moment—wait until the Americans take the initiative, until things are settled, before you rush into the East–West situation." To what extent was this a theme in the administration? What motivated it? How did the United States get away from that line of thought?

JONATHAN DEAN: There are those here who can comment with more authority on this subject than I can, but I might note that I did observe some nervousness in the new Nixon administration about the policy of the Federal Republic and a feeling that things were moving so rapidly that they could get out of control. In reality, I think, both governments wanted essentially similar goals. It simply took a while for their policies to mesh and for their leaders to realize that their goals, although described in different terms, were very complementary. This took only four to six months. Thereafter, cooperation and collaboration in a conscious and deliberate way were quite good.

MARTIN HILLENBRAND: When the Nixon administration came into office, it had not yet formulated a policy toward the Soviet Union. A lot of tough talk came during the first months, when President Nixon's visit to Europe took place. And it is true that Henry Kissinger, in particular, but others in the White House as well were providing background briefings, op-ed articles, and interviews with correspondents in which they expressed apprehension about and dismay at what they thought Brandt's government was doing. This was accentuated through some unfortunate visits made to Washington by West German governmental and party officials, who tried to engage in a war of "backgrounders." There was a general feeling in 1969 that Henry Kissinger and the White House generally opposed the direction that the *Ostpolitik* was taking.

The shift came, in my view, when it was time to draft the president's first annual report on foreign policy. It was in the process of writing this report that the idea of moving from an era of confrontation to an era of negotiation evolved. With thinking moving in this direction, and also with the initiation of back-channel contacts, meetings with Ambassador Dobrynin, and so forth, the atmosphere in the White House changed. In the State Department, to be sure, the attitude was more relaxed right from the start; in fact, papers were written that suggested that we should take advantage of the Soviet desire for a Conference on Security and Cooperation in Europe (CSCE) to extract whatever gains we could in other contexts. The White House only slowly became convinced that it was possible to negotiate advantageously with the Soviets. Basic to the actual negotiations was a State Department paper that, after rather heated meetings in the White House, was approved by the National Security Council. (Unfortunately, the press never quite caught up with the change in mood: as long as six months after the White House was reflecting a different attitude toward the idea of negotiating with the East, the press was still reporting White House reticence.)

Once the Federal Republic had successfully negotiated agreements with the Soviet Union and Poland, the momentum toward the CSCE and a mutual balance reduction in forces (MBFR) increased, especially within NATO. This in turn produced a more positive attitude toward negotiations on Berlin. The process itself was rather disorderly, with back-channel communications occurring at various levels between various individuals. But the real story of these negotiations is not likely to be written until vital information is declassified.[1]

KLAUS SCHÜTZ: With all due respect to Kissinger and other representatives of the three Western allies, it would not have been possible to reach any agreement on Berlin had the government in Bonn not set its *Ostpolitik* in motion. The Bonn government had to convince the other governments that something could be done. Before becoming governing mayor of Berlin, while I was still the state secretary in the Foreign Ministry, Brandt and I wrote down all the elements that, from our point of view, needed somehow to be resolved in any settlement of the Berlin question. The Four-power agreement met all of our requirements.

West Berlin played an important role, too. Its representatives convinced the government in Bonn to delay signing the treaties with Warsaw and Moscow until a satisfactory agreement on Berlin had been reached.

ANTONIUS EITEL: To what extent did the Soviet Union and Poland influence the Western position on negotiations over Berlin? The notes that the West presented to Moscow on August 6–7, 1969, were actually rather modest. In setting out the goals the West hoped to achieve through negotiations, such as improvements in transit provisions, these notes also offered concessions that suggested that the West was in a bad negotiating position. After the Moscow and Warsaw agreements had been signed, however, the Western position seemed to change enough to permit further demands and more ambitious goals. How real was this apparent linkage?

HELGA HAFTENDORN: Expanding a bit on Antonius Eitel's question, I should be interested to learn what changes in Berlin policy took place before the Brandt government came to power. The Western position in 1968 and at least up to the notes of August 1969 seemed to see Berlin as an isolated issue but subsequently viewed it in terms of the broader context of the CSCE and overall East–West negotiations. Moreover, it was only then that the West began to focus on West German initiatives toward the East.

JONATHAN DEAN: The genesis of the negotiations came in late 1968 in a discussion at which Willy Brandt, then still foreign minister, was trying to persuade his Allied colleagues that negotiations would be worthwhile since the Soviets seemed prepared to listen seriously to proposals. Our later negotiating position certainly improved rather rapidly with the conclusion of the Warsaw and Moscow agreements. Although perhaps not in August 1969, when we sent the notes to the Soviet Union, but by the time negotiations were beginning we had a pretty good idea of what we wanted to achieve. At the time I wrote a note to myself summarizing the goals which various Western participants sought. Almost all these goals were achieved.

How do we explain this transition? Our first steps were certainly rather more timid than what we subsequently proposed and obtained. Then came the mix-up at the outset of the Nixon administration, as some of the American principals began to realize that the West German government meant business with its Eastern policy, that it was not a rhetorical description of the FRG's posture but an actual policy that was being implemented. The rapidity of that development caught people by surprise. Later, however, they began to realize that West German and American goals fitted together. It was President Nixon, after all, who later in his administration was basing his policy on having achieved or being about to achieve "a generation of peace," and, by this time, he was clearly cognizant of this congruity of goals.

RENATA FRITSCH-BOURNAZEL: With respect to Shepard Stone's query about long-range Soviet interests in Berlin I would make two points.

First, the Soviet Union was rather ambivalent about its interests there. On the one hand, it had begun to realize that raising tensions in Berlin was counterproductive, especially since it had other policy areas that seemed to be more important at the time. But, on the other hand, the isolated position of West Berlin continued to give the Soviets a means for exerting influence over the Federal Republic, as well as an instrument for seeking more equality between the Soviet bloc and the West.

Second, and this has become even more apparent in the last year, the Soviet potential for threatening West Berlin's security and viability still provides its leaders with a deterrent to Western designs to undermine Soviet dominance in Central and Eastern Europe, not only the GDR. In December 1980, after the NATO Council had discussed the possibility of punishing the Warsaw Pact countries should Poland be invaded, the Soviets responded with threats to the implementation of the Four-power agreement on Berlin as well as the Basic Treaty signed by the two German states. They thus envisage a new kind of linkage between the implementation of these agreements and a certain quality of East–West relations in Europe.

DAVID KLEIN: Antonius Eitel asked what role the FRG's Eastern treaties played in the West's bargaining position. If we go back to President Nixon's speech in West Berlin on February 27, 1969, we find the kernel of the West's later stance: that further steps toward détente in Europe would require prior progress on the issue of Berlin. Moreover, it is true that there was a lot of unhappiness with the West Germans at that time: they were not only considered to be the last of the irredentists, and hence a potential danger to peace, but it was also not clear that they knew how to handle the Soviet Union.

The combination of the treaties with Poland and the Soviet Union, the opening of informal relations with the GDR, and the West German decision to stop trying to prevent third states from recognizing the GDR gave a great deal to the Soviet Union and the East bloc and thereby made possible a deal on Berlin. All this certainly did change expectations. These steps in effect ended the crisis that had begun with Khrushchev's ultimatum in 1958, since they gave the Soviet Union what it was seeking without having a peace treaty. It was a substitute for a peace treaty in Europe.

On a related point, one should not take too seriously all the peripheral maneuvering reported by Henry Kissinger and Kenneth Rush. In fact, a comparison of the final agreement on Berlin with the position paper prepared by the State Department and approved by the NSC shows a very close relationship. All the maneuvering on the side may have served ego needs, but not serious international purposes.

ROGER MORGAN: What role did American relations with China play in the Western bargaining position on Berlin? The news that Kissinger was to visit Beijing and would be followed by President Nixon seemed to help clear the minds of the Russians, although not immediately, and they began to be more amenable. If it is true, for instance, that even in 1961 the building of the wall was part of a long-term consolidation of the Soviet bloc inspired by the pressure of China, what can we say about a Chinese factor having played a part in moving the Russians forward in 1970 and 1971?

JONATHAN DEAN: China definitely played a role in Soviet efforts to consolidate its position vis-à-vis the West. It is remarkable that concern over China is something that anyone dealing with Soviet officials hears after virtually the first five minutes of discussion. I assume that Kissinger's visit to Beijing did have the effect of increasing pressure on the Soviet Union.

MICHAEL SODARO: Ambassador Dean, to what extent do you think that the GDR was trying to stall the negotiations? There are several indications that, from 1969 through 1971, Ulbricht was the fly in the ointment. Throughout 1969, for example, the East Germans were insistent that West Berlin lay in the middle of the GDR, on the GDR's territory. On one of the first public occasions when the Soviet Union indicated an interest in negotiations, however, in Gromyko's speech on July 10, 1969, before the Supreme Soviet, the position was taken that West Berlin lies geographically "in the heart of the GDR." Now, the term "heart" lacks a certain juridical status in international law, but it seems clear that the Soviets were rejecting the idea that Berlin lay on the GDR's territory.

Then, again, in his famous press conference of January 19, 1971, Ulbricht remarked that no agreement on Berlin could be achieved without some input from the GDR. Within a few hours, however, the Soviets affirmed very strongly that the four Powers were the only ones concerned with the Berlin negotiations. The fact that the serious logjams in the discussions were resolved only after Erich Honecker replaced Ulbricht on May 3 of that year suggests that, had it not been for East German obstructionism, agreement might have been reached much earlier.

JONATHAN DEAN: Signs of friction were definitely there, and at times Soviet officials spoke of the resistance of their allies and the delays it caused. This really continued right up to the final day, in the form of a dispute on the German translation of some key terms—a dispute in which the Soviets played a mediating role in favor of moving on to conclude the agreement.

KLAUS SCHÜTZ: Although Germans from neither side of the border were formally represented in the Four-power negotiations on Berlin, they made their presence very well known. We tried to help our allies make correct decisions on matters of extraordinary importance. On the question of whether or not West Berlin was a constituent part of the Federal Republic, for instance, FRG officials found an Allied order from the early 1960s that declared that it was not. Then, too, I was called on several times by Western negotiators to say how particular matters were viewed from Berlin. I imagine that people from the GDR were trying just as hard at very high levels to assist their ally.

The negotiators on both sides needed to be convinced on certain points. At the very beginning of the series of conferences, one of Ulbricht's closest associates wrote an article for the *Berliner Zeitung* in which he spelled out what the GDR expected from any agreement. A comparison of this article with the agreement itself suggests that the latter produced nothing not already considered in the former. The GDR had to convince the Soviet Union on several matters. But a lot of convincing was required on our side, too—not only of our Western allies but the opposition in Bonn.

A question of current importance is the durability of the Berlin agreement in the face of some Western move, such as installing medium-range missiles in the Federal Republic, that the Soviets strongly opposed. Would the Soviet Union increase pressure on Berlin? I personally tend to believe that, although the process is not complete, the neutralization of Berlin from the other tensions in Europe has gone very far. Even in periods of cold-war tension, a written agreement with the Soviet Union is better than no agreement at all, and the agreement we have has brought a large degree of security.

HANS OTTO BRÄUTIGAM: A unique feature of the Four-power agreement is that, although it consists of a set of separate principles to which the signators agreed, there are sharply conflicting interpretations of what these principles mean. Thus it confirms the Four-power status of Berlin without resolving the conflicting views of the meaning and substance of this status. At the same time, the agreement contains very specific rules of conduct on access to West Berlin, Federal German presence in the city, travel arrangements, and so forth. The Four-power agreement is best viewed as being based on a balance of interests that require the maintenance of conflicting views on questions of principle. To maintain this balance of interests it may be wise, although sometimes very uncomfortable, to take account of gray areas which give a certain flexibility to the agreement's implementation. In response to Ambassador Schütz's question about the durability of the agreement in times of conflict, I am hopeful that it will be possible to maintain the basic balance of interests—although what would happen in the event of a very serious East–West crisis no one could say.

MARTIN HILLENBRAND: The language of Article 4 of the final protocol attached to the Berlin agreement provides that, in the event of a difficulty in applying its provisions which any of the four governments considers serious, or in the event of nonimplementation of any part of the Four-power agreement, that government has the right to draw the attention of the other three to the agreement's provisions and initiate the requisite Quadripartite consultation to ensure that observance takes place. There was a time in the mid-1970s when the West was concerned that the Soviets might resort to that procedure: on several occasions Ambassador Abrasimov seemed to be hinting that, if we did not behave better, the Soviets would resort to this final protocol to call a review conference that would, at least theoretically, reopen the Four-power agreement. They did not do so. But the protocol nonetheless exists. If we ever get to the stage where they think a basic change in Western policy has taken place, they do not need to violate the agreement, at least initially. All they need do is call for a general review conference under Article 4 of the final protocol and then take off from that point.

Turning to Dr. Eitel's question about the modest note of August 1969, I would say that, historically, it should be regarded essentially as a "throw-away" note. It came before the formation of the Brandt government, at a time when the Nixon government still expected Kurt Georg Kiesinger to continue indefinitely as chancellor, and it sought to respond to the pressure Foreign Minister Brandt was exerting for action on Berlin, but without actually committing the West to Four-power negotiations. There was little conviction on the part of the three Western powers that the note would lead to negotiations or would even receive a positive response. And, of course, it was quite a long time before any response came at all.

Another thing that has led to a certain amount of misunderstanding and criticism is the fact that Brandt's *Ostpolitik,* which involved a fundamental shift of the FRG's traditional policy toward the GDR, caught the Western allies unprepared psychologically. After all, for some twenty years they had rushed to the barricades every time the Hallstein Doctrine was invoked. Suddenly we were being told that the Hallstein Doctrine was dead, that it could no longer be enforced, that the Indians were about to recognize the GDR. All the baggage of twenty or more years of psychological conditioning suddenly was no longer relevant. West Germany's turnabout caused hesitancies in Western capitals if for no other reason than that most bureaucracies are very sluggish in changing fundamental attitudes. It took a while before the bureaucracies in Paris, London, and Washington were prepared to go along with the West German government in its changed attitude toward the GDR.

SHEPARD STONE: When you say that we were caught by surprise when the FRG changed its policy, are you suggesting that Chancellor Brandt and his colleagues did not keep you informed or were not explaining it well enough?

MARTIN HILLENBRAND: It is my impression that we were kept reasonably well informed. The problem was that the doses of information were pretty large and, initially, indigestible. When Egon Bahr first told a meeting of senior Allied officials that the Hallstein Doctrine was, in effect, no longer enforceable and that India was on the verge of recognizing the GDR, the news sent shockwaves through the three capitals, for we had not recognized that the Hallstein Doctrine was on the skids to such a degree. This essentially psychological problem ultimately worked itself out, but it cost a year of recrimination, doubt, and hesitancy about the *Ostpolitik* that could, perhaps, have been avoided had it been described in a less abrupt fashion and without seeming to be such a fundamental shift in policy.

KLAUS SCHÜTZ: Brandt's *Ostpolitik* was neither planned in secret nor put into effect from one day to the next. It was the result of a long process of rethinking, some of which was surprising to many of us in the government at the time. In June 1969, before the national election that brought the Brandt coalition to power, an article I wrote after visiting Poland about the need to recognize the Oder–Neisse boundary was severely criticized by the Social Democratic party. Willy Brandt, however, said, "I read the article tonight, and it wasn't too bad"—and, of course, a half year later his government took precisely this step.

The point is that the policy shift was part of an ongoing process. In such circumstances it is sometimes difficult to keep your friends, allies, and even coalition partners informed about the latest thinking because one is not completely sure what it is. Some people, like Egon Bahr, were more forthright in explaining their thinking to a more or less private circle, but I do not think even Bahr realized that senior officials in the West were shocked by what he said.

SHEPARD STONE: It is interesting to learn that it was not only the West that did not inform the Germans about its intentions, but that, once in a while, the West Germans did not inform each other.

JOHN KORNBLUM: David Klein earlier suggested that the Four-power agreement on Berlin created a modus vivendi that was equivalent to a general European peace treaty. This point deserves more attention. The Berlin agreement's confirmation of Four-power rights and responsibilities, together with the Moscow and Warsaw treaties, made many other things possible. These included the development of relations with the GDR, the negotiation of an inter-German transit agreement (initiated by Bahr even while the Four-power negotiations were going on), later on the inter-German Basic Treaty, the entry of both Germanies into the United Nations, the conclusion in November 1972 of the little-known Quadripartite Agreement in which the Soviets reconfirmed some practices concerning Berlin, and eventually the final act of the Conference on European Security (CSCE).

The Berlin agreements provided a basis for the Federal Republic to pursue its very important goals vis-à-vis the East in a controlled fashion resting on consultation rather than pursuing these same goals unilaterally. I doubt that any West German administration, irrespective of which party is in power, would give up these goals. Moreover, with the passage of time it was to be expected that the federal government would continue to try to improve its relations with the East. The modus vivendi which came out of the package of agreements provided a framework—and, what is more, a consultative framework—for doing this.

FRANCIS MAC GINNIS: Certainly, at the outset of the Brandt government the Allies faced a radically different West German policy, one that required getting used to. When we look at the Quadripartite Agreement, however, it would seem that it was the Federal Republic and the Berliners who paid the price rather than those Allies. Klaus Schütz was correct in saying that the Soviet and Polish treaties, initiated by the Federal Republic, were absolutely crucial to the success of negotiations on

Berlin. So, too, was the Federal Republic's willingness to recognize the GDR. And, in the text of the Quadripartite Agreement itself, the Allied commitment to the Soviet Union, never before given by treaty, that West Berlin would continue not to be a constituent part of the Federal Republic entailed a price that the Allies could not pay except at the request and desire of the Federal Republic. The FRG's willingness to pay such prices provided a good deal of motivation for East Germany as well as the Soviet Union to accept the package and pay something in return, such as improvement of the access routes.

ANTONIUS EITEL: Permit me to reemphasize the important role played by the East German leadership in Soviet bloc policy. The Western press sometimes implies that the Kremlin gives out orders and Ulbricht or whoever else is in charge in one of the satellite states simply follows them. This is not the case for the GDR. Both the GDR and Ulbricht, who, after all, had personally known Lenin, were given great weight in Moscow. When we hear about the difficulties faced by the GDR in the Berlin negotiations and how these were overcome, we realize the nature of the role played by its leaders, especially Ulbricht. The Soviets did not simply overlook something to which the GDR voiced strong opposition. They renegotiated it. The same thing is true today with respect to Honecker.

SHEPARD STONE: Ambassador Dean, was it your feeling that, during the negotiations, the Soviets were really paying attention to the GDR?

JONATHAN DEAN: Yes, definitely—and I have seen that since 1971 as well.

ANTONIUS EITEL: Ambassador Schütz asked whether the Soviet Union is prepared to violate the Berlin or other agreements. I have the impression that the Soviets are very careful about deliberately violating such agreements. In Bonn politicians and the press are very quick to speak of flagrant and violent violations of the Basic Treaty or Berlin agreement; and, if they are more sophisticated, they add that not the word alone, but the spirit of the agreement was violated. One can think of some specific cases where violations did occur and others where, even if we did not agree with it, the GDR could provide some justification for delaying traffic or whatever. By and large, however, the positive outcomes of the Berlin agreement have greatly outweighed the effects of such violations.

MARTIN HILLENBRAND: For an authoritative listing of such violations up through late 1976 I would recommend the article by Günther van Well, the head of the political section of Bonn's Foreign Office: "Die Teilnahme Berlins am internationalen Geschehen: Ein dringender Punkt auf der Ost–West-Tagesordnung."[2]

HANS OTTO BRÄUTIGAM: While I have absolutely no doubt that there were violations of the Four-power agreements on Berlin, some of them more serious than others, and while I have no doubt that we made some mistakes as well, I do not think that this is the essential question. Both sides needed a period of learning. Most of the mistakes and violations occurred in the first five years. Since then, despite some possible exceptions, both sides have acted with a certain restraint. We do not do everything we believe we can and have a right to do, and I think it is fair to say that the GDR does not do everything it believes it has a right to do. This mutual restraint is the most essential principle underlying the proper functioning of the Four-power agreement, for it ensures the maintenance of the very delicate balance that the agreement set up. It is in this respect that the agreement has made a very great contribution to the overall stability, to the vitality and future of the city.

KLAUS SCHÜTZ: Taking into account the nature of this balance, let me return to my earlier question. If something such as the installation in the FRG of American medium-range rockets should convince the Soviet Union that the overall balance has been disturbed, would the Berlin agreement stand? I think it would. It is stronger than some people thought it would be, because it has encompassed much learning and ten years of actual experience. But, when the GDR says that it might change something or reconsider certain aspects of the agreement, what does that mean? How far can the East Germans go in this respect? I do not think that such questions can be answered today, but Western governments certainly must consider possible answers.

DAVID KLEIN: The East bloc functions with a built-in restraint that has always been there. These countries can stand only a certain amount of tension. If they want to take on more, then they must think very seriously about the level of control they have—and this may mean more liberal policies. This is what keeps them honest. For this reason I do not think they can afford excessive tension now or in the next couple of years in the GDR or Poland.

SHEPARD STONE: Are you saying that if the Pershing missiles, which were originally requested by Chancellor Schmidt, are stationed in West Germany, the Berlin agreement could stand the test, or will the entire context change?

DAVID KLEIN: I think the Berlin agreement will stand the test. The question is whether or not the West European governments can do so.

JOYCE MUSHABEN: Ambassador Dean, given the ten years of experience with the Four-power agreement, and given the extent to which both Germanies have shown themselves to be loyal allies of their respective patrons, are those superpowers not prepared to let the two Germanies negotiate with each other in the event of future tensions or problems? Or will they once again get together to deal with each other on behalf of the GDR and FRG?

JONATHAN DEAN: One of the strengths of this complex of agreements is that it provides a framework for either inter-German or Four-power negotiations or both without affecting the overall legal status. This has been shown in the treatment of complaints over possible violations of the agreement. In my opinion, both the FRG and the GDR have pushed their own interpretation of the agreement a bit hard. In one case, that of the new GDR currency regulations in August 1980, I considered that an actual violation occurred that warranted intervention by the Western powers. More generally, each of the six governments now has a contractual relationship with Berlin, and each of them can play a contractual role according to rules that have been set out. I think that this possibility is really the great advantage of the Four-power agreement.

5 From the Wall to the Quadripartite Agreement: Some Underlying Trends

Dieter Mahncke

It is appropriate, twenty years after the building of the wall in Berlin and ten years after the conclusion of the Quadripartite Agreement, to examine these events as well as the city's current status and future prospects. These dates are closely related. Just as it is not possible to sketch out a perspective from which to view the future without a keen sense of the past, so too it is important to avoid viewing the Berlin issue in isolation. It is one facet of the more general conflict in Europe between East and West; and it reflects in manifold ways the political, economic, and social aspects of this conflict. In looking at Berlin in this broader temporal and spatial framework, I shall present four sets of arguments.

Effects of the Wall

First of all, the building of the wall in August 1961 must be seen as the beginning of significant political and intellectual changes in East and West.

In the GDR the construction of the wall introduced a process of economic advance and some political stabilization. Not only did it stop the ever-increasing flow of refugees and loss of skilled technicians and professionals, it also meant that the population was forced more conclusively than ever before to come to terms with the existing situation and to adopt a modified attitude toward the country in which life had to be coped with. For the GDR the wall thus meant the beginning of a period of economic growth and slow, albeit limited, political consolidation.

In the West the construction of the wall had equally significant effects—psychological effects above all but eventually also concrete political effects. Two factors were especially important: first, the impression that the West had suffered a defeat and, second, the sudden realization for many that German reunification was obviously not to be expected in the immediate future. Although it was not possible to deduce unequivocally from any official statement by the three Western powers that their guarantees—viability, security, Allied presence, welfare, access—extended to East Berlin, vehement discussion on this point flared up after the wall was built. The question was raised as to whether, by their repeated championing of the city's Four-power status, the Western powers were not obligated to provide freedom of movement throughout Berlin and, still more so, whether they were not obligated to keep their promise to guarantee the "freedom of Berlin."

However one answers these questions, the result was the same: in West Berlin as well as in West Germany the wall created widespread disappointment about the Western allies, especially the United States—indeed, the criticism focused on the United States—and doubt about their reliability and even their ability to honor their promises. (It is interesting to speculate in this respect about the extent to which these disappointments and doubts may have been the basis of a growing anti-Americanism, one that sprang up first in Berlin.)

The wall also made people conscious that German reunification would only come about, if at all, as the result of a very long process. Due to an evident misunderstanding of Adenauer's clearly long-term policy aimed at reunification, which until then had found support among all political parties, after August 13, 1961, there was a growing feeling especially among Social Democrats, Free Democrats, and a significant section of the press that the previous policy had failed, that what was important now was to seek a new policy based on the new realities. This sentiment developed into a policy of détente, one result of which was the Four-power Agreement on Berlin of September 3, 1971, as well as the related inter-German arrangements.

Détente and Negotiations on Berlin

Second, the story of the negotiations on Berlin reflects in various ways the détente policy of the 1960s and early 1970s.

Since the mid-1960s the West, building on its internal stability and external strength, was increasingly interested in more intensive and better contacts with the East. Various motives played a role in this. One motive was concern about the danger of accidental war. This meant primarily a need for arms control. It also touched on Berlin at least insofar as it seemed necessary to limit and defuse this possible source of conflict. A second motive was the Western wish to improve the overall situation of West Berlin, primarily economically and psychologically. Not only had there been repeated crises, especially regarding access routes, but in the course of the 1960s there had appeared a number of critical analyses of the city's situation and its future prospects. To be sure, the generally pessimistic tenor of many of these studies seemed exaggerated. Nevertheless, it seemed necessary to reduce the psychological strain under which the city suffered as a result of continual situations of crisis and to improve its economic prospects.

Consequently, the Quadripartite Agreement sought not only to improve access to West Berlin, enhance its security, and make it less subject to crises, but also to reduce West Berlin's isolation. This last goal was to be accomplished by regaining access for West Berliners to East Berlin and the GDR; advancing the integration of West Berlin into the cultural, sports, and economic exchange programs of the Federal Republic of Germany with the East; and, possibly, attaining for West Berlin a special role as the pivot in this East–West exchange.

The two most important goals of the East's policy within the framework of détente were: first, stabilizing the communist political system in Central and Eastern Europe and, second, extending economic relations between East and West as a means of obtaining vitally needed economic assistance from the West for the Soviet Union and its East European partners. The East expected to approach these goals primarily within the context of the West German treaties with the Soviet Union, Poland, Czechoslovakia, and the GDR, as well as by means of an all-European security conference. To obtain these agreements, however, the Soviet Union and the GDR had to compromise on the questions of Berlin and inter-German relations. The Federal Republic of Germany had announced that without a satisfactory agreement on Berlin it would not ratify the Eastern treaties, and both the Federal Republic and the NATO Council made their agreement to a Conference on Security and Cooperation in Europe (CSCE) contingent on a prior arrangement for acceptable inter-German relations. Thus, from the Eastern point of view, negotiations on Berlin were in the first place a response to Western demands, a necessary concession in order to achieve other aims.

Of course, this does not mean that no specific goals were sought in

Berlin. These goals—in line with Soviet Berlin policy over the years—were in essence twofold. The first was the exclusion of East Berlin from the negotiations and concentration on West Berlin. This turned out to be one of the initial problems of the Four-power discussions. It was eventually circumvented by avoidance of the expression "Berlin." The first (general) part of the Quadripartite Agreement speaks of "the relevant area," and the four powers point out that they have come to this agreement "irrespective of the differences in legal views" and "without prejudice to their legal positions." These formulations uphold the Western position, even though all substantive provisions of the agreement concern the "Western sectors of Berlin."

A major aim of the Soviet Union had always been a reduction of the engagement of the three Western powers in Berlin. The first and second Berlin crises are testimony to this. What had, in fact, been achieved by these attacks was a strengthening of Western cohesiveness and commitment to Berlin. Thus, between about 1962 and 1964 a shift in Soviet policy becomes visible: the attacks are now concentrated on the West German presence in Berlin and on the ties between the Federal Republic and Berlin. The wearing crises of the 1960s were primarily concerned with this issue, Soviet hopes obviously being to weaken the vital links between West Berlin and West Germany and to encourage conflict between the Federal Republic and its Western allies over Berlin.

This, then, was the second main goal the East carried into the negotiations: a weakening of the ties between Berlin and West Germany.

The Quadripartite Agreement

Third, the Quadripartite Agreement on Berlin and related inter-German arrangements are, from the Western viewpoint, the most concrete result of détente. Despite initial difficulties and some continuing shortcomings, major Western aims have been achieved.

The improvements refer mainly to four areas. First, the psychological strains on the population of Berlin deriving from the repeated crises and threats have been eliminated. Second, travel between West Berlin and West Germany has been eased significantly. Third, access to East Berlin and the GDR has been reopened for West Berliners. And, fourth, the external representation of West Berlin by the Federal Republic throughout the world has on the whole been accepted despite initial and occasionally minor new difficulties.

Of course, the success of the Quadripartite Agreement does not mean that there have been no further difficulties or Eastern violations of the agreement. In addition, there is always the possibility that the very threat of reversal could become an instrument of blackmail against the West, in particular against the Federal Republic of Germany.

Furthermore, it has been pointed out that most of the concessions on the part of the East are unilaterally reversible. Although this is true, it must be seen that both the treaty itself and the experience of more than ten years of successful interaction would make difficult any attempt to end this relationship, and the West would certainly see it as a strongly negative signal.

More controversial than these four areas is the assessment of the Quadripartite Agreement with regard to the ties between West Berlin and the Federal Republic of Germany. With the Quadripartite Agreement the West accepted a formal limitation of West German federal presence in West Berlin. To be sure, all ties between West Berlin and the Federal Republic not expressly forbidden may, according to the agreement, be "maintained and developed." To obtain Soviet agreement to this principle, however, the West had to withdraw certain forms of federal presence and give the Soviets some voice in determining which were to be permitted, which not. Moreover, the other forms of federal presence have not been carried through without controversy either, as events have shown.

In addition, the Quadripartite Agreement asserts clearly that West Berlin is not "a constituent part of the Federal Republic of Germany and [is] not to be governed by it." Here, too, the West has given a voice to the Soviets. Such a say existed earlier, of course, on the basis of Berlin's Four-power status, but the Quadripartite Agreement to an extent breathed new life into the Soviet Union's right (while in effect diminishing that of the West in East Berlin).

The Western option of integrating West Berlin unilaterally into the Federal Republic—which, with slight limitations, is already possible under West German law—is curtailed by the Quadripartite Agreement. By this I do not mean that this option was necessarily attractive, for in the past there was more to be said against it than in its favor. Rather, the opportunity to choose this option in the future is greatly reduced.

It should be pointed out there is a growing tendency in West Germany to speak of West Berlin as if it were a separate entity. The earlier habit of speaking of either the "Federal Republic of Germany" as implicitly including West Berlin or else the "Federal Republic of Germany, including Berlin (West)" has declined. Television newscasters, for example, talk about traffic from West Berlin to the Federal Republic of Germany, and many similar examples may be found. While I do not want to overdramatize this and similar developments, neither should their psychological impact be underestimated, for changes in terminology often presage symbolically a changing attitude that has political relevance.

A final point refers to the status of East Berlin. Although the West formally interprets the Quadripartite Agreement as operational in the whole of Berlin, it can hardly be denied that the GDR has made some progress in its effort to incorporate East Berlin. The GDR's claim that East Berlin is its capital is accepted by the West in practice. Despite its formal reservations, the West has demonstrated this acceptance by, for example, establishing embassies in East Berlin.

Even more important—and really quite an astounding concession on the part of the West—is the fact that during the inner-German negotiations the West accepted the GDR government as a negotiating partner on Berlin as a matter of course, while the East insisted on negotiating not with the West German federal government, but with the West Berlin Senate.

A Modus Vivendi

Fourth, despite the obvious success of the Quadripartite Agreement, it has not resolved the Berlin question. What we now have is an acceptable modus vivendi.

The basic conflict between East and West in Europe continues. Neither during the negotiations nor in the resulting agreement nor through their behavior have the Soviet Union and the GDR indicated any willingness to compromise on the crucial questions of status. The conduct of the negotiations, the agreement, and the subsequent behavior point rather to a consistent application of the East's policy on Berlin.

Absence of an Overall Perspective

At the same time, the West does not have a clear-cut notion of how it sees the long-term development of Berlin. We do not have an alternative to Soviet intentions and hopes other than a continuation of the status quo in Berlin. This may be a great deal; it may even be sufficient. But it is a rather static view, and it is by no means certain that it can be maintained over the long haul.

It is, of course, correct to say that what has been important in the Western view since 1948–49 was holding on to West Berlin. But Berlin was also an essential element in the long-term plan for German reunification that, even though it had not borne fruit by the end of the 1960s, still provided a great deal of psychic support for the city and its population. Berlin was the "bastion of freedom" or the "West's island-outpost in the red sea of communism." The fact that the wall and the Quadripartite Agreement, as well as some general moves toward détente in Europe, sharply reduced the value of this function was bound to have a long-term effect on the psychology of the city. The question today, therefore, is whether or not it is necessary to replace this old perspective with a new one, and, if so, what should the new perspective be? Can this perspective be an isolated one for Berlin (West)? Or must it be fitted into a broader Western policy of dealing with the Soviet Union? And if that is so: Do we have such a broader policy? Do we have any idea of how we would like Europe, Germany, and Berlin to look, say in fifty years' time?

Discussion

RICHARD MERRITT: Did the West in fact give up a great deal in signing the Quadripartite Agreement? Recognizing the new realities in Europe provided the West with an opportunity to clear the brush and get on with the business of the future. Indeed, it was one of Chancellor Brandt's greatest contributions to détente that he could persuade his allies to take such a stance.

JONATHAN DEAN: It is correct to argue that the agreement provided a modus vivendi rather than a solution to the Berlin question. No one expected an ultimate solution of Central European issues from these talks. That was not their framework, not their task. But their modus-vivendi character is an advantage. Besides defusing the situation in Berlin, a main virtue of the agreement is that it confirmed the provisional nature of the situation in Eastern Europe and left Berlin as a wedge that holds the door of the future open in Central Europe, just as acceding to the Eastern desire to establish West Berlin as a separate entity or even incorporating it into the GDR would have closed it. These political objectives were achieved.

The Quadripartite Agreement did not give the GDR additional status. It says explicitly that the Soviet Union accepts responsibility for the access routes. The subsequent inter-German transit agreement, in turn, refers to the Quadripartite Agreement as the source of its authority for negotiating on this and other points. The underlying Four-power authority inherent in the complex of agreements far outweighs and, I would say, even nullifies the GDR's desire to be regarded as responsible and sovereign on these matters. Similarly, although the West has as a practical matter accepted the role of East Berlin as the capital city of the GDR, that acceptance had nothing to do directly with the Berlin agreements. It was rather part of the overall complex of agreements that ultimately brought the two German states into the United Nations, regulated traffic between West Berlin and West Germany, and so forth.

Whether or not the Federal German presence was weakened in West Berlin through the agreement, as contended, is a much-debated topic and one on which people have various views. In my view, there was simply a trade-off, giving up some symbolic appearances, which did not have a great deal of practical value, in return for a more solid course of development for the city in the future, for obtaining at least some degree of Soviet recognition of the Federal Republic's role not only in having agencies in West Berlin but also in representing the city abroad. This overseas representation, certainly a mighty jump forward from earlier Soviet views on this point, is now generally reflected in international practice. This practice amounts to a de facto recognition of the fact that the Federal Republic represents the western sectors abroad.

What about the much-discussed issue of a "function" or perspective for West Berlin? Is this question well-founded? From a philosophical view, we might well ask if it is necessary for a large, modern city to have a political function or role above and beyond providing a framework for the life of the people who live there? Aside from that question as to whether or not the question of function is a legitimate one, however, I would say that West Berlin does have an international function in the sense of maintaining the principle that the situation in Central Europe is a provisional one. Anything else depends on what we mean by the term "function." If we mean by it the services that a city can perform for some other body, then the logic of geography indicates that Berlin could provide many intensified commercial and financial services for the GDR—albeit perhaps not those spoken of to date. We might look to Hong Kong as an example where, despite a great deal of mutual antagonism and uncertainty about its relationship with the People's Republic of China, a flourishing business takes place.

KLAUS SCHÜTZ: Before responding to some of the major questions raised by Dieter Mahncke, I should like to record my impressions on two other points. First, it was not the view in the Foreign Office that the West was dealing from a position of strength in the late 1960s. There was a feeling that we had to do something to get the discussions on Berlin moving once again. Second, it would be wrong to suggest that West Berliners were anti-American in the years we are discussing. American commandants often told me that West Berlin was the only place in Germany where the American forces could still hold parades; the wall, if anything, led Berliners to try to be as close as possible to the Americans. It meant being pro- rather than anti-American.

Now, what role did Berlin play in the FRG's policy of détente? When Brandt's coalition government came together in the fall of 1969, its members did not know much about each other. Social Democrats were sure about neither the Free Democrats nor some of their own party members. It was a situation in which those of us who were responsible for dealing with the Berlin question could undertake some initiatives, but early efforts to do so encountered not only opposition from those who were prepared to hold on to the status quo (such as leaders of refugee organizations) but also a lack of focus on the part of those who knew something should be done but were not sure what it could be. What we were sure of was that any plan for détente had to include action on Berlin.

Our task, as we in Berlin saw it, was to stamp Berlin into any negotiations that might be initiated. We tried to do this every step of the way, up through the signing of the Quadripartite Agreement. One instance of this was our success in impressing on the government in Bonn the need to refrain from ratifying the Moscow and Warsaw treaties until substantial progress had been made on the Berlin question. This stance led to controversy with Bonn (although not with Brandt), some of it lasting until the signature of the Quadripartite Agreement. Eventually at least a provisional resolution of the Berlin question was accepted as an inherent part of any effort Bonn might make toward détente.

DIETER MAHNCKE: Ambassador Schütz, could you locate the point in time at which this acceptance came—for instance, after Bahr's return from Moscow?

KLAUS SCHÜTZ: It would be difficult to say exactly when it came about. Whenever I was in Bonn, and this was practically every week, I said over and over again that the Berlin question needed to be included in the process, that it would be foolish to think that any treaties could be approved if it were not. There would have been too much opposition otherwise, first and foremost from the Christian Democrats but also from a strong group within the Social Democratic and Free Democratic parties. Now, I do not mean to suggest that we forced a consideration of Berlin into the process. What we did was to raise people's consciousness to the level where it was inevitable that they would include this issue.

Regarding the role of West Berlin, all I can say now is what I tried to say during my last years in that office, though not with much success. Simply keeping a city the size of West Berlin together is a big enough challenge. Why must it have some other function? There was a time when we sought such a function—West Berlin as the city of détente, West Berlin as a cultural center, and so forth. It did not work, and it will not work. In fact, I think that the failure to come up with a function that the city was uniquely qualified to exercise is in part responsible for the pessimism that has frequently cropped up about the city. Each failed attempt left us thinking that the Americans had let us down or that Bonn had let us down or that groups within the city itself had let us down.

There was hardly ever a time when people in West Berlin looked around themselves and said, "You know, it is a miracle that the city continues to exist, given all its troubles, and we really enjoy living in such a city." There were simply too many forces within and without the city insisting that West Berlin *should* have a unique mission. When one considers the problems and crises in the rest of the world and then turns to West Berlin with its two million inhabitants, foreign workers, squatters taking over empty apartment buildings, and all the rest, it should be a cause for rejoicing that this incomparable city continues to thrive. Instead, we are expected to go about looking for some new role, a new mission.

No, this is not the answer. West Berlin simply does not need to have a special role. We don't need to do more than simply survive in the midst of a communist system—a free city that is in itself quite strong, that continues to be regarded by people all around us, including Poles and other Eastern Europeans, as a beacon of freedom.

RENATA FRITSCH-BOURNAZEL: Peter Bender wrote in 1981: "The West Berliners accepted their lot so long as they were important, however much threatened, and so long as they had a clear mission to fulfill on behalf of German unity. Both of these conditions have disappeared in the last two decades, after the wall was built in 1961 and still more since the Four-power Agreement of 1971."[1] What Bender was pointing to is the problem of identity for West Berlin. While this problem may exist for West Germans, too, there it is more one of adaptation than anything else, and is clearly possible. For the West Berliners, by contrast, the problem is one of existence and finding a new role to play.

West Berlin's links with the Federal Republic are a two-edged sword. Insofar as they bring security they are positive, but they are also constraints in the sense that they restrict the city's freedom of action. Even so, such arrangements may be the best we can expect given the current circumstances. It is not clear to me why Dieter Mahncke should expect more from the modus vivendi in Berlin than from other such arrangements concluded during the era of détente. Such arrangements are the very essence of détente. It has never meant the end of conflict but rather a limiting of its scope and the forms in which it is carried out. These are the rules of the game in the era of détente.

Regarding Shepard Stone's question about the long-term aims of the East, I cannot agree with Ambassador Schütz that the Soviet Union would like to see West Berlin absorbed into the GDR. The continued existence of the city serves to deter the West from exerting pressure elsewhere.

DAVID KLEIN: Dieter Mahncke has raised an important question about the future of West Berlin. The events that led to the fall of Dietrich Stobbe's government in 1981 indicate the nature of the problem. West Berlin is not an ordinary big city. It is basically a small town which has the function of a big city, and part of the problem is devising means for keeping the trappings of a big city. This, in turn, cannot be done unless there is a clearly conceived perspective regarding West Berlin's purpose. Now, it need not be the driving purpose that the city once had, but someone must provide a function and a reason to bring talent to West Berlin. The political turmoil in early 1981 was especially interesting because, ultimately, the three political parties had to send someone from West Germany to take charge in West Berlin—a fact which nullifies Dieter Mahncke's assertion that West Berlin is written off as a separate entity. Rather, it indicates the close relationship between the two areas. Someone must begin to think in terms of how the city can be kept going despite the fact that it sits there in a normalcy that is not very normal for any big city.

RICHARD MERRITT: If I understand Dieter Mahncke correctly, he was saying that the costs involved in maintaining links between West Berlin and West Germany are not merely symbolic but also real. It cost West Germany quite a bit of energy during the political crisis of early 1981 to pull West Berlin's chestnuts out of the fire. And it costs the Federal Republic a great deal of money to maintain West Berlin in the style to which its citizens have become accustomed. The question I would ask is: when will the West Germans say that the costs of sustaining West Berlin are simply too high? Or are some saying this already?[2]

DAVID KLEIN: Surely, no German politician is willing to take such a stance publicly.

HANS OTTO BRÄUTIGAM: Dieter Mahncke seems to be assuming that a major goal of the Four-Power negotiations was the full incorporation of West Berlin into the Federal Republic. This would be unrealistic, because it would weaken the Allies' sense of responsibility for the city, which is something definitely not in the FRG's interest. We have struck a rather good balance between Allied and German responsibilities for the city. It is in our interest to keep this balance as it is.

Ties between West Berlin and West Germany were certainly an important element in the Four-power negotiations. It would be a mistake, however, to see these ties primarily in terms of the Federal German presence. Such a presence is important, especially symbolically, but the question of whether there is one federal agency more or less located in the city is not the essential one. What really counts is the continuing integration of West Berlin into the Federal Republic's legal, social, economic, and financial system. In this respect we have had no problem. More problematic, although still not a danger, is the organization—but not the principle—of West Berlin's overseas representation. In short, the concept of ties is well established in the Four-power Agreement.

Regarding Berlin's role, the core of the issue is giving the people in West Berlin and West Germany the confidence that the city is quite worthwhile as a place to live in and is highly likely to remain so in the future. This means realizing the expectation that living conditions not only will continue to be attractive but will be at the same level as any other large city in West Europe. It is therefore essential to tackle the internal problems facing the city today. By this I do not mean shifts in governance, for such events could characterize any other metropolis in democratic society. Rather, the danger is that the continued existence of very difficult internal problems may escalate to crisis levels because of the political climate in the city. Even if Berlin does not have a special role to play, its climate is rather different from that in other big cities in the country. It is still influenced by the wall, which prompts a very emotional reaction to anything that happens in East–West relations. Then, too, feelings of insecurity may appear much more quickly and in a more massive form in Berlin than elsewhere. Hence it is all the more important that all political forces in the city stand together to deal with the problems West Berlin is facing today.

SHEPARD STONE: But the city cannot solve its problems alone. Every big city, whether it be New York, Paris, or somewhere else, depends on people coming in from outside the city. It is fine that, during the governmental crisis of 1981 and subsequently, the various parties sent a few politicians to Berlin, but what is needed is a constant infusion of new blood from all parts of the Federal Republic. The internal problems of West Berlin are those of the Federal Republic as well.

FRANCIS MAC GINNIS: Dieter Mahncke has asked whether or not the West paid too high a price for the Quadripartite Agreement. As I suggested earlier, since it was the Germans who had to pay the main price, it is ultimately they who must answer such a question. The Allies, or at least the British government, saw the price to be concessions to reality and the results to be very much worth it. It was most emphatically not a settlement, and I believe that none of the Allied governments ever published a thing which called it that. It was a limited modus vivendi. The occasional gray areas and infringements notwithstanding, it has worked very well.

ANTONIUS EITEL: While there are surely shortcomings in the agreement on Berlin, as Dieter Mahncke has pointed out, the overall balance is a good one. I was especially interested in Ambassador Schütz's remark about the lack of planning on a working level regarding the various agreements with the East. He was probably referring to the political levels of the government. On a lower level, in the Foreign Office, for instance, there was some planning. From Ambassador Schütz's remark I conclude that plans that included the Berlin question never made it to those higher levels (although many of the things we proposed were subsequently adopted).

Regarding the place of Berlin in the East–West negotiations, I would note that it was mentioned in Moscow as early as January 1970, during the first exchange of views. The problem is only that it was raised by the Soviet side, which was probably trying to circumvent Four-power negotiations on this issue. The West German side felt that we could not accept the invitation to discuss it because Berlin was too big an issue and the Soviet Union too imposing a negotiating power. Instead, the Germans simply pointed out their vital interest in Berlin but their limited competence to speak for it.

Later, after the Western allies and Bonn had gone back and forth on the question of who should negotiate what with whom, German spokesmen raised the issue again with their counterparts in Moscow. This time it was the Soviet Union, which by then had agreed to Four-power consultations, that declared itself in no position to discuss Berlin with the West German delegation. The latter nevertheless stated the FRG's position as one of its concrete interests. Thus Berlin was, from the very outset, in the minds of the negotiators.

While I would agree with Ambassador Schütz that there is no need, and indeed it is probably a bad idea, to look for a special role for Berlin, and that normality is the best role it can play, the comparison with Hong Kong is instructive. Given Berlin's geopolitical situation, a bit more ferment is needed than might be the case in, say, Düsseldorf or Hamburg. Without that extra something the point of comparison might be Macao rather than Hong Kong. The latter has managed to make itself vital to other countries whereas Macao has not. It is something similar that Berlin needs if its position is not to deteriorate.

DIETER MAHNCKE: May I insert two additional questions into our discussion? First, during the Four-power negotiations, was any effort made to establish the city government of East Berlin as a negotiating partner for West Berlin's Senate? The status that the GDR obtained for East Berlin was, in my view, a more important concession than the decision to establish embassies there. The second has to do with the external representation of West Berlin. The fact that the Federal Republic of Germany represents West Berlin overseas is accepted throughout the world—except in the East, which continues to balk, albeit less and less so. In the communications accompanying the signature of the Quadripartite Agreement the Western allies asserted their agreement that, for certain purposes, the Federal Republic could represent West Berlin abroad, whereas the Soviet Union merely stated that it would raise no objection to this practice. Is the Soviet formulation, which seems to be the stronger of the two, properly understood in the West?

JOHN KORNBLUM: As far as the letter accompanying the agreement is concerned, that was a construction we worked out. The first part of it should not be seen as describing what exists now; we did not agree to anything new in this part. The second part, which has the Soviet Union not objecting to the existing situation, is not interpreted as constitutive.

JONATHAN DEAN: The question of representation was the most difficult balancing act of all because, as Hans Otto Bräutigam pointed out, it seeks to balance Four-power responsibilities with the Federal German role and ties with Berlin, and, where Berlin's interests are being represented abroad, we are certainly in the international arena of Four-power responsibility. But a good practical solution was found which preserved the legal status while providing day-to-day help for Berliners abroad. This issue came up early in the negotiations, was adumbrated, but then, toward the end, really got hot. I am still somewhat surprised at the degree to which the Soviets were willing to accept this concept of representation by the FRG.

As regards actual practice, the acceptance by the Soviet Union and its allies of the Federal Republic's representation of West Berlin presents a mixed picture with respect to their own territory. Moreover, they contested the point in a number of Third World countries, with the result that there was far from automatic acceptance of the FRG as the representative of West Berlin. For the most part, these controversies have now been regulated. I might add that, in several cases, the Federal Republic would seem to have pressed its side early and hard, risking a negative reaction from some of these Third World countries. Nonetheless, there now exist grounds of principle that did not exist before, and which permit the FRG to pursue this form of representation in the future.

JÜRGEN ENGERT: The problem of identification mentioned by several participants exists on both sides of the wall. In the GDR today there is little or no identification with East Berlin on the part of various groups in the population (we might almost speak of tribes). There is in East Berlin a "capital-city bonus," similar to the tax preferences enjoyed in West Berlin, and the living standard there is considerably higher than in the rest of the GDR. This is felt very deeply outside the city.

The GDR's leadership has not been successful in the measures it has taken to foster a national sense of identification that includes East Berlin. An example: in East Berlin there was a soccer team in the People's Army, called Armee-Sport-Klub (ASK), which received tremendous support from the state in terms of both financing and manpower. It nonetheless played before empty stadiums. There was another team, Union Oberschöneweide, which had long existed in East Berlin and was not even in the major league but rather one of the minor leagues. Even so, when it played the stadium was full. The difference in the popular reception of these two clubs was so great, the demonstration effect so crass, that the government felt constrained to transfer Union Oberschöneweide to the provincial town of Frankfurt-an-der-Oder, some fifty-five miles to the east of Berlin. It was hoped that its absence would make it easier for East Berliners to transfer their allegiance to the army team.

Just as the gap between West Berliners and West Germans is a problem for the West, so, too, the gap between East Berliners and East Germans is problematic for the leadership of the GDR. Walter Ulbricht would have had an easier task of creating a national identity for the GDR had he moved the capital to Leipzig or Dresden instead of leaving it in East Berlin. One may look for the roots of this all-German identity problem in longstanding traditions, but the point is that it continues to the present day.

JOHANN BAPTIST GRADL: The relationship between the Berlin and Cuban crises needs to be underscored. The fact that the Americans were able to prevent the Soviets from installing missiles in Cuba in 1962 was viewed in Berlin and elsewhere as a victory over Soviet expansionism. It encouraged the West to consider whether or not the time was ripe to seek a better climate of relations with the East. But we were also concerned about Berlin. Should it not be possible to protect Berlin against repeated Soviet efforts to control or at least isolate it, then the Soviets would achieve a major triumph, one that would be so much in the public eye internationally that they could say, "In the last analysis we are the stronger power." We in Berlin (and in the Federal Republic, too, for that matter) would not accept either of these outcomes.

After the Cuban experience the Federal Republic initiated efforts aimed at the renunciation of force as an instrument of national policy. In 1964, Ludwig Erhard's administration talked directly with Khrushchev about bilateral negotiations, and an exchange of notes continued until 1968 under the chancellorship of Kurt Georg Kiesinger. The goal was to create a climate in the Federal Republic in which it would be possible to reduce Berlin's potential as a point of crisis and soften the effects of the wall and the armed border through Germany. I am not certain why this effort collapsed. But one day in January 1968 a note came from the Soviet Union which contained eight or nine points, all of which dealt somehow with Berlin and aimed at breaking off the ties between Berlin and the Federal Republic. When asked by Chancellor Kiesinger what my views were, I responded that only one point was acceptable: the very first one, which stated that, in the future, no Bundestag committees having anything to do with military affairs could function in West Berlin. Although the exchange of notes continued, the tone and content of this particular one indicated that the Soviet Union was not then prepared to yield on its desire to control all of Berlin.

This Soviet rebuff, of course, did not stop our efforts to resolve the Berlin question. In spring 1969 Vice-President Spiro Agnew, speaking before the Bundestag, declared that Berlin had to be protected, that no untoward events should be permitted to occur there. This netted him an overwhelming ovation—but, at the same time, everyone recognized that the Soviets would be unrelenting. It was this recognition that accounted in part for the willingness of the opposition to cooperate with Chancellor Brandt's Social Democratic–Liberal coalition. We drew up precisely formulated ideas, participated in discussions on the points our Allies might be encouraged to pursue, and so forth.

The result, ultimately, was the Four-power Agreement, perhaps the most essential reason why the Eastern treaties came off. Because of it we in the opposition were willing, albeit with heavy hearts, to let the Eastern treaties go by. There was always the question of what would happen from the German or the international standpoint if Berlin were to be removed as a point of discussion? Moreover, now that the negotiations had moved ahead as far as they had, who could assume responsibility for stopping the Quadripartite Agreement, whatever its defects might be? We were driven mainly by the desire to end the Soviets' use of Berlin as an instrument of political blackmail. By and large I would have to say that this goal was accomplished.

MARTIN HILLENBRAND: Dieter Mahncke asked whether or not there was any philosophy or organized body of thought behind Brandt's *Ostpolitik*. Antonius Eitel has already mentioned that in the Foreign Office's planning staff there was a certain amount of coherent thinking on the subject. Another stream of thought that made a contribution came from the group around Leo Bauer, those associated with the Social Democratic newspaper *Vorwärts,* whose clearly articulated philosophy influenced Willy Brandt and certainly Egon Bahr, as indicated in his formulation, "change through coming closer" (*Wandlung durch Annäherung*). This perspective bears directly on Dr. Mahncke's question of whether or not there are alternatives to merely continuing the status quo in Berlin or permitting the city's assimilation into the GDR. The argument, which may seem unrealistic, is that the series of agreements represented by the *Ostpolitik* could gradually bring about a change in the situation of Eastern Europe so that, at some point in the future, the Soviet Union might conclude that its security interests no longer require the kind of consolidated hold over Eastern Europe and particularly East Germany that it now considers essential. At that point, perhaps two decades or so from now, Berlin would again be able to resume its rightful place as the capital of a reunified Germany.

Turning to the balance of advantage and disadvantage in the Fourpower Agreement, I would say that the history of the negotiations should not be forgotten. We have already heard how closely the Federal Republic was integrated into the review process and in the preparation of positions. It should also be noted that there were certain points along the way where, at least on the American side and I suspect also on the part of the French and British in some cases, the reluctance to make concessions was overcome by pressure from the German Federal government to get on with the negotiations. We accepted these pressures as representing a balanced evaluation of all the pros and cons involved in the negotiations. A detailed review of the full history of the negotiations, when it becomes available, will reveal a number of instances where we were told that we were pettifogging and delaying the negotiations by being too tough and asking for further concessions from the Soviets.

Part 3 Berlin in Its New International Context

6 Twenty Years of Berlin History

Martin J. Hillenbrand

Any review of Berlin's history since 1961 must begin with the fact that in that year the city was the focal point of confrontation between the Soviet Union and the Western powers. Nikita Khrushchev had launched the crisis with his ultimatum of November 1958, and for five years Berlin was destined to be a center of attention for the world press and for the highest levels of government. At stake was the credibility of the Allied, and ultimately the American, guarantee of the city's security.[1]

The summer began with the meeting in Vienna between Kennedy and Khrushchev. That gathering was not only tense for the American president, it was also highly educational. It was followed by a period of intensive Allied consultation culminating in an American decision to call up the reserves, to strengthen U.S. forces in Europe, and to increase arms expenditures. Then, on August 13, 1961, construction of the Berlin wall began. From the outset it was clear that the wall was a Soviet-approved East German response to the seemingly endless flow of refugees from the GDR, which in the last days of July and early August had reached panic proportions. For some time the feeling had been growing on the Western side that the GDR would have to undertake something to stop the loss of its population, but the precise action of building a wall along the boundary between the eastern and western sectors caught the West generally by surprise.

Whatever the weight of arguments about failures of Allied intelligence and the unwillingness of the occupying authorities in West Berlin to take effective countermeasures,[2] the wall was immediately effective in ending the mass movement from East to West Berlin. It also radically and permanently transformed one of the important roles that West Berlin had played until the summer of 1961—the role of *Treffpunkt Berlin,* as a meeting place for those from the East and the West. Its special situation, its greater freedom, and its prosperity had made it both a magnetic attraction and a destabilizing influence in the GDR and to some extent in all of Eastern Europe. The wall changed all this. Although West Berlin radio and gradually television could still penetrate into East Germany, the absence of virtually any personal movement from East to West made a rethinking of West Berlin's function inevitable.

The Changed Crisis

The Berlin crisis, of course, continued. Despite the ignominy attached to it, the wall was effective and in due course that very effectiveness was one of the reasons why the crisis came to an end in the fall of 1963. It would be wrong to impute to it, however, as some commentators have done, almost exclusive causal responsibility. The objective of getting the Allies out of Berlin so that the entire city could become a part of the GDR continued to be a primary Soviet objective. There was, for two more years, severe harassment of Allied and German access to the city, and the bilateral talks on Berlin between Secretary of State Dean Rusk and Soviet Foreign Minister Andrei Gromyko, held periodically in New York and Geneva, ground to an inconclusive halt by the summer of 1962. The Cuban missile crisis of early autumn 1962 undoubtedly contributed to the eventual end of the confrontation, but here again the perceptions of those dealing with the problem at the time in Washington, London, and Paris were not all that clear. It was only in the autumn of 1963, a year after the missile crisis and after serious interference with the access of Allied convoys on the *Autobahn* in October that the Soviets gave up and in effect stopped pressing their claims against a continuing Western presence in Berlin.[3]

The evident Soviet change of tactics that took place in autumn 1963 suggests that the Soviet Union recognized that threats, pressures, and harassments could not drive the Western allies out of Berlin and that it hoped that new and more subtle approaches could produce better results, at least over time. There is no reason to believe that Soviet long-range objectives with respect to the city had changed, despite the relief provided by the wall. A relative lull took over and, by the end of the decade, as the move toward détente gained momentum, the Soviets seemed more and more willing to subordinate their Berlin objectives to more immediate goals.

After five years of strain and tension, which had put it in the center of world news, the city entered a difficult period of psychological adjustment. The sense of drama and purpose that the earlier years had provided was now gone, and the Berliners had to adjust to a new and more prosaic era. The excitement which the pre-wall freedom of movement from East to West had brought to the city was also gone, though ironically enough the wall, as a man-made monstrosity, became a major tourist attraction. Commentators began to speak of the provincialization of West Berlin, and critics even began to note a certain slackening of energy and creativity in its highly diversified cultural life.

Economically, the city continued to fare well as an integral part of the West German market. As the economy of the Federal Republic grew and prospered so the economy of the city grew and prospered at a parallel pace. The special set of subsidies that the latter enjoyed was considered an essential part of the obligation that the government in Bonn owed to the symbol of the ultimate goal of German national unity, and it is worth noting that, over the years, those subsidies that come out of the federal budget have never really been a subject of serious controversy. To be sure, the headquarters of several major German firms have been moved away from Berlin but no significant transfer of manufacturing facilities has taken place. The Berlin mystique provided a potent argument for German management to retain those facilities despite the continuing uncertainties of transport which the isolated and exposed position of the city necessarily entailed.

Another problem that a number of observers began to note sprang from some alarming demographic trends showing the median level of the population growing older and recruitment of younger workers and managers from the West largely stagnating. Given the structure of the city's population after the war and the loss of its rural hinterland, experts had long anticipated an absolute decline in inhabitants. But the reality of a shrinking city was difficult for many Berliners to accept or comprehend. The trend was, of course, to accelerate during the 1970s as the older groups in the top-heavy population pyramid began to die off. It should be noted, however, that the city never developed a serious shortage of labor since Berlin firms stayed in the forefront of rationalization.[4]

With the departure of Willy Brandt from Berlin in 1966 to become foreign minister in the Grand Coalition under Chancellor Kurt Georg Kiesinger, the city lost its last governing mayor who was at the same time a major political figure in his own right. A succession of well-intentioned but lesser SPD governing mayors was unable to provide the kind of inspirational and innovative leadership that the city required. In addition, there developed a kind of unhealthy dependency on the generous subsidies provided by the Federal Republic—a subsidy mentality that led to an unwarranted tolerance of waste combined with an easy assurance that the pipeline would never run dry. The process, vividly described by the untranslatable German word *Verfilzung,* created a sort of safe haven for mediocre politicians who set the dominant tone for the city's public life.

That much having been said, there is little evidence that the western sectors of Berlin were run notably worse than other leading European cities, and there were always a few bright spirits who gave some sparkle to the cultural, economic, and even political life of those sectors. Then, too, West Berlin was a part of the larger world picture, and the movements and the troubles of the 1960s and early 1970s found their counterparts in the city. Thus student and young faculty unrest and radicalization had full play at both the Free University and the Technical University—a development that led to a dramatic decline in their reputations, particularly that of the Free University. City officials responsible for education were no more effective in dealing with the chaos in the universities than were the beleaguered faculties and administrators. The problem in Berlin was accentuated by the inordinate number of radicalized students that flowed to the city, some to escape conscription into the Bundeswehr, others attracted by the new reputation of the Free University as a place where anything went and where the intellectual demands were relatively low.

The occupying powers did not like these developments, but could do little about them. It was a sad irony that the Free University, whose origins owed so much to American generosity in the early postwar period, should have become a center of anti-American agitation, and that the John F. Kennedy Institute should have become dominated by leftist elements. But these disturbances, as unpalatable as they may have been, had surprisingly little influence on the basically positive attitude of the Allies toward the city, or for that matter on the fundamentally broad support of the bulk of the population for the continuing protective presence of the Allies, particularly the Americans.

And on the other side of the Atlantic, very few Americans argued that, if Berlin university students represented the sentiments of the Berliners (which to those on the spot they obviously did not), then the occupation should simply end and the city be left to shift for itself. One of the constants of the postwar period has been the strong American support for Berlin and the willingness to provide without qualification that continuing form of guarantee which the presence of some 6,000 American troops afforded. Even during the heyday of Mansfieldism and the call for a reduction in American forces in the Federal Republic, the need for an indefinite military presence in Berlin was never seriously questioned. Nor has the precise size of those forces ever been an issue; it has in fact never been seriously discussed since the Geneva conference of foreign ministers in 1959. Indeed, in 1961 President Kennedy increased the size of the garrison by sending an additional battalion to the city; it was later withdrawn.

As the crisis of 1958–63 demonstrated, the security of West Berlin also had an additional NATO dimension. Not only would any attack on the city inevitably be of direct concern to the Alliance and involve British, French, and American forces, but by a somewhat involved series of interrelated agreements and declarations, there are important NATO guarantees for the city. This is true even though the three garrisons are not under NATO command, and the occupying authorities have been meticulous in banning directly related NATO activities in the city. Time and again the unique case of Berlin has demonstrated that countries and their leaders are willing to assume responsibilities toward the western sectors because of their overriding political importance without having that degree of control and involvement that they would normally demand.[5]

The Quadripartite Agreement on Berlin

With the SPD electoral victory in the fall of 1969 and the formation of the Brandt government in Bonn, a new era began for Berlin. The chancellor was determined to push ahead with his *Ostpolitik,* and he saw negotiations over Berlin as an integral part of that process. The early reception in the White House was cool, and National Security Adviser Henry Kissinger missed few occasions to express his disquiet about the whole business.[6] The State Department was considerably more relaxed and at an early point saw both a possible, if somewhat remote, opportunity to improve access to the city and the futility of trying to hamper by verbal assault what was obviously a considered and determined new direction of West German policy. It became clear at an early stage that Soviet willingness to make concessions on Berlin would ultimately determine whether or not the whole complex of agreements that was to be the concrete result of the *Ostpolitik* could be completed and ratified. Whether accepted in theory or not (and the Soviets were openly unhappy about the concept), the political realities were such that both sides had to emerge from the negotiations with real gains for their own views.

The Four-power negotiations on Berlin began on March 26, 1970. The prospects did not appear particularly good. Both sides began by restating their long-established positions, embodied in some fifteen years of exchanging notes and protests, and it seemed as if never the twain could meet. The subsequent story of the Four-power negotiations is a highly interesting one, both for historians and international lawyers. Political and legal issues relating to the city's postwar history have been uniquely intertwined. On the one hand, the great note exchanges between the Soviets and the Allies were conducted essentially in legal terms. On the other hand, Soviet arguments occasionally reflected their clearly superior position given the geographic location of Berlin. However, discussions of this period too frequently dwell on the political confrontations between East and West, without much regard for the underlying legal issues that both sides used to justify those confrontations and that served as the basis of their verbal disputes. These seemingly endless discussions are an integral part of the complicated background that must be understood for a full appreciation of the peculiar equilibrium of positions finally achieved in the Quadripartite Agreement on Berlin.[7] The Western powers proceeded on the assumption that, while the security of the city rested ultimately on the political determination of the Allies to maintain their position, their legal position had to be airtight and that any challenge to Allied rights would be demonstrably in violation of the rights of conquest along with the early implementing agreements that had been made with the Soviets.

One aspect of Berlin's politico-legal history that has been a source of difficulty between the Federal Republic and the occupying Powers is the precise relationship of the city to West Germany. Finding a definition of this relationship that was acceptable to both the Eastern and Western sides became an important prerequisite to the Quadripartite Agreement as well as a source of continuing controversy. From the beginning the Allies insisted that as occupying Powers they could not accept the three western sectors as an integral part of the Federal Republic. Thus in 1949 the three Allied military governors refused to accept the provisions of Articles 23 and 144 of the Basic Law, which implied that Berlin enjoyed voting membership in the Bundestag or Bundesrat, or that Berlin was governed by the federation.[8]

While Allied authority in Berlin forced them to accept this limitation, German officials and particularly federal judges were never happy with it. They developed the doctrine of the legal unity of Berlin and West Germany, a doctrine which the Allies accepted at least to a degree by permitting the separate adoption of federal laws and treaties by the West Berlin government. They could not, however, permit extension of the authority of the Federal Constitutional Court in Karlsruhe in a way that implied that decisions of the court were automatically applicable in Berlin even when they ran counter to Allied legislation, or attempted to extend the competence of the court or of federal law beyond that permitted by the occupying Powers.[9] Thus, in a very real sense, a politico-legal history of Berlin must concern itself primarily with the law of the occupying Powers, their rights and obligations, and the challenges to them by the Soviet Union. Given the economic dependence of the city on the Federal Republic, there has always seemed to be something artificial about Allied insistence on their prerogatives, but experience has shown that in a very real sense the continuing security of the city depends on the maintenance of these distinctions. There was indeed a time in the mid-1950s when some Allied officials argued that the Western occupying powers could gradually let the exercise of their rights with respect to Bonn and the Berlin city government lapse into desuetude, but the Khrushchev challenge and then the negotiation of the Quadripartite Agreement demonstrated how essential their maintenance was. One of the ironic consequences of that agreement has been a revitalization of certain military government functions in Berlin to ensure that inconsistent actions do not take place.

At about the time the discussions among the four ambassadors in Berlin appeared to be at dead center, certain events occurred which were to have a direct impact on those negotiations. Despite White House doubts, the West Germans had pushed ahead rapidly and concluded the Moscow treaty with the Soviet Union, followed by a treaty with Warsaw. At the same time, the Soviet leadership was mounting a major campaign to convene a Conference on Security and Cooperation in Europe (CSCE), and the NATO countries in turn were urging a Conference on Mutual and Balanced Force Reductions (MBFR). Reinforcing these various developments was the compelling desire of the German Democratic Republic to obtain that full measure of official recognition that it had been so long denied by rigorous application of the Hallstein Doctrine and the willingness of the Federal Republic's allies to support that doctrine whenever the need arose. So it was that, by the end of 1970, a network of mutually reinforcing causal factors was operating to motivate a breakthrough in the Berlin negotiations. The West Germans were refusing to ratify the Moscow and Warsaw treaties until agreement had been reached in the Quadripartite forum, success in which was also essential for full recognition of the GDR. The NATO Allies refused to move toward a Conference on Security and Cooperation in Europe until the negotiations on Berlin had succeeded. Pressure was not, however, directed solely at the Soviets. The *Ostpolitik* had acquired considerable momentum of its own, and West German urgings to move the negotiations along were also aimed at the British, French, and Americans.

By early 1971 these forces began to converge. At about this time the White House had decided to get on the bandwagon as well, since the advantages of détente had been accepted. While the Department of State continued to carry the burden of day-to-day development and coordination for the American position, and of coordination with the other negotiating partners, Henry Kissinger developed a back-channel relationship with the Soviets that he describes in some detail in his memoirs.[10] His activities provided not only a source of mystification and irritation for the British and French, but also considerably confused the internal processes of the U.S. government. Whether they were necessary to achieve the agreement that was finally reached is at least open to discussion.[11] Certainly, a procedure that involved direct communication between one section of the government, in this case the White House, and the negotiator in the field, Ambassador Kenneth Rush, without keeping the secretary of state informed, was not calculated to contribute to clarity or precision.

In any event the prospect of success in the negotiations did not become apparent until 1971, when both sides recognized that they could not obtain from the other acceptance of its own legal position with respect to Berlin. Thus, the controversial issue of whether the agreement applied to all of Berlin or merely to the three western sectors was "resolved" by use of the vague expression "relevant area." The opening portions of the agreement contain such language as "Taking into account the existing situation in the relevant area" and "Without prejudice to their legal positions."[12] Other such language which represented mutual forbearance was contained, for instance, in Part I of the General Provisions, which states: "the Four Governments will mutually respect their individual and joint rights and responsibilities, which remain unchanged," and "the Four Governments agree that irrespective of the differences in legal views, the situation which has developed in the area, and as it is defined in this Agreement as well as in the other agreements referred to in this Agreement shall not be changed unilaterally."

Finally, after a dramatic July and August, the four ambassadors reached agreement on August 23, 1971. Formal signature by the four took place in Berlin on September 3, 1971. While all this was going on, the citizens and indeed the government of West Berlin were able to play only a very passive role. They knew that important negotiations were underway that would vitally affect the future of the city, and the Allies and federal government did their best to keep the governing mayor informed, but the input and the momentum came from elsewhere. The Berliners were not entirely happy about some of the Western concessions made along the way when they learned of them, but improvements in the access regime were so clear and indisputable that scarcely anyone in the city was prepared to challenge the final results of the full agreement.

What the Agreement Says

Because of its overriding importance, it is worth noting some of the principal features of the Quadripartite Agreement. In many respects it was a peculiar document—a sort of umbrella completed only by a group of subordinate agreements. Interestingly, those subordinate agreements had been negotiated between the Federal Republic and the German Democratic Republic, neither of which was a party to the basic agreement; even so, they were an integral part of the overall agreement with presumably the same legal force, at least to the extent that each of the two parties would hold the other (the three Western allies or the Soviet Union, as the case might be) responsible for any alleged violations.

The first point that needs to be made is that the title of the agreement itself became a revelatory issue between the Soviets and the three Western powers. While the latter in their official documentation used the designation "Quadripartite Agreement on Berlin," the heading of the document actually signed by the four ambassadors in Berlin on September 3, 1971, was simply "Quadripartite Agreement." This represented the type of pragmatic compromise to which we have referred and without which it would have been impossible to reach agreement.

After the General Provisions, some of the language of which we have quoted, the most important provision from the Western point of view is the declaration contained in Part 2 by the government of the Soviet Union that "transit traffic by road, rail and waterways through the territory of the German Democratic Republic of civilian persons and goods between the Western Sectors of Berlin and the Federal Republic of Germany will be unimpeded; that such traffic will be facilitated so as to take place in the most simple and expeditious manner; and that it will receive preferential treatment." It also provided that detailed arrangements concerning this civilian traffic would be made by the appropriate German authorities (this agreement was contained in Annex 1 to the Quadripartite Agreement).

Further, the French, U.K., and U.S. governments declared in Part 2, "The ties between the Western Sectors of Berlin and the Federal Republic of Germany will be maintained and developed, taking into account that these Sectors continue not to be a constituent part of the Federal Republic of Germany and not to be governed by it." The detailed arrangements concerning the relationship between the western sectors of Berlin and the Federal Republic of Germany were set forth in Annex 2 to the agreement.

Part 2 also contained a declaration by the government of the Soviet Union stating: "Communications between the Western Sectors of Berlin and areas bordering on these Sectors and those areas of the German Democratic Republic which do not border on these Sectors will be improved. Permanent residents of the Western Sectors of Berlin will be able to travel to and visit such areas for compassionate, family, religious, cultural or commercial reasons, or as tourists, under conditions comparable to those applying to other persons entering these areas." It was noted that detailed arrangements concerning travel, communications, and the exchange of territory (primarily Steinstücken, but also some other small areas) would be made by the appropriate German authorities and described in Annex 3.

Finally, Part 2 stated that representation abroad of the interests of the western sectors of Berlin "and consular activities of the Union of Soviet Socialist Republics in the Western Sectors of Berlin can be exercised as set forth in Annex 4."

These four annexes, spelling out the details of the points made in Part 2, are in the form of communications from the government of the Soviet Union to the French, U.K., and U.S. governments (Annex 1 and Annex 3); or conversely in the form of communications from the French, U.K., and U.S. governments to the government of the Soviet Union (Annex 2 and Annex 4). This somewhat peculiar format arose out of the fact that the Soviet government was in effect acting as a conduit for the transmission to the Allies of GDR commitments, while the

Western allies were acting as a conduit for the transmission of FRG commitments. The actual language of these annexes was, of course, agreed among the four negotiating powers, together with two agreed minutes.

Berlin Since 1972

The history of Berlin since 1972 is largely intertwined with the operation of the Quadripartite Agreement. While the Berlin economy continued to behave generally in tandem with that of the Federal Republic, the visible improvement of access and movement of people and goods did much to remove that element of uncertainty that had previously added extra risk to any venture in the western sectors. There was no great spurt in economic growth, as some anticipated, but there was a sounder basis for long-term investment and planning.

Moreover, the possibility of large-scale movement of West Germans and West Berliners into East Berlin and the GDR (the reverse, of course, was not possible except for the aged and the generally unwanted) improved the psychological climate in and about the city, at least to the extent that the visible monstrosity of the wall permitted. And even though East Germans could not come to see it for themselves, a great number of them could observe life in the West via television and could draw their own conclusions.

At the same time, the exhaustion of political forces in the western sectors continued. The Berliners were not badly governed, but, with the excitement and the challenge of earlier days gone, routinization took over. Officials went through their normal paces, but with few exceptions imagination and creativity were not much in evidence. The usual round of festivals, fairs, and other events went on, but participation in them, even for the occupying Powers, sometimes seemed more of a required chore than something to be done with zest and for positive advantage. While there was frequently talk of withdrawing from such annual events as Green Week, the Allies knew that they had to make a show of presence lest their absence be interpreted as a sign of waning confidence and loss of commitment to Berlin and its institutions.

The demographic and human aspects of the city also showed some dramatic changes during the 1970s. The movement of foreign workers into the city, mainly Turks, transformed the physical appearance and sociology of certain portions of Berlin. Some parts of Kreuzberg came to resemble a Turkish city and the problems of education, language, and general cultural conflict became part of the normal problems with which city officials had to deal.[13] In addition to those foreign workers who entered the western sectors legally, an illegal flow of Turks, Pakistanis, and others continued through Schönefeld Airport in the GDR. Committed as they were to the principle of free movement across the sector boundaries, neither the occupying Powers nor the Berlin civil authorities were in a position to stop this flow, thus adding to both the unemployment and the assimilation problem.

During the 1970s the western sectors also witnessed a number of other urbanological developments that contributed to the burden of public administration and to the prevailing feeling that problems were piling up beyond the capacity of the public authorities to handle. For example, the western sectors seemed to have a larger number of drug addicts than most German cities, and there was a higher estimated death rate for heroin users in Berlin, although in recent years there has been some equalization of these disparities.[14]

The implementation of the Quadripartite Agreement, while generally satisfactory and clearly an improvement over what had gone before, was not without its difficulties. The Soviets were determined to prevent any activities that in their view tended to further the incorporation of the western sectors into the Federal Republic and maintained a steady fusillade of protests against the appearance of German officials in the city, meetings of federal political groups, or anything else that seemed to imply the existence of political ties between Bonn and Berlin. While, as we have seen, the Western powers had been willing in the Quadripartite Agreement to reiterate their standard position that the three western sectors were not a constitutive part of the Federal Republic and were not governed by it, they maintained that the language of the agreement permitted all ongoing practices that were not specifically prohibited by the agreement; prohibited were any activities by the federal president, the federal government, the Bundesversammlung, the Bundesrat, or the Bundestag that would constitute performance in the western sectors of constitutional or official acts contrary to the principle that these sectors continued not to be a constituent part of the Federal Republic of Germany and were not governed by it. The Soviets refused to accept this and, in effect, attempted to turn the clock back. The numerous Soviet protests listed in the GDR publication *Das Vierseitige Abkommen über Westberlin und seine Realisierung, Dokumente 1971–1977*[15] is impressive for the number and frequency of items relating to the Berlin–FRG ties. Yet, it should be noted, despite all this diplomatic grumbling, the Soviets never took any serious countermeasures of their own, nor did they more than vaguely threaten on one or two occasions to invoke paragraph 4 of the Final Quadripartite Protocol, which provides that:

> In the event of a difficulty in the application of the Quadripartite Agreement or any of the above-mentioned agreements or arrangements which any of the four Governments considers serious, or in the event of nonimplementation of any part thereof, that Government will have the right to draw the attention of the other three Governments to the provisions of the Quadripartite Agreement and this Protocol and to conduct the requisite quadripartite consultations in order to ensure the observance of the commitments undertaken and to bring the situation into conformity with the Quadripartite Agreement and this Protocol.

The Soviets did, however, permit the GDR on several occasions to impose controls on access in obvious retaliation for activities in the three western sectors that they did not wish to see take place. Thus, there were processing delays in June 1978 and selective denial of entry to three busloads of *Junge Union* members, and when President Carter visited Berlin on July 15, 1978, there were delays on the *Autobahn* because he was accompanied by Chancellor Schmidt.[16]

One area in which the Soviets could be even more obstructive concerns the right of the Federal Republic to represent the three western sectors in international organizations. The Soviets have taken numerous opportunities in international bodies and in international contexts to try to diminish the relationship between the Federal Republic and West Berlin. They have refused to grant adequate inclusion of West Berlin in proposed agreements between the Soviet Union and the Federal Republic on scientific and technical cooperation, cultural exchanges, transportation questions, environmental protection, energy and health policy, etc.; protested the inclusion of West Berliners as members of delegations from the Federal Republic to international organizations and international conferences; hindered meetings of international organizations in Berlin if the membership includes the Federal Republic; sought to prevent the inclusion of West Berlin in agreements reached by the Federal Republic with international organizations; and took action against the inclusion of West Berlin in documents and publications originated by the Federal Republic in international organizations.[17]

It is pertinent at this point to speculate about Soviet intentions toward Berlin. One need not assume that the Quadripartite Agreement, with all the advantages it brought to the western sectors, represented an upsurge of altruism in Soviet policy. The agreement is part of a larger picture reflecting a reasonable balance of advantages and disadvantages. Previous attempts to intimidate the occupying Powers and the Berliners had clearly failed, and, with the protection provided by the wall, there were gains to be made by removing Berlin from the center of controversy, particularly since some of those gains (those associated with the general concept of détente) could not be realized as long as the city seemed threatened. Once the complex of agreements reached in the early 1970s was in effect, the Soviets were aware that, while they could bluster a bit and make things difficult here and there to remind the West that the geographical location of the city still gave them a great potential advantage, any serious pressure on the city would immediately work to their broader disadvantage. The occupying powers and their NATO allies have lost few opportunities to make this clear. The communiqué issued after each biennial NATO meeting of foreign ministers has something to say on the subject; the one issued on May 31, 1978, from Washington, D.C., made the point as follows:

> The Allies reviewed the developments concerning Berlin and Germany as a whole. They noted that since the Ministerial Meeting in December 1977, the situation in and around Berlin had been generally without serious disturbance, but that the difficulties had persisted in certain important fields. They reaffirmed the previously stated positions of the Alliance, particularly the conviction that the strict observance and full implementation of all provisions of the Quadripartite Agreement of 3rd September, 1971, are essential for the promotion of détente, the maintenance of security and the development of cooperation throughout Europe.[18]

Two further points need to be made as this is being written in late May 1981. When they decided to accept the stabilization of the Berlin situation a decade ago, the Soviets did not thereby necessarily sacrifice their longer range goals for the city. The western sectors of the city will always be an unacceptable anomaly for them. Its elimination would be to the advantage of both the Soviets and the GDR. Since neither pressure nor the sacrifice of other objectives had resulted in the desired goal, the Soviets seemed to have decided that time was on their side and that patience might prove a more acceptable and ultimately more profitable tactic. It may be that the Soviets believe the city's vital forces will become exhausted and the West will become increasingly less willing to support it, so that one day West Berlin will simply fall in their lap like a ripe apple. Be that as it may, they are presumably not unaware that its changing demography, urban problems, and a hoped-for upsurge of neutralist attitudes among a new generation of Berliners and West Germans may create a more propitious climate from their point of view.

There is also, of course, the question of whether or not détente can survive in the post-Afghanistan period as the Reagan administration in Washington attempts to formulate a more vigorous foreign policy. The western sectors would appear to be extremely vulnerable in a new era of increasing rather than diminishing tensions—if that is what is ahead of us—yet it is difficult to imagine what either side would stand to gain in the short or even medium run by any revival of the old controversies over Berlin. Certainly no one in Bonn or Washington would want that, although perhaps for somewhat different reasons. It is hard to see what the Soviets would gain by increasing pressures on the city except perhaps briefly to underline to the West the strategic advantage they enjoy with respect to the city. Obviously a complete breakdown in East–West relations would bring about a new situation, but forward planning for the city can realistically assume a somewhat more benign environment. Moreover, the western sectors have demonstrated in the past that, if they must, they can survive and even relatively prosper under highly unfavorable conditions as long as the necessary qualities of will remain on the side of the occupying Powers, the West Germans, and the Berliners themselves.

The Present Situation in the City

Nineteen eighty-one has proved to be a year of significant internal political change in the western sectors. For some time there had been a growing feeling that the SPD–FDP combination that had run the city for so long was running out of steam. It took a financial scandal, however, involving leading Senate personalities (though not Governing Mayor Stobbe himself) to topple the increasingly weakened structure. A desperate attempt to shore it up by bringing the highly regarded minister of justice in Bonn, Hans-Jochen Vogel, to succeed Stobbe as governing mayor, failed. In the election of May 10, 1981, which Vogel was forced to call, the CDU, led by Richard von Weizsäcker, won 47.9 percent of the total vote. With 65 seats in the Berlin legislature, the party fell two short of gaining a majority, however. The Social Democrats dropped to 51 seats, falling below 40 percent of the total vote for the first time in the postwar period. The attempt by von Weizsäcker to form a coalition with the Free Democrats, an action which had the approval of the leader of the Free Democrats in Bonn, Foreign Minister Hans-Dietrich Genscher, succeeded in winning the support of four FDP deputies, and on June 11, 1981, by a vote of 69 to 61, a CDU member became governing mayor of Berlin for only the second time in the postwar era.

The results of the elections of May 10 involved a desertion of the SPD by many of its old-line supporters and reflected both their disillusionment and the widespread feeling that it was time for a change. The personality of von Weizsäcker, a man of clear integrity, was obviously an asset for the CDU. Observers also pointed to the 7.2 percent vote achieved by the Alternative List as indicating growing repudiation of the political establishment, especially among the young. In the past, Berliners had not been inclined to waste their votes on minor protest parties.

Where all this will lead is not clear, but the situation certainly does not warrant gloomy prognostications about the future of the city's political system or its economy. The system has demonstrated its ability to change, something that at least a few critics had regarded as unlikely. The economy, as we have noted, will always be closely linked to that of the Federal Republic. In a period of relative stagnation there, such as we have today, the economy of the city can hardly be expected to expand. Yet, as long as the federal subsidy system continues, the western sectors will have the advantage of a certain insulation against any dramatic decline. Given the existing pressures on the federal budget and the widespread feeling that the subsidy mentality has become a source of complacency and relaxed standards, there will undoubtedly be some tightening up. It is hard to imagine, however, that there will be any serious challenge in the Bundestag to the principle of continuing subsidization to preserve this important national and international symbol.

Many other things need to be done to insure a prosperous economic future for Berlin.[19] Some steps have already been undertaken, but there will be a continuing need for creative innovation, and maximum use must be made of those advantages that the western sectors now enjoy. For instance, the city must be a pacesetter in the structural adaptation and productivity already achieved by parts of the Berlin business community in this era in which all advanced industrial countries are facing the need for structural change in their economies as permanent shifts of comparative advantage take place in the world.

The very least that can be said is that venture capital should be able to flow into the city on the basis of reasonable risk. Many uncertainties afflict modern industrial societies as they enter the last portion of this century. These are not unique to Berlin. The problems that are unique to the city, even if they cannot always be solved, are not inherently the type that preclude a reasonably assured economic future, provided the requisite degree of innovation and leadership is available.

Postscript

Since 1981 there has been little change in the fundamental situation of West Berlin. Some critics have noted further provincialization of political and cultural life, but the standards of theatrical and musical performance remain high and the museum life of the city remains unparalleled in Germany. The ethnic minorities, particularly the Turks, continue to present problems of assimilation and social adaptation, and the basic German population of the city is still demographically stagnant. On the other hand, there is some indication that efforts to make West Berlin a center of high technology are beginning to bear fruit. In recovering from the recession of recent years that all of Western Europe has experienced, the increase in new investment in the city during 1983 was considerably above the rate of the Federal Republic.

With a few minor exceptions, the Soviet Union and the German Democratic Republic continue to observe the Quadripartite Agreement on Berlin with all of the consequent advantages of free access to and from the city. There was concern that the deterioration of relations between the two superpowers during the first Reagan administration, and particularly the initial deployment of Pershing II missiles, in the Federal Republic late in 1983 to which the Soviet Union reacted strongly, might result in increased pressure against West Berlin, but these fears proved unfounded. The interesting recent improvement in relations between the Federal Republic and the German Democratic Republic, if it continues, cannot help but provide an additional factor of stability for the city as the GDR becomes increasingly dependent on West German subsidies—many of them connected with access to Berlin—as a major source of badly needed hard currency.

All in all, therefore, West Berlin remains viable as we approach the middle of the present decade. None of the basic problems imposed by geography and history have been solved, but its assets provide grounds for hope that the city will be able to continue playing a politically and symbolically significant role.

7 The West Berlin Economy

Wolfgang Watter

I shall discuss the economic development of West Berlin—its past, its current situation, and its future—in terms of three key economic indicators: population structure, labor force, and gross national product (GNP).

West Berlin's Economy Since the Wall

On August 12, 1961, the day before the GDR built its wall, West Berlin had a population of 2.2 million, a labor force of 1.015 million, and a GNP (in 1961) of about DM 30 billion.

The wall, it may be surprising to hear, had no significant impact on these figures. There was to be sure considerable short-term turbulence: 1962 was a bad year for the West Berlin economy, but in 1963 the rate of growth in GNP came nearly to that in the Federal Republic as a whole. The next two years saw growth rates of 6.4 and 5.7 percent, respectively, with the latter figure being even higher than that for the FRG.

The political consequence of the wall was a considerable increase in the economic assistance given to West Berlin by the federal government. Karl Schiller, who came to the city as its senator for economics, created a system of "push and pull," aimed at pulling capital to Berlin and pushing investment and thus economic growth. This policy included substantial credits, tax allowances for employees and employers, and a negative tax, that is, a rebate in the neighborhood of 20 to 30 percent (which was nontaxable) for fixed investments.

The wall also affected the city's work force. First of all, it meant the immediate loss of some 50,000 workers who lived in East Berlin and crossed the border every day to work in West Berlin—the *Grenzgänger*, or "border commuters." A remarkable surge in productivity, which showed the possibility for real growth in this regard, nonetheless compensated for the loss. Second, and even more important, was the stoppage of migration from East Germany. From 1951 to 1960 more than 300,000 East Germans moved to West Berlin to live and work. Third, the age structure in West Berlin indicated that the work force would decline still more in the years to come. Hence, to stabilize the situation in West Berlin, it was necessary to attract West Germans and foreigners to the city.

Over the course of the 1960s, then, there were three main trends. The size of the population remained nearly stable. At the beginning and at the end of the decade West Berlin had a population of roughly 2.2 million. It lost about 100,000 Germans—a consequence of the city's poor age structure—and gained about 100,000 foreigners. More serious was the decline of the labor force from about one million to 930,000 (in contrast to West Germany, where the size of the work force remained nearly the same). The growth in GNP over the decade was a little bit more than four percent in West Berlin, a little bit less than five percent in West Germany—a difference of about one-half of one percent.

The conclusion of the Quadripartite and related agreements created what might be called excessive hopes in West Berlin. The situation there was simply not normal for a large city. The outflow of population was greater than the inflow; the manufacturing sector and other producers neither established many new firms nor created many new jobs in the city. Further, since the mid-1970s saw an economic slump in the FRG as a whole, it can be understood that it was not a time for expanding programs that already existed in West Berlin or setting up new ones. The result was that there was no inflow of fixed investment during this period. As far as demographic trends are concerned, an annual surplus in the city of 20,000 deaths over births (about one percent of the total population) resulted in a net loss to the labor force of some 15,000 workers, or about two percent of the work force.

The three economic indicators, then, point to a deteriorating situation for West Berlin in the 1970s. With respect to population, there seemed to be no way to stop the decline that had set in. The population dropped by 200,000 to about two million. Moreover, the city lost about 100,000 jobs during the decade. And, whereas the growth rate in the FRG as a whole was 2.8 percent, in West Berlin it was 2.1 percent—a remarkable difference of 0.7 percent that meant about a quarter less growth in the city.

The end of the 1970s, that is, 1979 and 1980, presents a somewhat more optimistic picture. The loss of jobs was slight, roughly the same in West Berlin as in West Germany. The gap in economic growth between the two areas also narrowed.

West Berlin at the Outset of the 1980s

We may briefly characterize the current state of West Berlin's economic situation as follows. The city now has a population of some two million and a work force of 835,000 (as opposed to a million two decades ago). Its gross national product in 1980 stood at DM 53 billion. West Berlin thus had about 3.4 percent of both the FRG's workers and its GNP. Moreover, West Berlin is intensively integrated into the economic and financial system of the Federal Republic: about 80 percent of everything manufactured in the city is delivered outside, 70 percent into West Germany and 10 percent abroad. The key figure of federal assistance stood at DM 9.5 billion in 1980 and will reach DM 10 billion in 1981. (These amounts may seem high, but they are not much more than one-half of one percent of the FRG's gross national product.)

Future Trends: 1981 and Beyond

The crucial aspect of West Berlin's future development (as it was in the past) is demographic: the age structure and nationality of the population. In the mid-1970s 15 percent of the city's population was under the age of 15 and 22 percent aged 65 or older. Comparable figures for the entire Federal Republic were 23 percent and 13 percent, respectively (and the latter figure, for those aged 65 or older, was 14 percent in the FRG's urban centers). These figures are a clear indication of an overaged population in West Berlin. Of the current population, about 10 percent are foreigners, half of them Turks. This has meant the emergence of foreign ghettos, and, since now every fourth baby born in Berlin has foreign parents, a sharp skewing of the city's age structure.

The Deutsches Institut für Wirtschaftsforschung, located in West Berlin, recently projected some long-range consequences of current demographic and economic trends. One main finding was that a further decline in population is inevitable: it could sink to as low as 1.67 million by the year 2000. The key variable in what actually happens is the city's exports. The more it is able to export, the higher will be the level of employment, especially in the manufacturing sector, which accounts for most of the exports; the higher the level of employment, the greater will be the size of the population. (The Berlin Senate, I should add, chose to accept the Institute's higher projection of 1.77 million in 2000. Its reasoning was as follows: in the coming years there will be large age-cohorts leaving school and entering the work force, and, of course, no one wants to tell them to leave Berlin to find work elsewhere. The task, then, is to find jobs for them in West Berlin. The Senate sees this as a political task that must be accomplished to maintain the city's viability, to ensure that employment figures will not decline so rapidly and neither will the size of the population.)

These considerations raise the question of what can be done to improve West Berlin's economic climate. There are, at the outset, some things that should *not* be done: search for new slogans to describe the city's "mission," an endeavor that is fruitless; or seek increased federal assistance. The city already gets a great deal of money from the federal government. What is needed is to reflect on the structure, not the amount, of this assistance, and, more generally, not to treat the issue as a sacred cow that cannot be disturbed.

Several measures could improve the economic situation. First, there should be a greater effort to attract new firms to West Berlin. Although this point is not undisputed, it seems that the federal assistance program for such firms is very attractive indeed. The problem is that these advantages are virtually unknown in the right circles. Second, there must be a more systematic program for training and retraining workers. At present the program in West Berlin operates at a much lower level than that in West Germany. Third, working and living conditions in the city should be improved. Of approximately a million dwelling units in West Berlin, about 100,000 (or 10 percent) do not have their own baths or toilets. Similarly, the infrastructure for workers should be made comparable to that in Munich or Hamburg. This means more facilities for recreation and the like. Fourth, political stability will improve the appearance of the city. The domestic political turmoil in recent months has not been conducive to bringing new investors to Berlin. Progress in all four respects is necessary if people are to choose West Berlin as a place in which to work and live.

Discussion

SHEPARD STONE: If West Berlin actually had more jobs available, would it be possible to attract West Germans, or are those who come likely to be foreigners?

WOLFGANG WATTER: If the city has good, modern jobs, then it should be possible to attract West Germans. Despite recent improvements in the age structure and the loss of 50,000 workers, however, there may still be more workers than jobs. What is needed is to retrain available workers and at the same time create new, high-quality jobs.

RICHARD MERRITT: It would seem that every new firm set up in Berlin means one new firm that is not set up in Düsseldorf or Frankfurt. Presumably, then, there are other industrial and economic regions in the Federal Republic that are competing with Berlin for new firms and jobs. To what extent is this felt in the planning for West Berlin's economic future? How long will these cities tolerate a federal aid structure or anything else giving preferences to firms that locate in Berlin?

WOLFGANG WATTER: The question of West Germans' sensitivity and good will toward West Berlin is a difficult one. At the moment, as the city's economic commissioner, Robert Layton, has discovered, there is very tight competition for investment capital. His efforts to attract investments to Berlin have encountered opposition from other regions, such as Brunswick, that are also in economic difficulty. The facts are that gross social product is declining everywhere, and unemployment is high. What the resulting social unrest will do to programs of federal assistance for West Berlin I do not know. My best hope is that the reemergence of growth rates in the neighborhood of six percent, as we had in the mid-1960s, will ameliorate the problem before it gets severe.

RENATA FRITSCH-BOURNAZEL: Is there any possibility for new discussions on Chancellor Brandt's earlier idea of economic cooperation with the Soviet Union, most particularly in the energy field? I am thinking of his plan to extend the East bloc's power network from Kaliningrad (Königsberg) all the way to the Federal Republic and West Berlin. A second question is whether or not a contingency plan exists should there be a new blockade or other difficulties in Berlin. How much coordination in this regard is there between West Berlin authorities and the Allies?

WOLFGANG WATTER: West Berlin's electrical energy flows through what the industry calls an "island system." That is, the city must produce its own electricity; it draws none from the GDR or anyplace else. At the time there were discussions about importing Soviet electricity into West Germany the West Berliners insisted that the line go through the center of the city, right through the Brandenburg Gate in effect. The idea was that any East German effort to apply pressure on West Berlin by cutting off the city's electricity would simultaneously cut off the flow of electricity to West Germany. Such a step would be such a serious intervention into Soviet–FRG relations that the GDR would not risk it. The Eastern position was that a line directly through Berlin did not make economic sense, that it would be better to have the line run from Königsberg directly to West Germany, with an offshoot providing electricity to West Berlin. It was precisely this that negotiators in the West did not want.

HANS OTTO BRÄUTIGAM: At the moment there are no Soviet–German talks on this point. It does not appear that the Soviets will take the initiative, and we certainly shall not. The earlier discussion, I should add, concentrated primarily on the problem of price. Since we never resolved that one, we did not move on to any serious discussion of how the line should be constructed.

There were also soundings in the GDR about the possibility of using West German aid to build a power plant there that could supply both West Germany and West Berlin. Although this idea has real possibilities, the talks got nowhere because it raises touchy political problems for the East Germans. It would mean in effect that the East Germans would be contributing in a very important way to the viability of West Berlin. The idea is not dead, however. The East Germans seem to be shifting their focus from the political aspects of such a power plant to its possible economic benefits for the GDR. It is out of the question right now anyway, because the Federal Republic does not have the money to fund it.

SHEPARD STONE: David Anderson, would you tell us whether you, Francis Mac Ginnis, and our German friends have a contingency plan for the next blockade?

DAVID ANDERSON: I am sorry to say that David Klein must have taken it with him when he left Berlin. Returning to Wolfgang Watter's comments, I must say that I found his conclusions remarkably optimistic. My own view about the next ten or twenty years is much bleaker. Even if, for example, the projection of 1.7 million people in West Berlin in the year 2000 turns out to be correct, about a quarter of them will be foreigners, mostly Turks. Even if no new Turk were to move to the city from today onwards, projections based simply on the birthrate among the Turkish population in West Berlin and their propensity to bring family members to live with them indicate that there will be 300,000 Turks in West Berlin in a couple of years, and most of them are not likely to be skilled workers. The Berlin Senate must come up with solutions to the problems likely to arise from this demographic development. For instance, regardless of how touchy the issue may be, the Senate leadership will probably have to consider repatriation. The other measures mentioned—quality work force, higher productivity, infrastructural change, political stability—do not match the dimensions of the problem posed by foreign workers.

WOLFGANG WATTER: The city has not received very interesting proposals on what to do about this problem, to the extent it exists. Even repatriation would cost enormous sums of money—much more than is currently available. Moreover, as Ambassador Schütz pointed out in an earlier context, if the foreign workers were to leave, who then would do the dirty work Germans do not want to do?

RONALD FRANCISCO: Is there really cause for pessimism about West Berlin? We always hear comparisons between Berlin and Frankfurt or Munich or Hamburg, and it may well be that Berlin suffers in some respects through such comparisons. But if we put Berlin into the broader context of all major cities in advanced industrial societies—in the rest of Western Europe, in Eastern Europe, and especially in North America—then West Berlin does not appear to be in such bad shape.

I would also suggest that our emphasis on goods-producing industries is misplaced. Economists have recently focused considerable attention on what are called "post-industrial societies," meaning those in which less than 50 percent of the gross national product stems from goods-producing industries and more than 50 percent from services (including government employment, transport, trade, and so forth). West Berlin crossed this threshold in the mid-1970s.[1] I am therefore dismayed when I read how pleased Berlin officials are that so many BMW motorcycles or various kinds of razor blades are produced in the city. It sounds as though they are trying to achieve pre-eminence in a kind of economic system that no longer exists in post-industrial societies.

Berlin should rather use its opportunities to develop high-technology industries. A possible basis for such a development might be the Hahn-Meitner Institute for Nuclear Energy. Another, in the business of the "new biology" that is raging in the United States, is the Institute for Molecular Genetics. Another area of rapid growth is computer software: writing computer programs and selling them on cassettes to users throughout the world. Why should people now working in Stuttgart on computer translation, for example, not be relocated in West Berlin—possibly with the support of the European Communities, which has all kinds of translation problems? The point is that the city has the potential for unlimited growth. It has a good climate, culturally and intellectually as well as physically. What is needed is to bring people here to set up and operate high-technology industries.

SHEPARD STONE: Let me note that, four to six times a year, the directors of research institutes throughout West Berlin gather at the Aspen Institute Berlin to discuss precisely this point: how can the city's scientific community help improve the economic situation of West Berlin, particularly in the new areas of high technology of which Ronald Francisco was speaking.

WOLFGANG WATTER: Developing high-technology industry in West Berlin is an excellent idea. There are, however, some barriers to overcome. One task is to try to persuade competent people to move to Berlin. Another is to know how to use our resources to finance the industries themselves. This may mean taking risks which are unacceptable to some: cutting subsidies for the razor blade manufacturers, for instance, in the hope that, without putting them totally out of business and thereby making the economic situation worse, we can use the money to support high technology. To date there has not been much enthusiasm in the city for taking such long-term risks.

MARTIN HILLENBRAND: There is a certain artificiality about talking of West Berlin's economy in future terms, divorced from the rest of the world. What we are experiencing and shall continue to experience during the rest of this century is a real crisis of structural change. The shift of comparative advantage away from the old industrialized countries to the new industrializing countries will mean a difficult process of adjustment for all advanced industrial societies, including the Federal Republic and the United States. These changes form the context within which planning for Berlin must be performed, for the Berlin economy will stagnate or flourish pretty much as that of the Federal Republic stagnates or flourishes.

What does this mean in practical terms for West Berlin? First, its economy as it has developed looks worse in many respects than it actually is.[2] At the same time the West Berlin economy has certain advantages that are not generally appreciated. It is slightly ahead of the Federal Republic in terms of rationalization, for instance. In an era when technology is replacing labor-intensive forms of production, the absence of excess labor in Berlin relative to other parts of the European Communities may be an actual advantage; it has already driven Berlin firms, as the productivity figures after the wall cited by Wolfgang Watter indicate, into a rationalization that is generally ahead of that which has taken place in West Germany. If this is the path West Berlin will follow, as I think it must, then the population figures are not so important in economic terms as they may be in the sociological, demographic, and urbanological sense. (Incidentally, given the experience of the Ford plant in Cologne, where most of the work and some skilled labor is performed by Turkish guest workers, we should not be gloomy about the prospects for training at least a portion of the Turkish population in Berlin.)

What is more important than attracting labor to West Berlin, except in certain skilled categories, is the need to attract capital investment. Capital investment in the city in the late 1960s and early 1970s was misdirected. The Berlin preferences, such as tax breaks, led to a great deal of investment in housing by people in West Germany who did not move to West Berlin to live. This in turn produced a speculative boom, an artificial upward surge of property values, and all the rest. As the experience in the United States has shown, that is a very unhealthy way to use capital resources. How capital formation in West Berlin can be moved into productive as opposed to speculative uses, however, is a good question.

A final point, which also suggests the artificiality of considering West Berlin as a separate entity, is that the city's energy problem is in fact part of a worldwide energy problem. Berlin's insularity and its reliance at least to some extent on nonindigenous sources of energy pose special problems to be sure. But it seems very likely that, unless there is a technological breakthrough of which no one is yet aware, both the advanced industrialized and the developing worlds will move by the late 1980s into an era of overall energy shortage that will have an impact on general economic activity. Planning in West Berlin seems to be ignoring the estimates provided by the International Energy Agency and the big oil companies. Building such information into the city's planning is necessary irrespective of whether or not the Soviet bloc's electrical network is extended from Königsberg through West Berlin into West Germany. This task, considering what West Berlin's energy needs in the late 1980s and 1990s will be and where they can be met, points again to the interlaced economic and political aspects of any long-range planning for the city.

HELGA HAFTENDORN: I have two comments. The first deals with the size of the public sector in West Berlin. The figures cited by Wolfgang Watter seem to include both the public sector and public administration. The large size of this public sector—widely considered inefficient compared to other administrations in the Federal Republic—covers up some hidden unemployment.

The second refers to the city's work force and an apparent contradiction in some of the arguments Wolfgang Watter has made. On the one hand, he pointed out that the changing age structure is creating a growing labor force, which means that it may not be so desirable as it once was to attract West Germans to the city. On the other hand, there is the hope of attracting more refined industries. I would question whether or not the work force for the latter kind of industry is present in West Berlin. Such high-technology centers as Silicon Valley in California are characterized by three factors: the availability of trained manpower; possibilities for mobility; and an infrastructure of housing, education facilities, and the like. I am not certain that these are present in West Berlin. There is of course the Technical University, but I am not sure how much it could contribute. Mobility is limited because of Berlin's insularity. And the cost of housing appropriate for high-technology workers is skyrocketing. All of this means that the kind of work force one would want to attract finds it more comfortable to live and work in West Germany than in West Berlin.

WOLFGANG WATTER: The percentage of Berlin's work force in the civil service (excluding the municipal services such as the Berlin Transport Authority, BVG) stands at 24 percent. This may seem to be high, but there are several reasons for concluding that it is not excessively so. First, as a large city, Berlin provides a great deal by way of public services. Second, maintaining the continued viability and even security of the city has meant expanding certain kinds of services. These include centers for learning and research, and also federal institutions (such as the Bundesanstalt für Materialprüfung, Bundesanstalt für Angestellte, and Bundesgesundheitsamt) that serve the political goal of tying West Berlin to the FRG. Finally, research conducted by the Deutsches Institut für Wirtschaftsforschung indicates that, while the civil service in West Berlin may be somewhat larger than that in Hamburg, there is little justification for considering the former excessive or inefficient.

SHEPARD STONE: I would not be so pessimistic as Helga Haftendorn about what West Berlin has to offer high-technology industries. Much of what is said about Berlin—that it is dying, that the most qualified people are leaving, and so forth—used to be said about Boston. But it turned out not to be true. One reason for this is that the Boston area abounds in good universities, the high level of which attracted the research industries on Route 128. West Berlin has the capability to develop its universities and research institutes in a way that could attract highly qualified workers to the city.

MICHAEL SODARO: I should like to ask Wolfgang Watter, first, approximately how many jobs in West Berlin depend on trade with the East, and, second, more generally, what role has East–West trade played recently in West Berlin's economic life? Are there any projections for the future?

WOLFGANG WATTER: Since about 1970 only about one percent of all goods exported from West Berlin go into the GDR. This percentage has remained fairly stable. The city's imports from the GDR have grown from two percent in 1970 to six percent in 1979, but these figures, based on the cost of the goods, reflect to some extent price increases. The share of West Berlin's exports going to other Soviet bloc countries has remained constant at the one-percent level, while the corresponding share of imports grew from one percent in 1970 to two percent in 1979. These data indicate that East–West trade does not play a major role in calculations about West Berlin's economic position or in its job situation. The DIW has not paid much attention to this trade in either its current analyses or long-range projections.

JOYCE MUSHABEN: Richard Merritt earlier raised the question of the extent to which other West German cities are resisting federal measures that improve West Berlin's competitiveness in attracting new industry. The other side of the coin is that these measures, which seem to protect industries in West Berlin irrespective of their efficiency and productivity, produce a certain "subsidy mentality" in the city. Does the assumption that West Berlin must be kept viable lead the firms moving to the city to take it easy for a while and then leave when conditions no longer seem profitable to them?

WOLFGANG WATTER: Although it is impossible to get any precise estimate of its extent, we know that a subsidy mentality exists in Berlin. It exists at the level of the small firm, the entrepreneur who receives subsidies for five or six years and then decides, when federal authorities begin inquiring about their effect in making the firm self-sufficient, to give up the business. This may account for the fairly high rate of "failures" among small businesses in West Berlin. It is very difficult to say how widespread such a mentality is at the level of the large firm. Those already in Berlin certainly enjoy their subsidies. Moreover, according to the DIW's calculations, practically any large West German firm could move to Berlin and, despite higher transportation and other costs, make a greater profit. Confronted with such calculations, most firms still say, in effect, "Okay, we would have more income and some tax benefits in Berlin, but we don't want to move there." Subsidies may help to overcome such resistance. It would nonetheless be less than charitable to suggest that a firm which, fully cognizant of all of Berlin's problems, decides to move there anyway is guilty of having a subsidy mentality.

ROGER MORGAN: How important to the West Berlin economy are its links with the European Community? There are some very conflicting opinions about this. On the one hand, it has been said that the city has obtained important loans and grants through the European Investment Bank, as well as access to certain economic facilities through membership in the Community. On the other hand, it has been said that this has not been a major factor in creating jobs or helping West Berlin's economy in general.

WOLFGANG WATTER: About 6 to 7 percent of the goods and services produced in West Berlin go to other European Community members. This figure is certainly higher than the percentage going to Soviet bloc countries, including the GDR. Although we might say that the same level of trade would exist in the absence of formal European Community institutions, and we might doubt their efficiency as a means for improving foreign trade anyway, these European Community institutions are very valuable from a psychological point of view.

KARL DEUTSCH: Ambassador Hillenbrand, the United States traditionally has quite different interest groups, even within the major parties. We have interest groups that consider Cuba, the Caribbean, and Central America to be very real, very near, and very important, and that may or may not care very much or even know very much about Berlin. If, in some future crisis, such interest groups should move the United States toward a blockade of Cuba, what are the chances that geographic parallels would be drawn between these two islands, each surrounded by and potentially subject to the main resources of the other superpower? That is, to what extent could the future of Berlin be affected by something most Berliners do not know much about and most people in Central America, the Caribbean, and Cuba do not know much about, namely, the creation of a new Cuban crisis?

MARTIN HILLENBRAND: The parallel is certainly suggestive, as it was in 1962 at the time of the Cuban missile crisis. At that time, while I was director of the Berlin Task Force, an amusing thing happened. Because the White House wanted to conceal what the crisis was about, they had me ostentatiously coming in through the front door of the White House so that the reporters would think it had something to do with Berlin. In any case, Berlin was very much a part of the planning for the Cuban missile crisis. We had a special Berlin group in the White House that met alongside the group focusing on Cuba, because it was expected at that time that the Soviets would react most probably in some way against Berlin. Well, they did not. Berlin was quiet. Nothing happened in the city. I do not know whether or not the United States would make the same assumption should there be in the next year or so another Cuban crisis with a blockade of Cuba. On the other side, too, should the Soviets decide to move against Berlin, they will have considered not only the Cuban parallel but also the broader implications of such a move. Beyond that, although it is pure speculation as to what they actually would do, they would not necessarily or automatically juxtapose Berlin and Cuba in their minds.

DAVID KLEIN: A recent event may serve to dramatize the continuing linkage of Berlin and Cuba in the minds of American decision makers. During the transition to the Reagan government, the question was raised about what the United States should do if the Soviets should take any of a number of possible actions against Poland. The suggestion was made that the United States had to look at Soviet vulnerabilities, such as Cuba. The response was that if the Reagan government considered pressure on Cuba, then it had better begin to worry about Berlin, because that is a Western vulnerability. The linkage remains current.

8 Berlin between East and West: Lessons for a Confused World

Jürgen Engert

In West Germany we are witnessing a romantic revival: the blue flower as the symbol of an undivided national movement. The old division between culture and civilization is being reestablished, thus provoking or at least increasing existential angst. Anyone who insists on taking a rational approach to things is considered narrow-minded.

In Germany's neighbor, France, nuclear power does not cause an uproar, regardless of people's ideological position. I do not wish to speak in defense of nuclear power or to denounce its opponents. I only want to draw attention to the discrepancy between these two countries: the one has always recognized the importance of placing rationality on an equal footing with intellectual and metaphysical needs, in order to make them civilized and logical; the other does not feel bound by this Latin tradition. Culture in France, unlike Germany, is not a separate sector placed high up above mean existence. This can easily be seen in the newspapers, whose cultural sections do not, as is true in most German papers, limit themselves to the "products of culture" in the narrowest sense of that term. In France, culture is civilization. This means the subject is broader. The world of change is perceived and contemplated in its diversity.

Berlin: German Prototype or Pariah?

What does this have to do with Berlin? I would suggest that Berlin is the quintessential German city, because it is the least civilized (in the

Western sense) and the most romantic. Konrad Adenauer, a native of Cologne, felt a deep mistrust for Berlin. He was the product of a town rich in culture, which competed with Paris in the late Middle Ages and retained genuinely close ties with France. Thus, although he was not a highly educated man, Adenauer was molded by Western European civilization, by its rationality and catholic universality. Adenauer, aware of the unfathomable depths and many imponderables of the German soul, located the antinomy in Berlin, the "pagan city," as he called it. After the collapse of Germany in 1945, he wanted to move the capital to the Rhine ("for there is old cultural territory"). He wished to anchor at least part of Germany firmly in the occidental tradition.

But intention has bowed to reality. At one time it seemed that Adenauer's wish, the permanent integration of the German Federal Republic into the West, was sure to be fulfilled, if only by institutional bonds. Today, as Germany regains its vitality, this integration is becoming increasingly weaker. When the cold war followed in the wake of the "hot" war, Berlin provided a foundation for the integration of West Germany into the European tradition and the bridge across the Atlantic was built here. The city (or, more precisely, part of it) became a symbol for this. But now Berlin is demonstrating symbolically again just how loose the ties are.

The question is: why here? After Prussia had been absorbed by Germany in 1871, Berlin lost its identity. This loss was a precondition for its rise as the metropolis of the empire and of European capitalism. It did not gain a new identity. Berlin's middle class was incapable of converting its economic potency into supremacy. The "Chicago on the Spree," as Walther Rathenau once called it, remained almost entirely without a firm shape or definition—an unfinished capital in the middle of an unfinished nation, which had been unable to achieve continuity after the ruptures and interruptions of history and which was therefore less able than others to cultivate the virtue of practical reason.

Berlin, although representative of this country, was never a source of identity for the German peoples. At the same time, its very incompleteness, its lack of an established framework, was highly attractive. This was the condition that in the 1920s led to the emergence of a cultural golden age, fed by uncorseted international forces. Creative and ambitious persons and nonconformists of every kind, as well as failures and adventurers hoping for a sphere of action or a place of refuge, were not forced to conform to any rigid way of life.

The year 1945 marked a turning point for the city. For geographical reasons, Berlin has always looked much more to the East than to the West. Berlin's ancestral hinterland lay in the East—in East Prussia, Silesia, and Pomerania. The East was the source of its population and vitality. Its industrialization would have been impossible without the farm laborers from east of the Elbe who were hoping for a better fate on the Spree. The loss of the eastern provinces in 1945 accompanied the departure of elites who had been kept there by the capital function. This bloodletting was as difficult to overcome as was the removal by the Nazis of the liberalizing Jewish element.

The East–West conflict nevertheless brought a measure of self-confidence not previously provided by history or guaranteed for the future. West Berlin represented the door in the Iron Curtain. It became the meeting point for East and West. It was the showpiece of Western civilization that countered the influence of Communist indoctrination and provided an outlet for psychological pressures.

In 1957 the Berlin Senate and the federal government introduced a form of subsidization whereby people from the GDR and East Berlin could buy tickets for culturally significant events in West Berlin at a one-to-one exchange rate. The result was that about 600,000 persons from the other part of Germany attended theater, opera, and operetta performances in West Berlin each year. As many as 85,000 came to concerts. Ten million inexpensive cinema tickets were sold to visitors from the East. One fifth of the visitors to museums came from the GDR. About 30 percent of the students at West Berlin's universities and colleges came from East Germany and received grants. West Berlin's public transportation system sold between 60,000 and 80,000 tickets a year for Eastern money. Tempelhof Airport was permanently open for flights to the Federal Republic, not only for refugees, but also for GDR citizens whose government refused them permission to travel but who could fly from and return to their home country, West Berlin. The annual Green Week agricultural fair and the German Industrial Exhibition also produced invasions from the GDR.

Moreover, although Berlin was divided, its people lived together. The border was clearly marked, but it was not internalized. It could be crossed without a permit. Controls were the exception and not the rule. Traffic flowed almost unhindered in both directions. Inhabitants of the streets that belonged half in the American and half in the Soviet sector were not separated by a barrier. Up until August 13, 1961, when the wall was built, 53,000 East Berliners worked in West Berlin, and 12,000 West Berliners had jobs in East Berlin.

The Real Meaning of the Wall

The wall forced Berlin to confront facts that it had until then been able to ignore. The western half of the city was thrown back on its own resources. It was a turning point without comparison. The difficulty of the new situation could initially be obscured by a declaration of hostilities. Such a declaration might have been addressed to the Western powers, or more specifically the Americans, who had not resisted the new battle line. Instead, attention was drawn to the foe standing threateningly on the doorstep, the East. Energy could be channelled—especially among the young, who were reluctant to make peace with the new reality—into activities like building tunnels under the sectoral border for refugees. German politicians cooperated with the Western allies and it was to their credit that the fragile situation which had arisen on August 13, 1961, did not erupt.

Politicians like Willy Brandt, Egon Bahr, Klaus Schütz, and Heinrich Albertz resisted the temptation to exploit the confusion of the moment for their own demagogic purposes. Unfortunately, the men in City Hall and the people of West Berlin had not given the city's situation enough thought before that date. Once they recognized the changed situation, Willy Brandt and Egon Bahr used the wall to justify their appeal for a new policy on Germany and *Ostpolitik*. What the Social Democratic–Liberal coalition set in motion in 1969 at the national level is inconceivable without the Berlin experience of Brandt and Bahr. It took a decade and more to make it clear that August 13, 1961, was a turning point in German postwar history, not only because it made Germany's split nationhood manifest, but also because it produced a specifically West German policy. At the outset this policy remained embedded in the West European and Atlantic framework as part of the generally accepted concept of détente. But it was easy to foresee that differing interests would one day force apart that consensus. This has since happened.

There is today a current of thought in West German intellectual circles that the "end of the ideological age" has arrived. It is no accident that a book with this title, by Peter Bender, was written in Berlin.[1] Supporters of the theory assert that communist ideology is no longer a mobilizing force behind the communist regime. The idea of world revolution as a Soviet export is, they say, dead. Moscow has reverted to being a mere superpower, intent on creating a conservative world order. The United States fares no better in this view: it merely uses ideology as an instrument to justify its egoism as a superpower in the Atlantic alliance.

The end-of-ideology theory also pays tribute to the convergence of interests in East and West and calls for a single, border-transcending European civilization, so that ultimately the ideological division and resulting animosity in the Old World can be overcome. Toward this end, nations must re-establish old relationships, with the West Europeans taking the first step.

The demand to "Europeanize" Europe includes new provisions for Berlin. The 1971 Quadripartite Agreement is seen as providing more freedom of action than has actually been taken advantage of up to now. It protects the ties between West Berlin and the Federal Republic—thanks to the city's integration into the latter's legal, economic, and financial system. Meanwhile the Western powers guard over its security. For this reason it should be possible to revive the idea of the city as a pivot between East and West. The Federal Republic cannot do more than continue to grant the city its heavy subsidies. It cannot give the city a new identity. Since the national question cannot be resolved in the foreseeable future, Berlin should grasp the opportunity to become international and not shy away from contact with the GDR and Eastern Europe. Berlin, not least on account of its geographic location, seems particularly suited to the role of pioneering a concept which the Federal Republic and Europe as a whole would take up: not the option of a Western formation, as it evolved in the postwar period, nor the option of the Eastern bloc, which is dominated by coercion. A third path is needed. Berlin could give the impetus for a new German identity—a pan-European identity.

Whither Berlin?

Since August 13, 1961, the search for a mission for Berlin has become a permanent cause. Until that year Berlin did not feel it was in danger of becoming isolated or extinct. The city had derived its certainty both from the fight against the communist threat and from its own influence on the GDR. This had compensated for the loss of its function as the capital city. And the West German hinterland had never ceased to express its solidarity with the soldiers in the trenches of Berlin. The construction of the wall disrupted all that. Today the city is looking for a function. It knows what it was, but it still does not know what it is, let alone what it will be.

The gap was apparent immediately after August 13, 1961. It is revealing that, only a few days after Berlin had been walled in, a plan to turn Berlin into a cultural center was conceived in City Hall. That this was the first thing to happen, before the politicians even thought about taking measures in any other area, illustrates just how hard the sudden spiritual emergency hit. It had to be dealt with swiftly to prevent Berlin from becoming cut off. The plans were monumental. A third university was to be added to the existing Technical University and Free University; it was to be a world university, or at least a European one. There was also to be a *Deutsches Gymnasium Berlin*—a secondary school for highly gifted pupils. West Berlin was spoken of as the "world capital of learning." Museums and orchestras were to be created. The Deutsche Oper was to become a "national opera," a super-Bayreuth. Organizations representing every important cultural body were to be set up with federal support and help from the Municipal League. The key to Berlin's well-being was seen to lie in the closest possible ties with the Federal Republic.

All these high-flown plans fell through. Many of them had been illusory. Others provoked resistance among existing institutions within and without the city. International projects were shelved lest they undermine Berlin's claim to being the German capital. Nevertheless, the plan for a cultural center did have some effect. In 1962 the Prussian Cultural Heritage Foundation commenced activity in the city. The museums under its care managed to have brought back to Berlin the objects that had been transferred to West Germany during the war. The German Cinemateque, the German Musicphonoteque, and the International Institute of Comparative Music Studies and Documentation were created. The Max Planck Society's Institute for Educational Research, the School Building Institute, and the Pedagogical Center came into being. The German Film and Television Academy and the German Institute of Development Policy were set up. The National Gallery, designed by Mies van der Rohe, and Hans Scharoun's Philharmonic Hall, built in the shadow of the wall, formed the central pieces of a new cultural center in the Tiergarten. The Free University acquired a large university clinic in Steglitz. The Institute of American Literature at the Free University was enlarged to become an interdepartmental American Studies Institute, later named after John F. Kennedy. It received grants (as did other organizations) from the Ford Foundation. In addition to these new developments, the Berlin Senate and the federal government concentrated on improving existing organizations.

This list, which is by no means comprehensive, shows that the city was assured an institutional framework. Emigration due to the wall and its consequences was kept to a minimum. Manpower was even attracted from West Germany because good employment opportunities compensated for the disadvantageous location. The loss of students from East Berlin and the GDR was more than compensated for by arrivals from West Germany. The slogan "Every West German in Berlin at least once" produced such a response that in the summer semester of 1962 the rector of the Free University had to turn people away: "The capacity of the Free University has been reached."

For young West Germans Berlin was an extraordinary experience. They had grown up in a world saturated with possessions but narrowly conceived, especially in the provinces where most of them came from. In Berlin they were plunged into a very different environment, where they experienced real danger that awakened in them a moral commitment. Perhaps some of those who aided escapes from the GDR, unaware of the risk, regarded their involvement merely as a continuation of their childhood cops-and-robbers games. Regardless of the motives, the rescue attempts were frequently made under extremely dangerous circumstances.

But the wall became ever more impenetrable. Freedom was not an empty delusion. It could be experienced directly. And it was the cause of freedom that led Free University students to resist the presence of illegal duelling fraternities at the university, and even to recall a chairman of the Student Governance Association who had been a member of such a fraternity. Students also protested a ban by the Free University's rector of the journalist Erich Kuby, who had argued in a lecture that the name "Free University" expressed *un*freedom because the university had been built only as a contradiction to the Humboldt University in East Berlin. The students saw the rector's action as a threat to freedom of speech.

From these relatively small beginnings there developed a youth and student revolt in the city that later spread to the Federal Republic and brought a cultural revolution in its wake. This revolution was not on a Chinese scale, but it broke with many forms of thought and behavior rooted in middle-class convention. It influenced the whole of West German society, especially its sexual ethics, relationships between the sexes, childrearing, and its attitude on the place of women in society. Authority could no longer justify itself by its mere existence. Young people gained in self-confidence and became increasingly articulate. Parents called upon to give explanations were often uncomfortable.

Again the Focal Point

Why did this begin in Berlin? To answer this question one must take a look at the city's social fabric. The German word *Gesellshaft* comprises the Middle High German prefix *ge-*, which expresses community relationship, and *Saal,* the term for the Teutonic one-room house. Thus *Gesellschaft* equals, as it were, "room-house-community." In West Berlin it includes just under two million people. Insofar as they are Germans, or more exactly native Berliners, people who identify with the city, they constitute a perfect whole. When John F. Kennedy let the words "Auch ich bin ein Berliner" resound from the balcony of the city hall, his name was to be associated at once with that of the famous Berlin character, Nante.

A lack of self-assurance combined with the dwindling solidarity beyond the city's bounds explains why West Berliners regard themselves as a special breed whose own peculiar character cuts across their differences. They may bicker and fight among themselves, but the quarrel is forgotten the minute a stranger tries to express any criticism. Then they are bosom friends. It is not just for pleasure that those more seasoned Social and Christian Democrats recall the past in which they governed together in Berlin's Grand Coalition. Anyone tolerating critical remarks from an outsider must expect public ridicule. If somebody goes so far as to pack his bags, saying that he can find his fortune elsewhere in West Germany, he will be accused of "fleeing from the bear-flag," the symbol of Berlin.

One might be tempted to assume that the members of this "room-house-community" of West Berlin communicate intensely with each other. But this is not so. The famous integration is bound up with an equally famous disintegration. There are several reasons for this. One often forgets that this half-city spreads across 185 square miles and that strong pockets of regionalism exist within its borders. The Zehlendorfer is only slightly interested in what is happening in Reinickendorf. He has his own shopping center and his own *Kietz* or village. Kurfürstendamm and Tauentzien Street are primarily showpieces for tourists.

The mentality of the Berliner has a proletarian quality—not in the negative sense of that word. Profession, money, fame fail to impress. It is a person's true character that draws one to him, not his appearance. A West German company that bought a firm on the Spree and set about marking off special parking spaces for the management had to turn this section over to general use again because it had damaged morale among the staff. Clothes are equally unimportant. Clothing shops (if they do not sell jeans, that is) have good reason to complain about how little importance is attached in Berlin to dressing. Elegance is the exception in this community.

How people spend their money is an indication of their loosening attachment to Berlin. Food and travel are two of the biggest items in the Berliner's budget. Since the Quadripartite Agreement, many have acquired a weekend or vacation house in the Federal Republic. The cost of real estate in the city is the highest in the Federal Republic, due to its shortage and because of Berlin's insular situation; this prevents people from satisfying the German longing for a place of one's own in the city itself. A number of Berliners have moved to Lower Saxony or Schleswig-Holstein. The family lives there, while father commutes to the city to work.

When it comes to community matters, a "subsidy mentality," by now a catchword, conceals a reduced sense of individual responsibility toward the city. The lack of patronage is a case in point. More money is and will continue to be earned in Berlin than is customarily thought. But there is a well-calculated reluctance to reveal such wealth. Nobody in the Federal Republic is supposed to get the idea that the "poor relative" is not so badly off after all. For the same reason, the wealthy are not moved to donate paintings to the city's National Gallery; such a display of wealth might be misinterpreted.

While many Berliners were loosening their ties to the city, numerous West Germans (especially young people) viewed West Berlin as a land of opportunity of another sort. There they could escape both the military draft and their parents' oppressive middle-class mores. Berlin, that unknown entity, was a shock to the family but a lucky bonus to the children. They were not disappointed. In Berlin they could submerge themselves unobserved into anonymity. They could communicate intensely with people holding similar views, crowded together in a city with a plethora of neighborhood bars and cafés open until all hours. Berlin's exceptional situation stimulated utopian ideas. It mirrored the feelings of the young: there must be change so that things can change for the better.

They began by rebelling against convention. But the beards, long hair, and nonconformist behavior provided evidence for the mistaken belief that these young people were communists in disguise—and the Berliner's liberalism does not extend to communists. In fact, the early rebels did not carry around the writings of Herbert Marcuse. They neither had plans for a "march through the institutions" nor did they advocate "power to the councils." They handed out flowers to policemen long before they took to throwing stones. They attributed the American war in Vietnam to the sexual hang-ups of the Americans. When Fritz Teufel was in court for the first time and was told by the judge to stand up, his reply was: "If you think it will help to establish the truth—certainly."

The New Left, making use of the ideological thought of the 1920s and of Karl Marx, advocated a "scientifically based idea of the truly human society." They set themselves up as leaders and viewed the human condition as trapped in a bureaucratic existence, manipulated by political and economic interests, devoid of any power. They knew better than everyone else. The truth was already established; all that remained was for the masses to recognize it. The moral protest was spurred on by the American war in Vietnam, by the formation in Bonn in 1966 of the Grand Coalition between CDU/CSU and SPD, and by the passage in 1968 of the Emergency Act. It found a platform in the universities, especially the Free University of Berlin. The university provided room where one could sit and arbitrate the fate of state and society. Politicians, first in Berlin, then in the Federal Republic, saw it as their most urgent task to resolve the conflict by keeping it in the universities. They wanted to set the city at ease. But this was putting too much strain on an institution: the universities, which were bound to a politically nonpartisan, pluralistic pursuit of truth, became battlefields of political egotism. They are still suffering the consequences today.

The rebels of the 1960s had three options once they had been forced to concede that they could not create a national movement: escape via resignation; the "march through the institutions" on a Social Democratic basis; or resorting to violence. The kidnapping in 1975 of Berlin's CDU president, Peter Lorenz, was the first of those terrorist acts which shook the Federal Republic to its foundations.

There is a close connection between the rebellion of the 1960s and the Alternative movement of the 1970s and 1980s in Berlin. Both rejected the structures produced by industrialized society and the division of labor. The students in the sixties wanted to establish an oppression-free base in the universities, just as the squatters do today in those run-down parts of Berlin, such as Kreuzberg, that are slated for urban renewal. Both are attempts to establish oneself for oneself. A publication of the Alternative movement states:

"Alternative" is for us synonymous with love of life and freedom. Love of life means respect for all kinds of life. Freedom means that each individual can do what he wants, as long as it does not restrict the freedom of other individuals. Both concepts mean the same thing. They preclude my oppressing others, especially weaker beings (children, subordinates, wage-earners, women, disabled and old people, animals), or my using force or exercising power over them. Both concepts also include my having my freedom and defending it against restriction by persons and institutions, and my learning to resist being dictated to from outside.

As in the 1960s, opinions differ on the question of force. Those who advocate striking back in self-defense do so with reference to the book by John Henry Mackay, *The Freedom Seeker*:[2] he who violates another human being's freedom is using force; if the victim fights back, this is no longer force. The counterargument is: "I may defend myself from restriction of my freedom, but in doing so I must attack the institutions which restrict my freedom and not the people in them. This forces me to use only certain methods: I must not use weapons and bombs. This does not condemn me to inaction, however, or simply to putting up with the worst violations of freedom. No! I can make those who threaten me look ridiculous," and so on.

In fact, the Alternative movement is disorganized, disunited, and contradictory in other respects as well. Its publication states:

> Self-determination and the greatest possible degree of freedom from force are preconditions for everything. People live together in small, decentralized, self-sustaining communities. The means of production are socialized; production is adapted to their needs. Humanitarian technology makes unalienated work possible. Decisions are made collectively by all those affected. The structures are divided into three parts: economy, law (politics), and free intellectual activity (culture) are returned to their natural condition (brotherliness, equality, freedom). It is a classless society, devoid of hierarchy, in which the distinctions between town and country, woman and man, intellectual and manual work have been removed. There is no state, there are no wars or prisons. What is it? A free cooperation among people who are aiming for the same objective, not by force but through feeling and talk and also seriousness. Action is concerned with tangibles (e.g., nuclear power stations, unemployment, changing conditions of production, rac-

ism). It raises the consciousness of the persons it is aimed at, and it is directed at their consciences. It is the universal weapon of social progress.

The Alternatives in Berlin actually comprise not a single movement as such but four groups: (1) romantic idealists; (2) the rootless—failures at school, at work, or in their personal relationships—who, without visible means or particular orientation, seek social integration; (3) negativists, for whom West Germany is synonymous with "Greenland," an icy, hostile social order, totally lacking in human warmth, whose ice floes are to be melted by a counterculture; and (4) militants, including violent individuals who try to use ideology to elevate their actions, as well as those intent on destruction for no apparent reason.

Before the election of May 1981 in Berlin, 65 percent of the people expressed the hope that the "Alternative List for Democracy and Preservation" would get into parliament. The majority of voters regarded this collection of "greens" (environmentalists) and reds, of idealists and ideologists (including even communist Maoists from formerly marginal splinter-groups) as having a legitimate right to seats and votes in parliament. That hope was not reflected in the election result, but it did signal a crisis of political culture. Political culture evolves out of the consensus that a society develops concerning its norms and proper conduct. These have proved themselves over time, constitute established wisdom, and are called tradition. Tradition is always conservative. "Conservative" should not be regarded, as is normally the case in Germany, as synonymous with reactionary. It is interpreted here as an attitude that is not obsessed with what happened yesterday, but which professes that which is always valid. Tradition, where it is effective, is the expression of a recognized principle that outlives changes in politics and in civilization.

Berlin's (and Germany's?) Identity Crisis

The social fabric of Berlin lacks such a tradition. Although the society appears to be satiated, it can suddenly be haunted by fears for the future. It is plagued by a depression that cannot be explained by rising oil prices and stagnating income. On the one hand, it is skeptical and pessimistic with respect to the political and social order. On the other hand, it expects its much-abused and insulted politicians to function as moral rearmers. It needs them to think for it and be its philosophers—a need that became evident during the 1981 Berlin election campaign. But politicians are not knights in shining armor rescuing damsels in distress. They are not psychotherapists. They, too, are part of this society, whose main characteristic has become an abhorrence of uncertainty.

We all face an identity crisis. Even the intellectuals will not be spared. They, so proud of their ability to reflect, are tempted to assign to politicians a task that they cannot perform. Politicians are not judges or dictators of good conduct. Their job is to ensure that a community functions. No more and no less. A politician may not use his power to turn his personal value system into law. For, what is power? It is the ability to produce obedience by commands, or if need be by force, a dangerous instrument that can only be kept in check by self-discipline among the powerful and self-confidence among the people. Anyone expecting politicians to give answers to questions about the meaning of life is leading them into temptation, which, if given in to, can produce totalitarianism. Neither the politician nor the state can decree what is good for the individual. In a democracy the state is a necessity, but it is society that really counts. And only society can form a consensus as to what is ethical conduct, what is morally good.

This involves individual effort. The state, however, has ceased to be a mere night watchman and has become responsible for general welfare and for the provision of comprehensive care and security. We have grown to expect the state and its politicians to provide spiritual care. The mentality of entitlement that has grown like a weed over the last decades has also made the intellect lazy. We have enjoyed letting others work for us, and now we would even like to be relieved of thinking. The churches stand open but few go inside. The Sermon on the Mount and the philosophers, who for thousands of years have been seeking the meaning of human life, are waiting to be read. But they are ignored. We do not even reflect upon our daily experiences. We let ourselves be overtaken by them. The consequence is that disagreeable matters and problems are seen to be absolute rather than relative. Depression and dejection result.

It is not just the young who have lost their bearings. Older people are lost, too. The crisis of youth and the associated generational conflict are talked of as the most prominent phenomena of the present day. Certainly, the confrontation between young and old, between utopia and conservatism, still exists. But over and above it there is an inner vacuum, regardless of which generation people belong to. The search for sails for the ship of life is not specific to a certain age group. A son squatting in

Kreuzberg and his father living in his freehold apartment in Dahlem, apparently separated by worlds, are really linked by a common homelessness.

What separates father and son is the difference in responsibility. Parents have to ask themselves what kind of ethical guidance they gave their children in the so-called years of plenty: had they been more and more inclined to take the easy option, even in their children's upbringing? Raising children requires that one take a definite position that children will rebel against. It enables them to test out and develop their own personality. Educators cannot pursue the youth cult. Society is fascinated by youth but forgets that it is a transitory phase. An intermediate stage is treated as if it were an absolute. We subordinate ourselves to the dictates of youth; we talk ourselves into being on the defensive; we become followers of Jean-Jacques Rousseau, the inventor of anti-authoritarian childrearing. Ideology has succeeded in fooling us into thinking that authority is a whip, mere force, although it really means power through respect. We cannot reproach the young for rejecting even legitimate authority. Adult inability to decide between ritual and disorderliness has been the cause of the squatter movement and student riots.

Once again it is the politicians and the state who are supposed to bail us out. But the children who live in Kreuzberg, who move in hordes across the Kurfürstendamm, who shout, "Germany, drop dead," are not the children of the state, nor have they fallen from heaven. Their parents, however, are quick to shun responsibility. And they are not the only ones sensing both helplessness and fear. When a group of masked figures bursts into a bar on the Kurfürstendamm to take chairs as weapons for the street, the customers obediently stand up. Later they grumble loudly about the failure of the police to intervene. Before the election of May 1981, one could hear people in the city talking about a possible civil war if the CDU were to win the election. There are still people who wonder, given the uproar in the city, whether or not it might be advisable to leave Berlin.

Anyone wishing to understand the undercurrents in the Federal Republic should look at Berlin. Berlin has become much more representative than it was in the 1950s, even though the distance, as seen from Stuttgart, Hamburg, or Frankfurt, has increased. Berlin is no longer alone in its quest for a purpose, in its uncertainty. West Germany can no longer derive its identity from its prosperity. People can no longer base their security on their terrace house or their second car. The seemingly unbreakable floorboards are beginning to disintegrate beneath their feet, and they are on the lookout for something to cling to.

Historical Awareness and Berlin's Future

It is dawning on Germans that the present has something to do with the past. After 1945 the Germans in West and East denied this connection. They wanted to forget, and make others forget, the terrible things that had happened in their name and were seen as a logical consequence of their history. They cut themselves off from these things. To make this easier they committed themselves totally to the present. The enemy and target of hate became the much-needed ally—for one side the United States, for the other the Soviet Union. In the Federal Republic memory was repressed; in the GDR it was narrowed by the communist Socialist Unity party.

An ahistorical, antihistorical way of thinking is confined to the present; at best it is interested in the future. It requires that we live from hand to mouth. It increases our confidence that anything is possible through technological progress. At the same time it destroys the knowledge that history is the lesson of the enduring limitations of the human race through changing times. This awareness of history, too, leaves its mark on people's attitudes. It silences those who boast that they live in the best of all worlds and those who claim they are doing what is inevitable. History makes things seem more relative by reminding us of mortality and eternity.

History is once again in vogue among Germans in both West and East. Historical exhibitions, such as those about the Hohenstaufens and the Wittelbachers, have become great attractions. Tribute was paid to Friedrich Schinkel in both parts of Germany. Martin Luther's birthday was an occasion for celebration on both sides of the frontier—in the GDR with a committee which had Erich Honecker as its chairman. In this way the two German nations are proving to be funnels of communication. Soon after the Prussian exhibition was announced in West Berlin, the GDR returned to its old position on Unter den Linden the mounted statue of Frederick the Great, banished in 1950 to the park of Sanssouci. Today the East German régime would not have demolished Andreas Schlüter's Berlin palace, which was badly burned in the war. In West Berlin today the Anhalter Railway Station, a symbol of the city, would be lovingly restored—were it not for the fact that it was torn down long ago.

This newly aroused interest in history should not, however, be mistaken for historical awareness. Historical interest is accidental. It grasps indiscriminately at anything distant, is fascinated by the unknown. The "throw-away society," which is swarming into the antique markets, is not after the objects sold there because they are souvenirs of a certain era. It is mere curiosity that draws them. An interest in history can lead to historical awareness, but this requires a minimum of knowledge that has been lacking in both parts of Germany up until now.

History as taught in schools once concentrated on past eras. Now the focus in the Federal Republic is on the post-1917 decades. GDR history is also torn out of context. It selects and violates events and persons in order to fabricate a logical sequence of history leading up to the GDR and testifying to its legitimacy. Good is that which serves one's own interests and damages the enemy. Two traditions were created: a progressive one for oneself, and a repressive one for the Federal Republic.

This basic pattern has remained. But it is now possible to detect some movement away from the simplistic and toward differentiation. It is especially the younger historians who want to refine their tools; the emergence of new generations, an important factor not just in the GDR, is accompanied by new forms of thought and behavior. Ingrid Mittenzwei, author of the first serious and noteworthy biography of Frederick the Great, made the following comment:

> Our view of Prussia was for a long time obstructed by the polemics which the revolutionary workers' movement had to adhere to in the nineteenth and twentieth centuries. This finding has nothing to do with the smugness of a later generation. The interest in Prussia, especially with phenomena such as the Prussian-German type of militarism, was absolutely essential after the catastrophe. . . . Prussia is part of our history, not just Weimer. A people cannot choose its own traditions; it must face up to them and it should do this in as many ways as possible.[3]

The Federal Republic likes to laugh at the difficulty the GDR has with its history. But is this justifiable in the light of its own uncertainty? When Dietrich Strobbe, shortly after taking office in 1977 as Berlin's governing mayor, conceived the idea of an exhibition on Prussia as a means to embellish his new government with a great event, he had no idea what an impact it would have at home and abroad. Prussia—the date of whose death (1871, 1933, or 1947) is very debatable, but whose actual death no one questions—this Prussia has been dug up from the grave to the rejoicings of some and the horror of others. It was not just an historical exhibition that was initiated—a political issue was created. Frederick the Great could not have dreamed that in the 1980s he would become such a topical and controversial figure for a German society.

Prussia as a lighthouse, signaling a safe harbor: Prussia as a siren, tempting us into destruction. And outside, beyond Germany's gateways, in the United States, in France, and in England, but especially in Poland, the skeptical question: what do these Germans suddenly want with Prussia? The ghosts of Tauroggen and Rapallo are abroad.

What can one do, caught between Scylla and Charybdis? One appoints a committee for the Prussian exhibition—internationally and ideologically balanced—and gives the show the careful subtitle, "Attempt at a Review." Not for one moment did anyone consider commissioning just one well-known historian to compose his portrait of Prussia, thus ensuring a compact treatment of the subject. For Prussia is a sensitive issue. Attempts to neutralize it were doomed from the outset.

This exhibition was nevertheless important for a city whose memory reaches back only to 1948, the year of the blockade. By showing the splendor and the misery of a great history, the exhibition helped us realize that the roots of this community reach far back and do not merely hang in space. This Berlin was and still is a center of Prussian and subsequently German history. Prussia may serve as a lesson: its virtues were transient, and they were perverted. But that bygone state can show this city and this country that they cannot stand their ground without generally accepted values and beliefs.

Historical awareness of Prussia will not bring Berlin a new identity. But it can help generate the spiritual strength needed to bear an extraordinary situation and to show tolerance toward the large cultural laboratory situated within Berlin's walls. The city has been relatively uncreative historically. But, because of the freedom it offered, it attracted creativity that had been born elsewhere but which could not flourish in its birthplace. Berlin as a catalyst—this is the key to its uniqueness.

9 Interpersonal Transactions across the Wall

Richard L. Merritt

At the core of the community is interdependency.[1] Interdependency, in brief, is a relationship at once mutually beneficial for those party to it and binding in the sense that the parties all would perceive a real loss were it to be dissolved. There is thus a commitment on the part of members of the group to the maintenance of that interdependency. Its nature varies greatly from group to group, just as does the degree of commitment to it. A fully integrated community will enjoy an economic division of labor, political and other institutions responsible for making decisions for the territory populated by the group, common facilities for and habits of communication, and sets of procedures for determining what is important, resolving conflicts, socializing children into the community, and performing a host of other day-to-day tasks. Other groups may have more limited purposes, institutions, and processes.

When interdependencies within a social group break down, we speak of *disintegration*. As is true of interdependency, the degree of disintegration is a relative matter. Moreover, both may have "spill-over" effects: steps toward or away from a high level of integration may be self-reinforcing and soon assume their own dynamic. The key to the disintegrative process is the collapse of people's commitment to the community's values, a decline in their willingness to make sacrifices in the expectation that the rewards of community life will significantly outweigh the costs.[2]

This paper examines integrative and disintegrative developments in postwar Berlin, especially in the period after the Quadripartite Agreement of 1971. The first postwar years saw the city, a single political community without significant cultural, ethnic, religious, linguistic, or other differentiation, arbitrarily divided into two competing political systems with sharply different political institutions, processes, and values. A question of both practical and theoretical interest is whether or not living in two separate but contiguous political systems will pull apart people who, before their political division, were pretty much like each other, viewed themselves as members of a single political community, and engaged in as much interaction as is normal in any metropolis.

Political Division and Human Interactions

Greater Berlin, one of the world's largest cities spatially and boasting almost four and a half million inhabitants in 1943, suffered three successive waves of disruption during the next half-decade. The first came when aerial bombardments and, in April 1945, intense street fighting reduced great parts of the city to piles of rubble, forced evacuations of over a third of its population, and crippled Berlin's communication and transportation facilities and such municipal services as the electrical and water works. This disruption, however, had a random effect on the eastern and western halves of the city, which were basically similar in their physical and socioeconomic structure. The effects of the second disruptive wave were distributed less equitably. In the two months between the city's fall on May 2, 1945, and the arrival of Western occupation troops on July 1, Soviet occupation authorities extensively dismantled its industrial capacity—especially in the sectors designated for American, British, and French control—for shipment to the Soviet Union as reparations.

The main dimensions of the third disruptive wave, the political division of Berlin itself, are well known.[3] The breakdown of Four-power cooperation in Germany led ultimately to the currency reforms in 1948, the subsequent blockade of the city, and the creation of separate governments not only for the Western zones of occupation (Federal Republic of Germany, or FRG) and the Soviet zone (German Democratic Republic, or GDR) but also, by fall 1948, for East and West Berlin. What ensued were quite conscious efforts to split the city's formerly unified infrastructure of municipal services, traffic routes, and public transportation and communication facilities. This took time, of course. For the most part, however, the task of infrastructural division was completed by 1952. Today, very few elements of pre-1948 Berlin's infrastructure, among them parts of the sewage system and Quadripartite control over air traffic, remain as living examples of an earlier, undivided past.

But what about the Berliners? How did they respond to the division of their city? Two aspects of behavior are particularly relevant here. One is their attitudes toward the political events and their consequences. Although attitudes as such will not be discussed in this paper, it may be worth noting that on both sides of the border mass opinion, originally hostile to the new status quo, gradually grew accustomed to it, whereas elite and official opinion was and continues to be divided.[4] The idea of the original wartime agreements defining Greater Berlin within its boundaries of 1920 as a single political unit continues to dominate in the West—that is, West Berlin, the Federal Republic, and their Western allies—whereas the Eastern position is that subsequent events nullified the Four-power agreements, turned the eastern sector of Berlin into the capital city of the German Democratic Republic, but left the western sectors as an anomaly, located on GDR territory but still occupied by the victors of World War II. Few in the West, however, and certainly not the American, British, and French commanders who retain sovereign control over West Berlin, are prepared to take any concrete action to support their legal claims that the entire city remains under Four-power rule. Elaborate interpretations of its underlying meanings notwithstanding, the Quadripartite Agreement of September 1971 had the effect of giving the status quo of divided Berlin a seal of acceptance (albeit not, at least in Western eyes, approval).

The second relevant aspect of the Berliners' behavior comprises possible changes in their habits. Even after the division of 1948–49, the border between East and West Berlin remained open, at least in principle. Citizens of one side merely had to board a subway or elevated railway to get to the other side, or else simply walk across at any of the eighty-six border stations that connected the two sides of the city. But, of course, what was possible in principle was limited in fact. Just enough arrests or other unpleasantries occurred to remind most citizens that crossing the border entailed some risk. This risk, however small, remained fairly constant from the end of the blockade in 1949 to the construction twelve years later of a wall that virtually ended all Berliners' travel to the other side of their city during the next eleven years. The Quadripartite Agreement of 1971 paved the way for inter-German agreements of the following year that reopened the border between East and West Berlin in a restricted fashion for West Berliners only.

Ideally, what we would like to know is how the Berliners actually changed their daily lives in response to these political events. Did they continue to visit friends who lived on the other side of the demarcation line in the years before 1961? If they lived in one half of the city but worked in the other, did they give up their job or their residence—both of which were scarce indeed in postwar Berlin—or did they try to continue as they had in the past? Did they go to the same movie houses, lakes, and shopping centers as before? What was the nature of the contacts they had with people from the other side of the city? Whom have West Berliners visited in the East since 1972? The most clear-cut answers to such questions would rest on information gathered at the level of the individual, information that does not exist or, if it does, has not been made public.

It is nevertheless possible to obtain a picture of how such transaction patterns changed by examining indicators of behavior at the aggregate level. For instance, given the fact that a third of Greater Berlin's population lived in the East, we would normally expect that an opera house located in the West but near the center of the city would draw a third of its visitors from East Berlin. If the actual percentage is less than a third, then it would seem reasonable to assume that the political division had had some impact on the composition of the opera house's audience. Even if we conclude that we do not know what quota of visitors would "normally" come from the East—since, perhaps, a taste for opera is strong only among certain social classes, and it turns out that most of the opera lovers live in one rather than the other half of the city—trends over time in the pattern of visits may indicate shifts in the flow of transactions between East and West Berlin. This example points also to the need to search for a multiplicity of indicators of any complex concept.

Indicators of personal interactions are important on several counts. Most relevant for present purposes is the fact that they indicate changing levels of community involvement on the part of the community's members. Accordingly, one hypothesis might say that the political division of Berlin did not significantly affect the predispositions of Berliners toward each other and toward their formerly unified political community; this is the official position espoused with respect to both Berlin and Germany as a whole. An alternative hypothesis derives from Ernst Renan's assertion of more than a century ago that nationalism is a plebiscite of daily living. Over time, the resident of a particular political system builds up a pattern of expectations, demands, and identifications relevant to that system but only tangentially so vis-à-vis other such systems. This line of thought, if accurate, would lead us to expect that transactions between East and West Berliners would have dropped off during the 1950s despite the continued possibility for personal contacts and that reopening the border in 1972 would have done little to restore the lost relevance that the other side of the city had for them.

This paper examines aggregate data on transactions between East and West Berlin during two periods. The first is from 1949 to 1961, that is, the dozen years after the city's political division in the wake of the blockade and before the construction of the wall stopped most opportunities for interaction. The second period covers the years since the inter-German agreements of 1971–72 reopened the border on a limited basis.

Decline of Community, 1949–61

The search for data on interactions from 1949 to 1961 between East and West Berliners could lead in several directions. This study concentrates on both official statistics and those produced by public and quasi-public agencies in the course of their normal operations but never published. The indicators examined are: (1) passengers carried by public transportation, 1937 and 1958; (2) Eastern visitors to West Berlin's municipal theaters, exhibition center, radio tower, and summer garden, 1950–61; (3) letters from the East to the station Radio in the American Sector (RIAS), 1950–61; (4) letters and packages sent between West Berlin and the East, 1952–60; (5) membership in the East Berlin organization of the Social Democratic party (SPD), 1950–61; and (6) sales of the daily newspaper *Telegraf* to East Berlin subscribers, 1950–60. A comparison of these various quantitative streams of evidence reveals striking convergence. Each curve declined during the decade of the 1950s. To be sure, they started out at various levels and declined at varying rates (with the steepest linear curve dropping 2.6 percentage points per year and the least steep about a quarter of a percentage point per year), but the overall trend of declining contacts between East and West is unmistakable. Moreover, in those cases in which there were clear-cut efforts by the West German government to revive flagging levels of contacts, the actual impact was brief before the curves began to decline again.

The composite curve in figure 9.1 shows these trends clearly. For each set of data listed above, the average "interaction rate" for 1952–60 was computed. Using this average rate as 100, the index figure for each year was then calculated. Figure 9.1 shows the average of these yearly index figures. For example, the average interaction rate for 1950, based on the available data, was 159, that is, 59 percent greater than the aver-

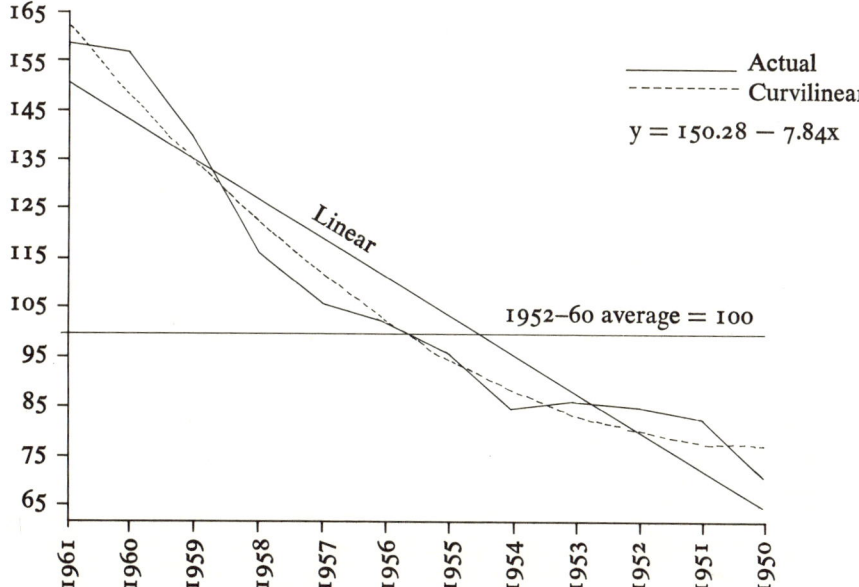

Figure 9.1 Decline of Interactions between East Berliners and West Berliners (index figures, average of 1952–60 = 100)

age for the decade. By 1961, as figure 9.1 also indicates, the average interaction rate was 70, or about 30 percent below the average for the decade as a whole. The best-fitting straight line declines almost 8 percentage points per year. A second-order curve, the broken line in figure 9.1, fits the data still better (although both are significant at the $p < .001$ level). It suggests that the rate of declining contacts was greatest at the outset of the 1950s, and then, by about 1958, flattened out considerably.

How can we explain this declining pattern of personal interaction between East and West in the divided Berlin of the 1950s? A part of the explanation doubtless lies in the changing character of the population concerned. For one thing, knowing that more than three million residents of the GDR fled that country during the dozen years before the Berlin wall was built, we can easily imagine that many of those most inclined to have extensive contacts in West Berlin were among the first to flee. Whether or not it was these contacts that led them to their decision is not of moment here. More to the point is the fact that, for every person who left the GDR for the West, there was one less person predisposed to have contacts in West Berlin. For another thing, it seems likely that the death of older Berliners reduced the number of those who had memories of an undivided city and the set of daily living habits that goes along with such a memory. Indeed, by the 1980s well under half of all Germans could remember living in a time when Germany and Berlin were not divided. Both these trends suggest that the mere passage of time served to reduce contacts across the city's arbitrary borders.

More generally, however, the data indicate that Berliners' expectations of and identifications with a single political community in the city were probably declining. Living in separate and mutually hostile political systems was taking its toll on a common sense of community. Here a number of purely practical barriers to social communication arose. First, it was difficult to find out what was happening in the other side of the city. Most of what one read in the press on the one side was negative, and it was virtually impossible to get newspapers from the other side of the city without actually going there. Radio reports might tell listeners about the more spectacular occurrences, without, however, giving them much of an idea of what the daily life in the other part of the city was like. What were people thinking about the events of the day? How were they planning to spend their holidays? What interests did their children have? These and a host of other questions could not be answered without visiting the other side. It was even difficult to find out what was playing at the theater or movie house on the other side. The media on both sides eschewed reporting on cultural events on the other side—unless, of course, something occurred that could be used as political propaganda.

Second, it was difficult during the 1950s to discount entirely the personal risk entailed in making visits to the other side of the city. West Berliners, particularly if they carried with them Eastmarks purchased at black market rates in one of West Berlin's many (and officially supported) exchange bureaus, always had before them examples of other West Berliners who had been detained and even imprisoned in East Berlin. East Berliners knew that visits to the West were officially discouraged. Those known to have too many contacts with the West might well find that they or their children were disadvantaged at the workplace or in school. In short, even though nothing was *likely* to happen—and, given the number of border crossings each day, the percentage of incidents was minuscule—the thought that something *could* happen was ever present. Such a thought doubtless discouraged many casual visits across the border.

A third barrier to social communication across the border comprised the imperatives of Berliners' daily lives. That is, West Berliners had to deal every day and in virtually every way with the political system of the West: its public schools, marketing procedures, tax laws, banking, telephone system, consumer products, newspapers, and everything else in their immediate social environment. The same was true for East Berliners. The practical relevance to them of the other side of the city was slight. Moreover, the probability that anything they did would have an impact in the other part of the city was slighter. In such circumstances the findings of social psychologists that levels of relevance are correlated with levels of both knowledge and interest would lead us to expect Berliners to become increasingly indifferent about what was happening "over there." Renan's "plebiscite of daily living" was day by day turning Berliners into either East Berliners or West Berliners.

The overall trend of declining interactions suggests that Berliners were learning to be different. In this sense it is the converse of the curve identified in other studies as the pattern by which a sense of community is learned.[5] Each aspect of behavior examined here in the aggregate moved steadily, albeit with fluctuations, in that direction. Governmental efforts to retard estrangement produced only a slight and temporary amount of regression, indicated by an upward swing in the curve. Nor is there any reason to think that the curve would have reversed itself had not the events of August 1961 taken place. By that time Berliners were well on their way toward complete separation.

Decade of Separation, 1961-72

If the 1950s, years in which the border between East and West Berlin was relatively open, were an era of declining interaction, what would the closing of that border in 1961 bring? We might expect—and East German authorities doubtless hoped—that virtually complete separation would whittle down the last vestiges of community. Alternatively, given the strong West German emphasis on maintaining contacts with relatives and friends "over there," we might expect a surge in the forms of interaction that remained possible. The reality, as indicated by available data, conformed completely to neither expectation.

The days after the GDR sealed off West Berlin witnessed a double hardening of the interpersonal boundaries between East and West Berliners. For one thing, the wall assumed ever greater proportions. Concrete slabs, bricks, and cement gradually replaced the barriers of wood and barbed wire; workmen, under armed guard, bricked up the windows of buildings directly on the border, evacuated their residents, and eventually tore down the buildings themselves; mined "death strips" as well as attack dogs became a common feature of what GDR officials called their "modern state border"; and the number of white crosses on the western side of the wall, each representing a refugee killed in the act of trying to flee the German Democratic Republic, grew virtually from day to day. For another thing, access to East Berlin on the part of West Berliners was restricted. In the first days of the wall West Berliners could come and go as they pleased. Soon, however, GDR officials, seeing the need to control this traffic, decreed that West Berliners would need special passes, obtainable from GDR offices that would be located in selected elevated railway stations in the West.[6] But Western authorities refused to permit these offices to be set up. With what must have been a great sigh of relief, the GDR then announced that this action by the West meant that West Berliners could not be permitted to enter East Berlin. Thus began a period of almost eleven years of sharply restricted personal contacts between East and West Berliners.

Two types of entry to East Berlin were granted to West Berliners during this decade. First, from December 1963 to June 1966 the GDR issued special entry permits during eight holiday periods. As table 9.1 shows, the Christmas and New Year's holidays attracted the largest number of applicants for these special permits. Over the brief two and a half years covered by these arrangements, it should be noted, the trend was definitely downward. Christmas visits per day declined by 25 percent from 1963–64 to 1965–66, and visits over Easter and Whitsuntide dropped by 10 percent in the single year from 1965 to 1966.

Second, beginning in 1964 West Berliners could apply for special emergency permits to enter the East in the event of a pressing family matter such as illness or death but also, on occasion, marriages. The criteria for granting these emergency permits varied over time, generally becoming more liberal. Even so, the high point in the number of emergency permits granted, as table 9.2 shows, was 1969, when an average of 269 permits were given out daily.

Although visits between East and West Berliners were sharply restricted between 1961 and 1972, it continued to be possible to send and receive mail. Indeed, the West German government officially encouraged this kind of maintenance of contracts, both in advertisements and circulars and through its policy of permitting tax write-offs for the value of packages sent to the GDR. Unfortunately, complete data on mail

Table 9.1 West Berliners' Visits to East Berlin and the GDR, 1963–66

Period	Christmas/New Year's			Other Holidays		
	No. of days	No. of visitors	Visitors per day	No. of days	No. of visitors	Visitors per day
Dec. 19, 1963–Jan. 5, 1964	18	1,242,810	69,045			
Oct. 30, 1964–Nov. 12, 1964				14	571,145	40,796
Dec. 19, 1964–Jan. 3, 1965	16	825,188	51,574			
Apr. 12, 1965–Apr. 25, 1965				14	581,470	41,534
May 31, 1965–June 13, 1965				14	501,515	35,823
Dec. 18, 1965–Jan. 2, 1966	16	824,014	51,501			
Apr. 7, 1966–Apr. 20, 1966				14	510,433	36,460
May 23, 1966–June 5, 1966				14	467,956	33,425

Source: "Bericht über die Durchführung des Vier-Mächte-Abkommens und der ergänzenden Vereinbarungen zwischen dem 3. Juni 1972 und dem 31. Mai 1973," Abgeordnetenhaus von Berlin, 6. Wahlperiode, "Mitteilungen des Präsidenten, Nr. 56," Drucksache 6/1013, August 3, 1973, p. 13.

flows have not been made available for the period after 1960. We may nonetheless get an idea of trends by looking at the exchange of large and small parcels. In 1967 West Berlin's postal system recorded 10.85 million such packages sent to or received from the GDR, but by 1971 this figure had dropped by 32 percent to 7.41 million.[7] (See below for the further development of this trend.)

Another indicator, albeit still more indirect, of contacts between East and West in Berlin is provided by attention patterns. In the absence of direct ties among people, mutual empathy may be the next best thing. Empathy, however, or the ability to put oneself in another's shoes, to see the world as the other sees it, requires an ample amount of accurate, up-to-date information. Without such information, one's image of the other remains rooted in some past time, unable to take account of what

Table 9.2   Special Emergency Permits to Visit East Berlin and the GDR, 1964–72

Year	Number of permits
1964	9,852
1965	29,860
1966	31,491
1967	58,745
1968	85,678
1969	98,210
1970	97,329
1971	84,758
1972 (annual rate)	64,130*

* The actual number from January 1 to June 3, 1972, was 27,159 permits; caution should be used in interpreting this figure, since it is possible that, anticipating a more open border after June 4, 1972, fewer West Berliners applied for permits in early 1972 than might otherwise have been the case.
Source: Same as Table 9.1.

is a dynamic and quite probably divergent living situation. Accordingly, examining the attention patterns of West Berliners may provide us with a clue as to their degree of concern with what is happening to their countrymen in the East.

An excellent source for such an examination of attention patterns is *Das Berliner Sonntagsblatt: Die Kirche,* published since the end of 1945 by the Evangelical Church in Berlin-Brandenburg. Of all the corporate bodies in pre-blockade Berlin, it was the provincial church that maintained its organizational unity the longest and sought most effectively to keep Berliners on both sides of the city in a single community. Even the construction of the wall did not break it apart. Church leaders in East and West Berlin conducted their business at church conferences elsewhere, or through intermediaries (primarily West Germans who were permitted to enter East Berlin). Still today, a decade or so after the provincial church bowed to pressure from the GDR government to have separate bishops and synods, an astonishing amount of coordination between the two branches takes place on a day-to-day basis.

The *Berliner Sonntagsblatt* appears weekly to inform the faithful about activities of the church. In the earliest postwar years it devoted most (76 percent) of its space on matters in Berlin-Brandenburg to a provincial body undifferentiated according to its Eastern or Western

Table 9.3 Attention to the Evangelical Church in Berlin-Brandenburg: Content Analysis of *Das Berliner Sonntagsblatt*, 1946–71*

Period	Total column centimeters	Undifferentiated church	East Berlin church	West Berlin church
1946–50	2344	76%	11%	13%
1951–55	3904	64	6	30
1956–60	3944	46	8	46
1962–66	4700	4	7	89
1967–71	6584	5	4	90

* Percentage distribution of space devoted solely to matters within the sphere of the *Evangelische Kirche in Berlin-Brandenburg* (and not to church matters elsewhere in Germany or the world). The term "Undifferentiated church" comprises items referring to the EKiBB without reference to its separate branches in East and West.

wings (table 9.3). The passage of time and growing division in both Germany and Berlin, which had very practical implications for the church, nonetheless brought increased attention to church activities pertinent primarily to West Berlin alone. After 1961, the image of a unified church in Berlin-Brandenburg was virtually dead (5 percent for the decade 1962–71). A flurry of attention to churches in the East immediately after the wall went up soon gave way to an overwhelming interest in churches in the West (90 percent in 1962–71). In the years immediately before the inter-German agreement reopened the border between East and West Berlin, attention to church activities in the East or cutting across the boundaries (8.4 percent in 1969–71) was about an eleventh of that devoted to the West (91.6 percent).

The data reviewed here point to a complicated picture of community in Berlin during the decade of almost total separation, 1962–71. Opportunities for interpersonal contacts between East and West Berliners were few and far between. In the mid-1960s, when visits to East Berlin during holiday periods were permitted, a substantial number of West Berliners obtained entry passes (table 9.1). The number of permits ranged from approximately one for every two West Berliners during the Christmas and New Year's holidays in 1963–64—the first opening in the wall since August 1961—to less than half that number during the Easter and Whitsuntide holidays in 1966. Insofar as such a brief time period reveals trends in interpersonal contacts, they were downward. The distribution of emergency permits to West Berliners (table 9.2) also hints at a declining trend even though, as the East German authorities discovered that such traffic was financially profitable, the criteria for issuing them were liberalized (table 9.2). The number of packages shipped to or received from the East as well as attention patterns in the weekly church newspaper (table 9.3) strengthen the impression that the trend of declining interest in the East among West Berliners was real and not the artifact of any particular analytic approach.

Ties between East and West Berliners were far from moribund, but the decade of separation did little to keep them alive. The initial outrage instigated by the wall may well have strengthened the will of East and West Berliners alike to defy the East German authorities who would keep them apart. But any increased activity in the months and years immediately after the wall was built appear as an upward aberration on a curve that is otherwise steadily dropping. Only a full opening of the borders, many thought, could arrest this trend toward increased isolation.

The New Status Quo

The Quadripartite Agreement of September 1971 laid the groundwork for at least a partial opening of the borders. On December 20, 1971, the West Berlin Senate and the GDR agreed, among other things, to permit West Berliners to visit East Berlin and the GDR for up to 30 days per year (and even more in some cases, such as illness in the family) and create offices in West Berlin to process applications. Although the traffic would be for the most part one-way, that is, for West Berliners only, the prospects nevertheless existed to reestablish ties severed or weakened during the 1960s. The significant question is how these West Berliners actually responded to the opportunity to reassert their sense of community across the wall.

One of the conditions of acceptance of the agreement in West Berlin was that an annual report would be written to outline developments and problems during the course of the previous twelve months.[8] An element of this reporting, the number of visits made to East Berlin and the GDR by West Berliners, is reported in figure 9.2. The data show two striking aspects. First, the number of visits per year declined over the last twelve years, from 3.72 million from June 4, 1972, to May 31, 1973, to 1.56 million between June 1, 1983, and May 31, 1984. A linear regression characterizing the shifts in the year-to-year figures indicates that the average number of visits declined by 177,600 per year—which means,

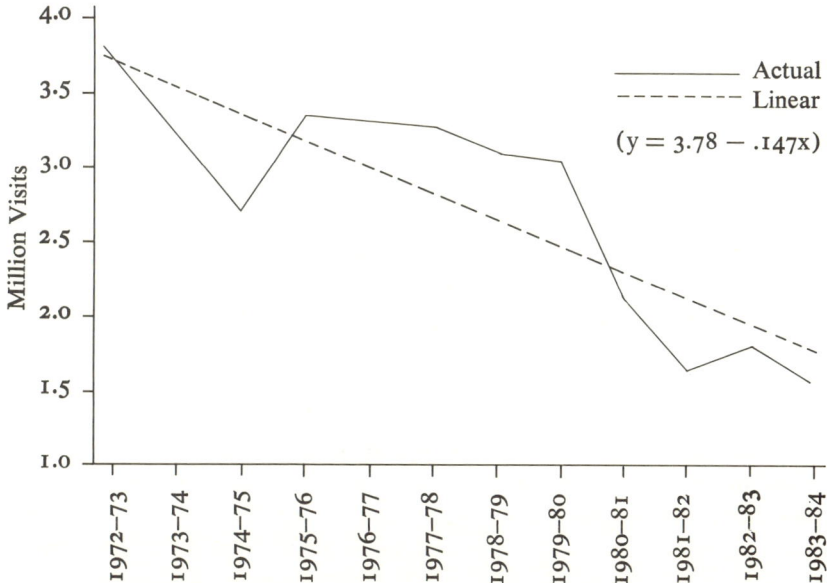

Figure 9.2 Number of Visits by West Berliners to East Berlin and the GDR, 1972–84

if we may extrapolate this trend into the future, that visits will drop to nearly zero by mid-1994.[9]

Second, there are two remarkable dips in the curve that cry out for explanation. The first was during the second and third years of the new arrangement. In both years the decline was about a half million visits. How do we account for this? For one thing, the figure for 1972–73 may have been extraordinarily high, as people rushed to take advantage of the agreement before it should be cancelled or to visit friends and relatives they may not have seen since 1966. (Actually, a preliminary agreement for Eastern and Whitsuntide 1972 had seen 1.24 million West Berliners visit the East.) For another thing, and doubtless more helpful in explaining the dip in the curve, during the second and third years the GDR both raised the amount of hard currency that any visitor to the East was obligated to exchange and also decided to make the financial provisions of the arrangement applicable to pensioners. The annual decline in the number of visits during the next five years was closer to the average. Even heavier costs imposed by the GDR on visitors beginning in the late summer of 1980 contributed to a second sharp dip in the curve.

A third trend, not visible in figure 9.2, is a decline in the number of visits lasting more than a single day and the share of these in the total number of visits. In 1972–73, almost every fourth visit was for longer than a day. By 1983–84, however, the number of longer visits had dropped from 854,000 to 290,000—a decline of 66 percent—and their share of the total number of visits dropped slightly from 23 to 22 percent. The share in 1979–80, at 16 percent, was even lower, which suggests that the greatest impact of the currency measures imposed in 1980 was on casual visitors. This fact would lead us to expect a slower decline of visits in the future than was the case in the first decade of the new arrangement.

Consistent with the pattern of personal visits is an even sharper decline in the number of packages sent to or received from East Berlin and the GDR on the part of West Berliners (figure 9.3). As indicated earlier, the number of such packages dropped from 10.85 million in 1967 to 7.41 million in 1971. By 1977 the number had dropped still further, this time by more than half (57 percent) to only 3.18 million. If this decline by an average of 794,000 packages per year in fact continued in a linear fashion, then the last package exchanged would have been delivered in the fourth week of May 1981!

Countering these trends, however, is an increase in telephone traffic

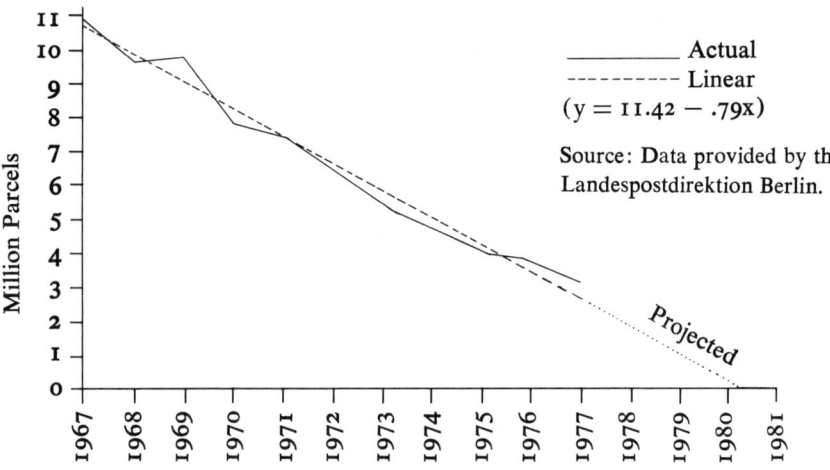

Figure 9.3 Parcels from and to East Berlin and the GDR, 1967–77

between West Berlin and the East. Except for a handful of emergency lines, telephone service between the two halves of the city was broken off in the early 1950s. Not until February 1971 was this service restored. The number of available lines nonetheless remained limited. It grew from 40 in October 1971 to 201 by mid-1973 and to 609 in December 1981.[10] In 1972–73 the daily traffic was roughly 8,200 calls to East Berlin and another 2,000 into the GDR; by 1981 these figures were 23,800 and 5,500, respectively.[11] In the latter year as many as 10.7 million telephonic contacts were made yearly between West Berlin and the East.

In a sense, the use of telephones may be replacing the mails as the chief means of communication between East and West Berliners. Neither a letter nor a telephone call has the same impact as a personal visit, to be sure, but either is a means for maintaining contacts when personal visits are impossible or inconvenient. The importance of such telephone calls for sustaining a sense of community nonetheless remains to be seen. Not until a sufficient number of lines have been available for some time to handle desired telephone conversations will it be possible to assess any trend. The most reasonable prediction to make is that, when ample lines are available for all who wish to telephone between East and West Berlin, and quite possibly even before then, the number of calls actually made will begin to decline.

The partial reopening of the border thus has not reversed the long-standing drop-off of interpersonal ties between East and West Berliners. Every indicator available for the past three decades—for the 1950s, when the border was fully open, for the 1960s, when it was closed, and for the 1970s, when it was partially open again—shows a pattern of decreasing communication.

All this does not necessarily mean that political community is dead in Berlin. In this regard a number of facts are important to note. First, although the level of contacts is declining, these contacts have not disappeared. It is likely that the decline will continue until only the firmest of familial ties or those of friendship remain. Second, there are signs that younger Berliners are interested in setting up new contacts with their age-cohorts on the other side of the city. Such contacts are likely to be of the sort that exist between the youth (and other groups) in any two neighboring countries whose residents speak a common language. Third, that the contacts which do exist have a political impact can be inferred from the decision of the GDR in summer 1980 to raise once again the financial costs for West Berliners and others crossing the border into the East. The result of similar actions in the early 1970s, not long after the new arrangements were put into place, was to decrease the flow of West Berliners by about a half million visits per year. The decrease from 1979–80 to 1981–82 was substantially greater—630,000 per year. Finally, it is possible, albeit not very likely, that political breakthroughs will reunite the city and reverse the trend of declining community.

The possibility of reversibility raises an interesting question: what would happen if Berlin were to be reunified today? Would not the old patterns of interactions, and with them the expectations, demands, and identifications associated with political community, simply re-emerge? In other words, have close to four decades of separation *really* made East and West Berliners distinct from each other?

In seeking to answer this question, it is tempting to think in terms of historical examples. Poles did not give up their sense of nationality despite a century and a quarter of division under alien rule, and similar nationality struggles were recurrent in the Balkans. Such examples, however, which would lead us to expect a sense of German nationality and Berlin community to persist for many decades to come, may be misleading. The classic cases of reunited nationalities occurred at times and in places in which there was a relatively low degree of organized complexity. Polish peasants in what were then the German, Russian, and Austro-Hungarian empires were fairly similar, more tied to the land and their peasant communities than to elaborate sets of imperial social communication systems. It is by no means clear that the Poland that re-emerged in 1918 was the result of spontaneous pressure from the masses, as opposed to an unusual set of international circumstances, effective organization by a small number of leaders, and the willingness of the masses to cast votes in plebiscites. How likely is it that a new international crisis would make the rest of the world accept a reunified Germany and/or Berlin? Moreover, another element in the Polish case, a unifying thrust by determined leaders may occur in Germany. What they will face, however, is not a mass of peasants independent of any large-scale and complex system of government and communication, but rather populations with strong sets of interdependencies that are mutually exclusive.

The latter is a more likely scenario for a Berlin reunified at some future time. If the city is politically amalgamated on the basis of new international agreements, it will be fairly easy to rebuild a unified municipal government, and with time it will be possible to construct the links to tie together divided water and sewage systems, streets and subway lines, and the like. More difficult to reconstruct will be the sentimental ties of community. Reunification in the year, say, 2000 will come more than a half century after the city's political division and almost 40 years after the appearance of the wall. By then there will be very few Berliners alive who will have a vivid memory of what it was like before 1945 and fewer still who will have any active contacts on the other side of the city. Changing residential, traffic, and other patterns by which people organize their daily lives will by then have produced two cities in a physical sense. East Berliners will be tied intimately to the social, economic, and political systems in the German Democratic Republic, West Berliners to quite different systems in the Federal Republic. Rebuilding a common set of expectations, demands, and identifications among Berliners will doubtless be a very slow process, quite possibly slower than that which had forced them apart in the first place.

What seems less likely in the present circumstances is that a nationalistic movement firmly grounded at the grassroots level will emerge to force the German governments or those of the victorious Allies of World War II to reunify the country (or, still less likely, Berlin alone). The precondition for such a movement would be the kind of social communication networks that the GDR government still seems determined to prevent. Free mobility within Berlin and Germany will probably remain an impossible dream until there are no more economic incentives for citizens of one Germany to flee to the other, until pacts have been reached for returning to their country of origin those who have left for political reasons (a possibility that most West German leaders would firmly reject now), and, more generally, until neither country poses a threat to the other. It is unlikely that, in the absence of free mobility, an effective social communication network will emerge in the two Germanies.

The prospects, at least for the foreseeable future, are for the division of Berlin to continue. As each year passes, the underlying basis of political community in Berlin as a whole erodes a bit more. East Berliners become more closely tied to a network of systems that tries as much as possible to ignore the existence of West Berlin, while West Berliners form stronger links to a network of systems in which nongovernmental processes in East Berlin are of little moment. In the place of community, estrangement is growing.

Discussion

SHEPARD STONE: It seems to me that television is providing a very significant contact between East and West in Berlin and throughout Germany. People in the East really do seem to be better informed than they used to be. And it is certainly clear to anyone who visits East Berlin between 7:00 and 8:30 in the evening that most people are watching television from the West. I have the feeling that at least the Berliners I know seem to know more and are a little bit closer than they were ten years ago.

JOHN KORNBLUM: In looking at contacts across the border we must remember that we are living in an increasingly provincial age. People all over the world simply do not care much about other people anymore. There are all sorts of indicators for this: less interest in German–American exchange programs, community involvement in the United States, even what is happening in the West Berlin boroughs other than that in which one lives. The fact is, everybody seems to be staying at home.

HELGA HAFTENDORN: I would like Mr. Engert to expand a bit on his views of the younger generation. Some of the previous speakers have suggested that a large proportion of the university student body is highly politicized, that the Alternative movement is a politicization of the young. That is not my impression. My impression is rather of a *ratlose Generation*—a difficult phrase to translate but, roughly, a generation in search of a purpose, in search of an identity, of moral values. To some extent Berlin has become the capital of the young Alternatives. My question for Mr. Engert is, What kind of impact do you think this will have on the city? A second and larger question is, What will the impact be on the political life of the Federal Republic?

JÜRGEN ENGERT: On this issue of the *ratlose Generation*, I agree completely. In fact, it permeates our entire social fabric and manifests itself in people's noninvolvement in political affairs, in an ahistorical attitude. The 1981 election campaign produced a totally new phenomenon: citizens asking politicians to answer philosophical questions dealing with the meaning of life. In other words, they were seeking to turn the politician into a psychiatrist or a guru who can help the individual find his way out of this difficult situation we are all in. People don't want to make certain kinds of decisions on their own, and they have no sense of identity with their community, no sense of responsibility toward others.

This lack of involvement and concern is emotional, manipulable, and therefore highly dangerous. And it is quite different from the New Left of the 1960s. It is closer to the actions of Fritz Teufel and the communards of those days, who were also more irrational and did not know where they were headed.

HANS OTTO BRÄUTIGAM: This fascinating discussion about Berlin's psychological condition strikes me as being a picture of the city from within the city. But much of what has been described as unique in Berlin—and may indeed have been more pronounced or become apparent at an earlier point in Berlin than elsewhere in the Federal Republic—strikes me as being part of a larger movement. It also proves that Berlin is in fact part of the Western world, of West Germany, Western Europe, the industrial world.

I would also like to comment on your suggestion, Herr Engert, that the Alternative movement represents the demise of our political culture. There is no question but that this movement creates tremendous problems for those who have played the political game according to its traditional rules. What strikes me as far more significant is the need for our established parties to rise to this occasion and come to grips with the issues raised by these people. Despite the difficulties all of this brings, I regard their presence in the city parliament as a positive thing, certainly better than if they were not represented and were acting as an opposition outside the governmental process.

JÜRGEN ENGERT: Yes, I agree. It does seem to me that, while Berlin is representative for all of the Federal Republic, things do come to a head in the city much more rapidly and intensely, perhaps because the inhabitants are less likely—or, because of their relative physical isolation, less able—to take off for a weekend of skiing in the winter or sailing in the summer. One reason for the existing situation is the fact that West Germany did not develop a positive political tradition after 1945. The way political parties behave and how they respond to our great national issues should indeed be discussed within the governmental framework rather than through an extraparliamentary opposition.

KLAUS SCHÜTZ: After I left this city I discovered many similarities between Berlin and Israel, but there are two very significant differences that relate to the theme of this conference. First of all, young people in Israel live in a state of constant danger and have taken upon themselves a responsibility, namely, to fend off that danger. All of them accept three years of military service followed by reserve duty. In Berlin that sense of danger no longer exists, as it did at one time. Second, and this is even more important, after the danger dissipated in Berlin, nothing was left. In Israel, regardless of how skeptical the young people may be, they at least have their sense of history, their traditions. In Germany the young can quite rightfully ask, What do I have in common with the history of those who set up Auschwitz? Or does my history belong with those who tried to kill Hitler? This is one of the most serious questions facing West Germans today.

The Alternatives distributed an interesting paper at this conference that contains a provocative statement on the German question.[12] Even though it may be difficult to estimate how widespread this sentiment is shared among those identifying with the Alternative movement, it is one deserving attention. I do not believe that any political party has really dealt with it before.

JÜRGEN ENGERT: That is a very important point. Among the nonorganized Left there have been discussions about this issue for several years now. Actually it began in the literary domain, where people have in fact been talking about the question of Germany's identity. And this is now happening in Berlin as well as in the GDR, especially among writers. The discussions are extremely intense, and a fairly permanent exchange of views has developed between East and West Berlin. This level of intensity, incidentally, is far more important than the number of times people cross the border.

RICHARD MERRITT: Without wishing to denigrate the importance of transactions at the elite level, including those among writers, any popular sense of common identity requires substantial and positive interaction at all levels. To have intense interactions requires first and foremost that there be ordinary interactions. The data show that these are dropping off as far as the mass of Berliners is concerned.

JÜRGEN ENGERT: The communication that takes place among the West Berlin youngsters who go over to East Berlin as part of their schools' exchange program, for instance, is far more intense than would be expected if they were going over just to take a look.

JOHN KORNBLUM: A different kind of consciousness is developing in Berlin, one that is not quantifiable. Indeed, it is not even describable. At the moment it exists among only a small group of people, and it accounts for the fact that an East German writer such as Sarah Kirsch can come to the West and express amazement at how familiar things seem. They discover that they are really still in the same country. This consciousness of community cannot be ignored.

RICHARD MERRITT: The same phenomenon occurs when Germans visit the United States. Everything seems very familiar, German intellectuals have told me, in large part because they have seen so many American films and television shows that the American way of life has become part of their own consciousness. Similarly, those visiting West Berlin from the East find many elements in common. The number and significance of these elements are nevertheless slowly and rather steadily diminishing.

JOHN KORNBLUM: While the United States is certainly a part of the West German political consciousness, the point is not that Easterners visit West Berlin and discover that the mailboxes are still yellow but rather that they get together for intensive intellectual contact. Germans do not have such contact in the United States. Indeed, why should they?

SHEPARD STONE: This intensive interaction among intellectuals in East and West Berlin has increased dramatically in recent years and cannot be underestimated.

Part 4 Living with the Wall

10 Living with the Wall
Richard L. Merritt

A central fact of modern political life is that Berlin and the world have learned to live with the wall.

Its construction in 1961 was without question one of the most spectacular events of the decades since World War II. The surpise and outrage it occasioned nevertheless gave way eventually to efforts to ameliorate its consequences and to some measure the conditions that produced it. After the Quadripartite Agreement of 1971 the eyes of the world turned to other matters. This did not mean, of course, that the longstanding "Berlin problem" had been resolved. It only meant that West Berliners and the various governments with a stake in the city's future had turned their active attention to more immediate concerns.

West Berliners and the Wall

There can be no denying the fact that the construction of the wall in August 1961 was a blow to West Berliners. It disrupted their lives in manifold ways. For some it meant the end of visits to relatives and friends in the East or of opportunities to attend theatrical and other events on the other side of the city. For many it meant the loss of services and employees, since approximately 50,000 East Berliners commuted regularly to jobs, especially low-paying ones, in the western sectors. For still others it meant the dissolution of church parishes and other associations of which they were members. Doubtless each of the two million West Berliners was affected more or less directly by the wall—not to speak of what East Berliners suffered.

Search for a new mission

At a more general level the wall threw West Berliners into a state of uncertainty. For more than a decade they had basked in the glory earned during the harsh days of the blockade and benefited from the city's tenuous position between East and West as the much-vaunted "bastion of freedom." The Western allies had promised to protect them; the West German government said it would never let them down. Yet it was precisely these promises that appeared to West Berliners to be among the first victims of the wall.

Of key importance was the question of the city's future. Did American lassitude in the first days after August 13, 1961, signal that country's desire to end its commitment to the defense of Berlin? Was the wall simply the first step in a larger Soviet strategy, a first step that would be followed by disruption of transit traffic between West Berlin and the FRG, harassment of the West Berliners themselves, or something even worse? Now that West Berlin was literally walled in, would an "island mentality" emerge, and what effect would that have on the population? The war of nerves that followed the building of the wall—poised tanks at Checkpoint Charlie, Soviet MIG fighter planes buzzing downtown West Berlin, arbitrary stoppages on the transit routes—did not make the answers to such questions look any brighter.

Amidst the morale-building exercises that ensued appeared a new kind of question: if West Berlin had now lost the function it served during the height of the cold war, what was its new mission to be? Febrile minds produced a variety of schemes to "save" the city. Not all these ideas were half-baked, and some were sufficiently well thought through that they could later be implemented. But the jumble of suggestions and the patent infeasibility of most created an impression of desperation that exacerbated the tension gripping the city's citizens.

While the search for West Berlin's new mission went on, West Berliners were gradually and quietly adjusting their lives to the new realities. The pain of loss diminished. New daily routines and patterns of thinking emerged. And, what is more, the economic well-being of the city and its people improved markedly from year to year. This prosperity resulted in part from new supports emanating from Bonn and in part from the sudden demand throughout West Germany for workers, a demand that had previously been filled by refugees from the GDR. But in still larger part it was due to the enormous economic growth of the Federal Republic as a whole (a recession in the late 1960s notwithstanding). If the goal of the East's measures in 1961 had been to undermine West Berlin's viability and demoralize its population, then they certainly failed. There were no mass flights from the city by West Berliners paralyzed by doubts and fears. Instead, they began to learn to live with the wall, even if they did not like it.

Awakening to a new reality

In short, normalcy set in. Significantly, however, this normalcy was not something to which the city was returning after an episode of excitement. Berlin had not led a "normal" existence since the beginning of the bombing attacks during World War II (and some would claim not since the Great Depression began in 1929). The city had barely crawled out from under the rubble when, in rapid-fire succession, its Four-power control structure broke down, the blockade of West Berlin and airlift began, and the city itself was split. The next dozen years saw West Berlin living in an artificial climate of hyper-excitement, a situation in which its citizens could feel that they were frontline soldiers in the crusade to save Western democracy. With the wall came the collapse of this sustaining myth and, as I have suggested, no new one to replace it.[1] Many West Berliners were experiencing normalcy for the first time in their adult lives.

The Quadripartite Agreement confirmed West Berlin in its new condition. Opening up the wall for visits to the East was without question important. West Berliners could renew weakened familiar contacts and once again visit their favorite theaters or lakeside restaurants in the East. But for most the years of desuetude and the habits of their daily lives in the West had sharply diminished the priority attached to such opportunities: highly significant in principle, they became far less so in practice. More important were the guarantees that West Berlin would be left alone to develop at its own pace, in conjunction with the FRG and under the protection of the Western allies, and that access routes to the West would be completely open. This certification of President Kennedy's "three essentials" enunciated in June 1961 enabled West Berliners to turn their full attention to internal matters. East Berlin and the GDR moved ever more into the background of most West Berliners' consciousness.

The two decades since the mid-1960s have found West Berliners coping with a new reality: that their's is a metropolis like many others, that, once the cold-war framework was put aside, their city faces most of the same problems, albeit with a slight twist, encountered by other metropolises in the West. The exigencies of international politics during the 1950s and early 1960s had at once shielded them from major social changes going on in the West and encouraged a siege mentality that pressured people to paper over differences in the interest of unity against the common enemy. The growing realization that those days were over enabled a raft of other matters to come to the fore.

West Berlin in the post-industrial age

Here I shall focus on only three broad areas of concern: making the city's economy as self-sustaining as possible; coming to grips with changing perceptions and social values, especially among the younger generation that had not known the privations of the Great Depression and had only dim or no recollections of the Nazi past; and dealing with the city's changing demographic structure. Each of these problematic areas has many ramifications that cannot be dealt with here, and each has impinged extensively on the others. All are problems shared in one way or another with every other West German city, but West Berlin's special situation casts them in a light that gives them a unique importance for the island city.

Economic structure In the years immediately after the end of World War II, Berlin lost most of the functions associated with a capital city that it had enjoyed during the previous three-quarters of a century.[2] By 1949 politics had moved to Bonn, commerce to Hamburg, banking to Frankfurt, and so forth. Because of its precarious situation and the past experience of the blockade, and because new industrial centers were arising in the FRG, industry, too, was reluctant to rebuild its former strongholds in the city's western sectors. Many of the city's most capable businessmen also moved to the West, where the main arena of activity was. In short, West Berlin was moving steadily toward the periphery of a booming West German economy.

The question successive West Berlin governments since 1949 have sought to answer is, how can the viability of the city be maintained given such trends? One important response has been to ensure that the federal government provided adequate funding to keep the city alive and healthy. This meant, first of all, direct subsidies to the city's budget that in some years amounted to over half the total. It also included federally supported low-interest loans and tax credits for business firms investing in West Berlin, especially those establishing productive facilities there, as well as a variety of economic benefits to individual West Berliners—including, in the period immediately after the wall went up, a "jitters bonus" to help people pay the extra costs for vacations in the West.

The negative side of this indispensable program was psychological: the emergence of a "subsidy mentality." On the one hand, it became easy for West Berliners to believe that the federal government should produce the cash for whatever they thought necessary. While in the last analysis the city's representatives had to battle for everything they got from Bonn, the reliance on federal support produced some irresponsibility in the priorities that were set as well as, on occasion, the public emergence of that combination of self-abasement and effrontery associated with begging. On the other hand, some West Germans have from time to time expressed resentment about the alleged proclivity of West Berliners for a "high life" financed from public coffers.[3] Such expressions in turn have spurred the West Berliners' fears that the FRG will eventually abandon them.

Successive governments hence sought to make West Berlin minimally dependent on federal subsidies. For a variety of reasons, however, success has not come easily. For one thing, tax and other preferences notwithstanding, business firms have found it more economically advantageous to locate in the West than in Berlin. For another, other West German cities such as Frankfurt and Munich were not keen to see these firms carry their activities and business elsewhere. Nor was the city's political leadership completely clear in its views about how to attract and hold industry.[4] Except for a brief period (1953–55), until 1981 Social Democrats controlled City Hall. The strong support the SPD enjoyed from organized labor and the ideological pressure within the party to elaborate social welfare programs had a dampening effect on business, and so did the government's ineffective handling of the rising wave of protest that began in the mid-1960s. Given all these hindrances, the remarkable thing is that West Berlin's economy has done as well as it has.

The years of economic uncertainty have brought structural change to West Berlin. Despite a gross social product that rose 18 percent in constant prices from 1970 to 1982, overall investment in the city declined by five percent (−12 percent for plant, +6 percent for equipment), and the number of employed persons shrank by 11 percent.[5] The number of people employed in production dropped by 35 percent over this period, the number in commerce 22 percent. In contrast, the size of the governmental sector has grown. In terms of state expenditures from 1970 to 1982 (in constant prices), the increase was 50 percent, while the number of government employees grew by 28 percent. The service sector has also expanded. From producing 19 percent of the city's gross social product in 1970, its share went to 24 percent in 1982 (an absolute increase in constant prices of 45 percent), and the number of people engaged in this sector grew by 12 percent. (The share of those employed in private households and not-for-profit organizations rose by 44 percent over the same period.)

The shift to a service-oriented economy would not be so worrisome to West Berlin's leadership were it not also linked to stagnation or even decline in the production sector. Economic growth in West Berlin has lagged well behind that in the rest of the Federal Republic. The Christian Democrats, who assumed command of a coalition government after the election of May 1981, have placed high priority on reestablishing a more balanced pattern of growth. It has indeed achieved some notable successes, such as attracting a computer production facility of the Nixdorf Corporation (which will employ some 6,000 workers) and a fiberoptics plant of Siemens (to employ 600 workers). Investment during the first eight months of 1984 was more than 14 percent greater than in the corresponding period of the previous year (and ten times greater than the growth rate in the Federal Republic).[6]

Even if the CDU government is successful in its high-tech gamble, however, West Berlin will be far from out of the woods. Its employment rate (which counts only those unemployed for less than a year—the others are put on relief rolls) of 9.7 percent is a percentage point higher than that of the FRG. Moreover, most of those not now working will be unqualified for the skilled positions opening up. Other demographic trends point to still greater social welfare costs in the future. The fact that the percentage of the population employed, for instance, dropped from 45 percent in 1960 and 1970 to 43 percent by 1982 suggests that in the future there will be ever fewer workers to support the population. And, of course, the projects set in motion to increase economic activity must in fact be realized before the CDU government can make good its claim that it is turning around West Berlin's economy.

Radical protest Just as Berlin grabbed the world's headlines in 1948–49 over the blockade and in 1958–62 over the ultimatum and wall crises, West Berlin did it again in 1967–72, this time because of the eruption of often violent waves of protest among especially the younger generation.[7] The protest movement was far from unique to West Berlin. Students at the Free University of Berlin in 1966–67 looked directly at the Free Speech movement in Berkeley as a model for some of their own thought and behavior, and in Paris a year later students (and others) came close to stopping the normal course of French life. Throughout the nonsocialist world young people were protesting the actions of their own and other governments. Even so, the student protest movement and what followed in West Berlin were unusual in the extent to which they tore apart the city's social fabric.

How do we account for the virulence of this protest movement and the reaction to it? Since 1948 West Berliners had been nervous about the intentions of the East and hostile toward those expressing views too close to the version of communism practiced in the Soviet Union and GDR. The initial insensitivity of both Kennedy and Adenauer to their psychological needs during the first days after the wall was built, however, left West Berliners wondering on whom they could really count in times of trouble. Intellectuals soon began to question the wisdom of kneejerk anticommunism, and before long students and others were voicing their concerns about the allegedly authoritarian nature of West German society (especially the universities), the perceived illegality of America's presence in Vietnam, the formation of the Grand Coalition that seemed to deny Germans any meaningful parliamentary opposition, and a host of other issues. Political leaders and administrators, by contrast, stuck to their earlier attitudes—and all too frequently the intolerance toward opposition that went with them—while those charged with the task of law enforcement found themselves utterly baffled in trying to deal with the new breed of political protester, a phenomenon not uncommon in other parts of the world.

Rhetorical and then physical violence escalated on both sides. By 1968 protestors were waging pitched battles with the police, and one government even fell because of its inept handling of the situation. Similarly, with professors as well as students locking horns on virtually every matter, the Free University was paralyzed. The West Berlin government eventually enacted legislation (later rescinded at the federal level) that turned over governance of all the city's institutions of higher education to tripartite bodies comprising equal numbers of tenured professors, teaching assistants and nontenured professors, and students. The damage done to the Free University during these years would carry over to the reputations of other institutions, most notably the Technical University, in ways that, for a while, made government agencies and private business shy away from collaboration with university researchers and reluctant to hire their graduates.[8] Meanwhile, some of the more disaffected youth were moving from protest to outright terrorism.

West Berlin thus became the symbol of the youth revolt in the Federal Republic. Cassandras saw in this development signs of the decline and final collapse of the city. Doubtless most citizens, however, envisioning nothing of the sort, simply wanted their government to use whatever means were necessary to reinstitute law and order. This readiness to go beyond the law in putting down the movement and incarcerating its leaders prompted a counterreaction among many liberals. Notable among these were some Protestant church leaders and even members of the ruling SPD, who favored some of the goals, if not the means, of the protesters and who could remember how the Nazis had used a similar desire for law and order to eradicate all dissent. Ambivalence and mutual mistrust among the city's political, intellectual, and spiritual leaders in turn created a new kind of crisis of confidence in West Berlin's future.

By the late 1970s the protest movement as such was giving way to other forms of dissent.[9] "Squatting" was one of these. West Berlin's peculiar economic structure, with its tax write-offs for investment in such things as housing, encouraged owners of older apartment buildings to let them deteriorate, tear them down, and then build new luxury apartments—all this at a time when a desperate shortage of low-cost and even middle-income housing existed.[10] The effect was that the poor were being pushed into the street or forced to pay much higher rents somewhere else. Another effect was that numerous apartment buildings, especially in the working-class districts of the city, stood empty or nearly so.

Groups of young people began surreptitiously and then openly to occupy some of these doomed buildings. Their claims to domicile gained a fairly wide hearing and substantial sympathy. Historic preservationists pointed out that many of the buildings could be saved and were in fact worth saving. Critics of the government's tax incentives argued that, through needless demolition and reconstruction, the landlords' private purses were being fattened at public expense. And many more lamented the plight of the homeless in a city where housing costs were skyrocketing. But, at the same time, the police were obligated to protect the landlords' property rights and throw out the squatters.

Once again the city witnessed pitched battles between police and dissenters, and once again the city's government failed to master the situation. From one apartment building occupied in March 1979, the number grew to 29 by January 1971 and as many as 165 in May of that year, the month in which new elections turned out the Social Democratic–Free Democratic coalition in favor of a Christian Democratic–Free Democratic one. The new government took energetic steps to solve the problem. During the course of the next three and a half years, implementing policies initiated by the SPD–FDP government and adding some of its own, the CDU–FDP government forcibly vacated some 60 apartment buildings (while squatters voluntarily abandoned 27 more) and concluded rental or purchase agreements that permitted the squatters to continue to live in and renovate the remaining 78. Peace has thus been restored—but at considerable costs in terms of both political strife (with one squatter killed and some 700 arrested) and financial outlays.

By the late 1970s, too, a new form of political protest was emerging throughout the Federal Republic. More or less distinct groups concerned with environmental protection, arms control or unilateral disarmament, women's rights, protection of foreign workers, greater social control over the means of production, and still other issues began to coalesce into regional movements (collectively termed the "Greens," or, in West Berlin, the Alternative List—the AL). Theretofore they had tried, separately and frequently outside the usual political framework, to affect policy making, generally without much success. Those who organized the loose coalitions hoped that a united effort working within the political system would stop the policies that in their view were taking Germany and the world to the brink of disaster.

From the outset there were many open questions about the Green movement. Could such a mixed bag of *naïfs* and ideologues actually stick together? Could they move from negativism about such matters as nuclear power plants or Pershing missiles to a coherent, constructive program? If the Greens were successful in getting into city councils or state and national parliaments, how would that affect the existing balances of power? Would they in fact carry through their pledge to eschew the traditional tactics of parliamentary government, such as participation in coalitions, as a means to prevent compromising their goals? It was particularly the announced antipolitical intentions of the Greens that worried most critics.

After failing to obtain parliamentary representation in 1979, the Alternative List gained 7.2 percent of the popular vote in 1981 and nine (of 132) seats in West Berlin's parliament. This made it the third largest party in the city. Although tending toward obstructionism at the outset, AL parliamentarians soon gained some respect for the boldness of their ideas, if not always for their practicability. Probably all West Berliners, for instance, are concerned about the environmental impact of growing automobile traffic. Few, however, are likely to accept the AL's proposal of November 1984 to move toward a complete ban on all private automobile traffic by the end of ten years. Even so, about three-fifths of the West Berliners with opinions on the Greens express a tolerant attitude,[11] and their percentage of the vote rose to 11.2 percent in the election of March 1985.

Again we see the recurrence of a phenomenon noted earlier. On the one hand, the Social Democrats are quite torn by the prospect of coalescing formally or even working together with the Greens. Those on the party's left wing are openly receptive to the ideas and some of the proposals that the AL has offered, whereas the conservative wing feels that too close an association with the Greens will damage the SPD's electoral chances and its ability to carry out policies that will maintain the city's economic viability and links with the Western allies. The business-oriented CDU, on the other hand, argues that the city cannot afford to chance having the AL in a position of power, since it will destroy the confidence of the business community and the Allies in West Berlin's ability to deal realistically with its own problems. To the extent that this perception contains a self-fulfilling prophecy, that those who are trying to help Berlin will back away should the Greens ever assume positions of responsibility, the prospect is one that concerns the entire community. Such considerations doubtless contributed to the voters' decision in March 1985 to keep the CDU–FDP coalition in power.

Politics of demography Vital to any metropolis is an active, creative population. In this respect West Berlin has faced a serious problem since the end of the blockade. First of all, it has suffered a constant loss of people, as practically every year those leaving the city for West Germany outnumbered those moving in the opposite direction. In only two brief periods, the mid-1950s and 1964–65, was there population growth. These spurts stemmed more from the influx of East German refugees in the earlier period and foreign workers in the later one than from the decision by West Berliners to remain in the city. From a population of 2.15 million in 1950 and 2.23 million at its peak (1958), the number of people in the city dropped to 2.12 million at the end of 1970 and 1.85 million in March 1984.[12] On the average, since 1958 West Berlin has lost 15,000 people per year.

This loss has not been distributed evenly across all sectors of the population. The number of West Berliners gainfully employed declined from slightly over a million in 1961 to 803,000 at the end of 1982. (Overall, including those unemployed and searching for work, the number of persons in the job market declined over this period by 14 percent.) Only the influx of close to 100,000 foreign workers has kept this number as high as it is. As I suggested earlier, a root cause of this decline in levels of employment was the drop in economic activity; by the same token the flight of skilled workers from West Berlin to West Germany was an important factor in decisions to shut down firms.

Breaking this vicious circle has been a major task each West Berlin government has set itself. With federal support the city has undertaken extensive advertising campaigns to persuade young West Germans to move to West Berlin, created job programs for new workers, and provided a wide range of economic benefits to those making the move; and, of course, the city has sought to attract new industry that would in turn bring in workers. Overall, as the figures cited above indicate, this effort has not been successful—although it is surely true that the situation would be much worse had the city done nothing. The first major breakthrough in decades came with the CDU-dominated government that assumed office in 1981. Its ability to bring new industry to the city is in fact creating jobs that will attract skilled workers from the West, but to date the effect has been little more than an upward blip in an otherwise downward curve.

Along with the general decline in the size of the population and working force has come another trend: an overaging of the population. Although the casual visitor to Berlin and even the longtime resident might gain the impression that most of the people seen on the street are young,[13] the share of citizens aged 65 or older (21 percent) is actually double that of the rest of the Federal Republic. (Among the non-foreign population, 23.4 percent are senior citizens as opposed to 1.8 percent of the foreigners.) This puts a heavy burden on the city in terms of social costs that will continue into the foreseeable future.

Another aspect of the loss of population is more difficult to put into numbers. West Berlin has found it difficult since the 1950s to attract strong leadership in various spheres. This problem became noticeable in the early 1950s, when the economic boom in West Germany led upward-striving businessmen to seek positions there rather than in politically and economically troubled West Berlin. Today, too, although many businessmen are keen to move to the city to enjoy its deservedly famous quality of life, more generally managing the branch office in West Berlin is seen more as a way-station en route to the top corridors of entrepreneurial power, located firmly in the West, than as a final destination.

By contrast, the heady days of the cold war gave important opportunities to politicians in West Berlin. The names of such men as Ernst Reuter and Willy Brandt became known throughout the world. But, as the city and its problems receded ever more into the background of German and world politics, potential leaders sought positions elsewhere as well. As had traditionally been the case, parties were forced to recruit their top leadership from West Germany—especially younger men in mid-career, whose successful handling of matters in Berlin might propel them into positions of national prominence. The latest example of this process was Richard von Weizsäcker, whom the CDU sent to Berlin to reconstruct the party and contest the election of May 1981, but who subsequently returned to Bonn to serve as federal president. West Berlin also imports leaders in the cultural sphere. In this case, however, the FRG's cultural pluralism and the city's high cultural *niveau* are sufficient to attract and keep the best.

In a way, such a pattern is typical of any metropolis: most are net importers of ambitious, creative people. A major difference in West Berlin's case is the changing perspective over time. It once was the city in Germany to which any young person with talent and ambition yearned to go. It is now, except in the cultural sphere, a secondary city, which serves as merely one proving ground among others for would-be national leaders, and one in which inbreeding and the special concern for security have hampered creativity. For most cities the status enjoyed by West Berlin would be highly desirable. It is only by comparison with the brilliance of its earlier days that the city suffers. But such a comparative perspective and the sense of disappointment it engenders are part of the Berlin *problematique*.

A second demographic issue of major concern is West Berlin's foreign population. Until the early 1960s the Federal Republic and West Berlin did not have many resident foreigners. The building of the wall, however, ended the flow of East German refugees needed to man the booming West German economy, and the country looked increasingly beyond its borders for new workers, especially unskilled workers willing to accept jobs that Germans did not want. As late as 1965 only one in a hundred employed persons in West Berlin was foreign. Within a decade the figure rose to one in ten, and by the end of 1982 every eighth resident was a foreigner. Half (48 percent) came from Turkey and another eighth (13 percent) from Yugoslavia.

Two events conspired in the late 1970s to turn the perception of these "guest workers" from an economic necessity into a social "problem" needing attention. One was a sluggish economy with its attendant unemployment. The percentage of the West Berlin work force out of work grew from 0.5 percent in 1970 to 3.3 percent five years later and 9.7 percent in late 1984. With so many people out of work, some began to ask, why not send the foreign workers home? Second, when West Berliners (and West Germans) looked around with their new sense of economic hard times, they discovered that the foreign community was really much larger than the number of foreign workers, for the latter were bringing their families to stay. Turkish ghettos were emerging. In one of West Berlin's twelve boroughs, Kreuzberg, 31 percent of the population at the end of 1982 was foreign (two-thirds of them Turks), as was a shade under half of the school children. Cultural differences, communication difficulties, and such issues as unemployed Turkish youths in the streets drew attention to the fact that West Berliners had in their midst a strong minority population.

West Berlin's situation is once again far from unique in the Federal Republic. Indeed, eight other cities have larger proportions of foreigners than does West Berlin, and one of them, Frankfurt-am-Main, has a ratio almost twice as high (23.5 versus 12.5 percent). These other cities, too, are still suffering from the stagflation of the late 1970s, as indicated by an overall unemployment figure of 8.7 percent in the Federal Republic. The major difference is that West Berlin has no suburbs, and hence nothing comparable to the "white flight" of American cities that characterizes West German cities as well. The higher proportion of foreigners in Frankfurt is thus an optical illusion if we take into account the whole of Frankfurt's metropolitan area.

Berliners are just as confused about how to deal with the foreign workers "problem" as are other West Germans. Some envision with horror the emergence of a permanent, Moslem minority that will change the very complexion of German society. Others see the introduction of foreign elements into German society as a healthy development, at any rate one that was inescapable if the country wanted economic growth. The CDU in West Berlin has pushed for restrictive legislation that would encourage the foreigners to return home—for example, refusing to grant an entry permit to any worker's child older than six years, and deporting any minor arrested (not convicted!) for a crime. The SPD has emphasized measures to help integrate those foreigners who want to remain in the city and to support those who find the adjustment difficult for economic or other reasons. Perhaps the current government's position was best summarized by its deputy mayor and minister of the interior, Heinrich Lummer (CDU): "A series of measures we have undertaken," he said in October 1984, "consciously exerts pressure for integration, consciously forces people to ask whether they want to remain in Germany or go away."[14] The opposition terms these same measures "scare tactics."

A third demographic issue, potentially very disruptive, is the recent influx of Pakistanis, Sri Lankans, Ghanaians, and others seeking political asylum. They get to West Berlin via inexpensive flights to Schönefeld Airport, located on the outskirts of Berlin in the GDR, whose officials then grant them transit visas into the western part of the city. (From the GDR's perspective, this serves the double purpose of earning hard currency from the flight and visa and disrupting West Berlin's political life.) Whether or not they can legitimately claim political asylum is an open question. Doubtless many are in danger at home because of their political activity or ethnicity, but, in the view of the courts, others, seeking work and a better standard of living, use political persecution as an excuse. Many, too, have simply responded to advertisements in their local newspapers guaranteeing them asylum in the Federal Republic if they buy a one-way ticket to Schönefeld and pay a fee to the broker organizing the trip.

Whatever their reasons and however they got to Berlin, the number of people from Third-World countries seeking political asylum has been substantial: 14,000 in 1981, 6,300 in 1982, 5,500 in 1983, and 9,000 in the first ten months of 1984.[15] Large numbers are denied political asylum and, lacking permission to reside in the FRG, are shipped home at West German expense. Those accepted are distributed among the various West German states (with West Berlin, which used to take 5 percent, now having a quota of 2.7 percent). A few do not actively seek political asylum or social support, but simply move in with friends until they can obtain residency permits.

The influx of asylants has been costly in a number of ways. Monetarily, the city's government budgets DM 60 million (approximately $20 million at the rate of exchange obtaining in fall 1984) for supporting them while they are processing papers and before they are sent to West Germany or returned home. Far more significant are the social costs. Their very presence is an irritant to those who feel that the asylants (and their recruiters) are taking advantage of legal loopholes and German humanitarianism. Others argue that, even if the asylants are not bona fide political refugees, as human beings they deserve a chance at a better life than they can obtain at home and that, indeed, Tamils in Sri Lanka and other ethnic minorities face the danger of oppression and even extermination.[16] Proponents of the latter view are increasingly active in organizing defense funds for new arrivals and even engaging in civil disobedience in the face of government efforts to close what it sees as the floodgate to unrestricted immigration.

The issue of asylants takes us back to the special nature of life in West Berlin. Other states are able to control their own borders and points of entry better than can the Germans in West Berlin. In fact, Sweden, France, Switzerland, and other West European countries have acted firmly to prevent Tamils and others from even crossing their frontiers. As a matter of principle, however, through its refusal to control traffic from East Berlin on the subway or elevated train, West Berlin keeps its border open and then must deal with the consequences. To force passengers to go through border controls would be to yield a point on the entire city's Four-power status—and in the long run dealing with the influx of asylants may be better than jeopardizing the basis of West Berlin's security.

Any of these questions—economic growth, radical protest, and adverse demographic trends—is enough by itself to consume the attention of a metropolis, and dealing with all three together demands energy and creativity. Other questions urgently require attention as well: the schools, environmental protection,[17] public transportation,[18] and so forth. The fact that these issue areas contain difficult problems to solve is not the result of West Berlin's position between East and West. Other cities face variants of the same problems. The difference is that they do not simultaneously suffer from West Berlin's insularity. A key element of West Berlin's "mission" in the mid-1980s and beyond is thus that of other metropolises, the one Aristotle prescribed two and a half millennia ago for the *polis:* to provide its citizens with the best chance possible to obtain and enjoy the good life. And yet, we cannot ignore the fact that West Berlin is not alone, that its role and responsibilities go far beyond its own borders.

West Berlin and Its Environment

Just as West Berliners, especially since the accords of the early 1970s that eased their daily lives and stilled some of their anxieties, have learned to live with the wall, so, too, the other political units that affect and are affected by the city's situation have made their peace with it. This is not to say that they are happy with the new status quo. If they could change it without suffering costs in other respects, they doubtless would do so. The point is more that the new status quo is the best they can achieve at present. Any attempt to move outside the narrow room for maneuvering currently acceptable to the parties would jeopardize not only existing understandings on Berlin but also the broader framework of détente in which they are embedded. The task of these parties is much more to ensure each other that they are playing by the tacit rules of the game so that they can concentrate on other, and from their perspective more important, matters.

The four Powers

From the perspective of the four victorious Allies of World War II, the essence of the Quadripartite Agreement of 1971 lay in three dimensions. First of all, it clearly maintained their rights and responsibilities regarding Berlin. This is turn gave them a legal basis to pursue broader policies vis-à-vis their German allies and Germany as a whole. Second, beyond reestablishing the fundamental principle of Four-power control, the accord represented agreement among the Powers to disagree on a wide range of other matters. They firmly put aside any attempt to unravel the legal snarls into which the original Four-power agreements had fallen or to seek common ground on Berlin's status in international law. They similarly wrote into the Quadripartite Agreement language that would subsequently be available for alternative explanations depending on which side of the wall one sat. Third, in signing the agreement the four Powers indicated their readiness to make practical concessions as a means to defuse the Berlin situation and enable the pursuit of other foreign policy goals. They were prepared to stabilize the status quo. None was prepared, however, to be insensitive to attempts by others to change that status quo to its own disadvantage.

United States Successive American governments have sacrificed too much to sit idly by while West Berlin's existence became ever more attenuated. The city became and remains a symbol of both the American willingness to support a people trying to maintain its freedom from communist aggression and the success that such an effort can enjoy. Since President Kennedy's famous address in 1963 on the steps of West Berlin's city hall, American leaders have felt constrained to visit the city, be photographed while peering over the wall, and issue statements admiring the West Berliners' courage and pledging support to their future freedom. It would be difficult for any new government in Washington to renege on such a longstanding commitment.

This United States commitment to protect West Berlin is not merely a matter of sentiment or desire to demonstrate steadfastness in the face of Soviet pressure. The city's Four-power status gives the United States a presence in both Germany and Europe. While no responsible American official since 1948 has ever suggested that U.S. troops be withdrawn, the mere thought that this might happen—the replacement of the Western (and especially American) military by some international force, such as a United Nations peacekeeping mission—is enough to send shivers up the spine of most of the city's inhabitants. This need for the American defense of West Berlin sharply limits the extent to which West Germany can ignore other American interests, and, indeed, such instances as the FRG's boycott of the Moscow Olympics in 1980 indicate that West Germany has been America's staunchest ally. Moreover, the existence of the U.S. garrison in West Berlin lends force to the United States' support for and dependence on the North Atlantic Treaty Organization. The dissolution of NATO would seriously jeopardize the city's existence. By the same token, the need to maintain troops in Berlin ensures a certain stability for NATO.

And yet the American presence in West Berlin is not unproblematic. The slow American response to the psychological needs of West Berliners after the wall was built shook their confidence in the United States. It is not by accident that, subsequently, the first and loudest voices protesting American policies (for example, in Vietnam) came from the walled city. A virulent anti-Americanism continues to characterize a significant portion of especially the city's younger population. The *Amerika Haus,* the United States Information Service's center located in the heart of the city, is to be sure no longer under almost constant siege, but even such events as the American presidential election in 1984 are sufficient to occasion protest marches, in this case against President Reagan's policy on arms control and toward Central America. In the presence of such overt manifestations of hostility, it is sometimes difficult to recall that the vast bulk of West Berliners stand squarely behind the United States and that the two must work in tandem to maintain the city's viability.

Soviet Union The status quo also gives legitimacy to the Soviet presence in East Berlin and the German Democratic Republic. Today, four decades after the end of the war, the Soviet Army maintains some 19 divisions in the GDR. Nor has the Soviet Union, several formal agreements notwithstanding, paid more than lip service to the GDR's full sovereignty. It has on several occasions, such as in summer 1984 when it forced Erich Honecker to cancel or delay a projected visit to the FRG, intervened directly into the internal affairs of the GDR. The disappearance overnight of its Four-power rights would, of course, not necessarily mean the withdrawal of Soviet forces. The contractual right to protect the GDR would remain, and so would the de facto ability to direct GDR affairs from Moscow. Soviet intervention in the absence of the rights and responsibilities accruing from Quadripartite agreements, however, would appear more likely as the exercise of naked force than a fulfillment of treaty obligations.

Continuing uncertainty surrounding the Berlin question also gives the Soviet Union opportunities to exert pressure on Western countries, especially West Germany and the United States. For more than a decade and a half major Soviet aims have included détente in Europe and reduced East–West tension on a global scale. The reasons for this are, of course, many, including economic difficulties at home and policy failures abroad (for example, with respect to China). It is also true, as the examples of Czechoslovakia in 1968, Afghanistan in 1979, and the Olympic boycott in 1984 demonstrate, that the Soviet Union does not give unconditional priority to a relaxation of international strains. In the event of conflict with the West, though, West Berlin's vulnerability presents a target of opportunity for mischief. Even in relaxed times Western states must always keep in clear view the possibility that their actions may trigger a Soviet reaction affecting, say, access routes to West Berlin.

Since at least 1978 the Soviet Union has not made significant use of this stratagem. It seems more interested in nourishing neutralist sentiments in West Europe—a spark of fire that a new Berlin crisis would quickly dampen. Similarly, it seems satisfied with the West's care in sticking to the letter of the various Berlin accords of the early 1970s, or, such as in 1978 when it was the West Berlin governing mayor's turn to chair the FRG's Federal Council (*Bundesrat*), with the West's explanation that apparent departures from these provisions do not in fact diminish Soviet (or even East German) rights. Soviet leaders clearly recognize that any unwarranted turning of the screws on West Berlin would be counterproductive, in the short run at any rate. But the continuing possibility to exert pressure is there for all to see.

Great Britain and France The maintenance of West Berlin's Four-power status guarantees both Britain and France that they will have their say in any future efforts to shape German and European politics. The French, in particular, have pointedly emphasized Quadripartitism. For one thing, it continuously legitimates the French claim as a "victor power" in World War II. For another, and this was especially the case during de Gaulle's heyday in the late 1950s and early 1960s, it gives France a basis from which it can seek to loosen what its leaders sometimes see as the FRG's overreliance on the United States. From the very outset France has stoutly resisted any diminution of its Four-power rights and punctiliously performed its Four-power responsibilities.

Like the Superpowers, both Britain and France stand to gain more than they would lose from détente in Europe. All four Powers see the smooth functioning of provisions worked out under their own collective aegis as the best means both to reduce the tensions inherent in the Berlin situation and to create an international climate in which they can pursue goals they consider more important than scoring debating points against each other over Berlin's status. Yet, all four are vigilant. They are quick to protest, and possibly take action against, measures that encroach on what they feel are their rights accruing from Four-power agreements.

The two Germanys

The FRG and GDR have sharply differing conceptions of the future of the land and people that once comprised a united Germany. The West German government persists in striving toward reunification, if not immediately, then eventually; it envisions Berlin as the capital of a reunified Germany. It once sought to accomplish this goal through a "policy of strength" that aimed, in effect, at intimidating the Soviet Union into "returning" East Germany to the "lawful successor" of previous German governments, namely, the Federal Republic. Beginning in the late 1960s, however, FRG governments have come to view détente as the proper path. Easing tension by explicitly disavowing any intention actively to seek territorial change, the new policy toward the East said, would at the very least improve the lot of Germans on both sides of the border. It might also create the conditions in which reunification would no longer be unthinkable—even to the Soviet Union.

The East German government, by contrast, persists in stressing the permanent separation of the two Germanys and its own sovereign right to control the whole of Berlin. It was Soviet power rather than the GDR's shrill truculence that made the first part of this goal a reality recognized by the entire international community. But gaining control over West Berlin has proved to be a more elusive target. The very détente that the FRG sees as a precondition to future reunification, the GDR views as a condition in which the former might be willing, nay, eager, to rid itself of the burden of West Berlin by agreeing to the latter's accession to its natural hinterlands, namely, the German Democratic Republic.

Neither vision is realistic at the present time. Leaders of both German states recognize this fact, of course, but expressing the vision keeps alive the hope (and possibility) that it might be realized some day. In the meantime they pursue a policy of détente, all the while keeping a distrustful eye on the other side. The result has been significant improvement in FRG–GDR relations, and the lives of Germans in East and West Germany have in fact been made easier. An incidental, but hardly trivial, result has been occasional concern on the part of one or the other Superpower that the two Germanys cozying up to each other can destabilize the status quo that ensures their conqueror's rights.

Federal Republic of Germany For the FRG a strong West Berlin, inextricably tied to itself, is an important symbol of the reunified Germany that is to be. Not surprisingly, then, the FRG has tried everything possible to integrate West Berlin into the Federal Republic politically, economically, socially, and constitutionally. The Allies blocked formal integration, both in 1949 when the West repudiated a constitutional provision incorporating West Berlin as a state (*Land*) in the federal system, and again in 1971 when the Quadripartite Agreement asserted explicitly that West Berlin was not to be considered a constituent part of the Federal Republic. These steps did not, however, stop the FRG from claiming full integration as its goal. Bowing to the realities of world politics, the FRG settled for a modus vivendi that, without ruffling the feathers of the four Powers, provided for full integration in everything but name and prepared the groundwork for immediate integration as soon as the occupying Powers should relinquish their position.

Creating the modus vivendi was not without its problems. The first years of the new régime under the Quadripartite Agreement saw the FRG taking steps, such as locating federal offices in West Berlin, that the Soviet Union interpreted as violations of the spirit if not the letter of the agreement. Soviet and East German threats and countermeasures were the response, with heightened tension the result. Eventually West German officials were able to persuade the Soviet Union that their intentions were not to violate agreements reached, not to cause trouble—that, indeed, enhancing the area of peaceful relations in Europe was one of the FRG's central goals. Thus encouraged, and no doubt preoccupied with other problems (Afghanistan, Poland, China) that would be exacerbated by continuing conflict on its Western perimeter, the Soviet Union and GDR settled into a more peaceable pattern of interaction.

Pursuing a policy of détente serves the FRG in other ways as well. It holds out the promise that, in a more relaxed Europe, the FRG would enjoy more freedom of action within the Western alliance, a greater chance to pursue its own interests outside the confining straitjacket of cold war considerations. It provides the government with a basis to counter rising domestic protest against an intensification of the arms race, with its attendant danger to European survival. (These combined to produce the FRG's position that a precondition for the installation on German soil of Pershing missiles had to be a serious effort by the West to reopen arms control negotiations.) With respect to West Berlin, taking its legalistic claims out of the spotlight enables the FRG to concentrate more intensively on practical assistance to the city and further structural integration.

The last of these steps is important. A central part of the Berlin *problematique* is psychological: the West Berliners' fear that they will ultimately be abandoned. It was the apparent evidence of this on the part of the United States and FRG that caused such bitterness in 1961. And, of course, a significant part of East German propaganda through the years has averred that, sooner or later, the West Germans will turn to their own affairs and leave West Berlin to shift for itself. The danger is the eruption of a vicious circle: fear of abandonment will lead West Berliners to flee the city, and the consequent loss of population and vitality will push West Berlin ever more to the margin of West Germans' consciousness. Strident support for the city's cause is one means to allay such concerns, but, as I have suggested, a confrontational tactic can exact a heavy price. Taking West Berlin out of the limelight can be more effective, if the opportunity it provides is used to improve the city's vital linkages with the Federal Republic.

Viewed from a different angle, the continued viability of West Berlin is a test of the FRG's political skill and credibility. No government in Bonn can even look as though it might abandon West Berlin or permit its situation to deteriorate significantly. The level of popular support throughout the FRG for sustaining the island city would not permit that, and, more broadly, should such decay occur, the FRG's long-range goal of reunification, the promise of which it holds out to East and West Germans alike, would ring hollow. The problem is that the FRG has other priorities as well. Difficult times might force it to swallow tremendous costs in terms of these other priorities for the sake of keeping its commitment to West Berlin and, in effect, all Germans. Similarly, the FRG cannot defend the city. That task remains in the hands of the Western allies in Berlin—again, at whatever the cost may be in terms of other goals the FRG might like to accomplish. In this sense the Federal Republic is a hostage of the Berlin situation.

German Democratic Republic   The GDR has traditionally sought to use West Berlin for a variety of purposes. The most important of these aimed at gaining for itself international recognition and hence greater freedom for maneuvering within the Soviet bloc. (In effect, one might argue, at least during the 1950s when GDR leaders feared that the Soviet Union through some plan for reunification might cede the GDR in exchange for something else it wanted, de jure recognition itself was seen as a means to limit the latitude of Soviet decision makers.) The popular outbreak that erupted in June 1953, first in East Berlin and then throughout the GDR, forced the Soviet Union to shore up Ulbricht's tottering regime. In 1961, too, by permitting and even encouraging the egress of its citizens, Ulbricht's government placed the Soviet Union before the choice of either permitting the building of the wall through Berlin or else jeopardizing the stability of the GDR and hence the entire Warsaw Pact structure. Similar steps aimed at tipping the Soviet hand led Brezhnev to replace Ulbricht in 1971. Even so, Ulbricht's successor continued to act in Berlin in ways that violated the spirit of the Quadripartite Agreement, at least in the West's eyes, and forced the Soviet Union to intervene in a moderating fashion. It is not for nothing that the Soviet Union is seeking to maintain its Four-power rights as a means to control its East German ally.

Concomitant with this drive on the GDR's part for greater independence without giving up Soviet protection was a continuing effort to make good its claim to sovereignty over the whole of Berlin. This goal, heard softly during the early 1950s and then loudly after 1958, gained Soviet verbal support but no serious action aimed at achieving it in the face of Western opposition. The very existence of West Berlin has a destabilizing effect on the GDR. But, at least until the Soviet attitude on the German question changes significantly, the best the GDR can do is to follow a strategy aimed at maximizing uncertainty in West Berlin. In recent years, for instance, as indicated earlier, it has facilitated the flow of political asylants to West Berlin, a city already plagued by high unemployment and social costs, and it has regularly supported student and other groups that would change the status quo in ways beneficial to the GDR. Such measures, along with the constant threat to the city's access routes, seek to hasten what GDR leaders see as the inevitable decline of West Berlin and its eventual fall, like an overly ripe apple, into the East German lap.

Such pressure is also useful for obtaining concessions from the Federal Republic. Although this strategy cannot be pushed too far, lest it occasion Soviet intervention, even the threat of certain actions, such as restricting traffic on the access routes or raising the minimal amount of hard currency that Western visitors to the GDR and East Berlin must exchange, is enough to force West Germany to reconsider its position on such matters as credits to the GDR, grants to the GDR to improve the transit highways, and the visibility of Federal officials in West Berlin. Then, too, the GDR gains financially from aspects of the city's situation. The clearest example of this is sewage, which the GDR accepts from West Berlin against the payment of a hefty fee and then uses commercially as fertilizer. The money which Western visitors must exchange, fees paid by the FRG for entry permits into East Berlin and the GDR ($65 million from December 1972 to April 1984), and federal subsidies of transit travel to and from West Berlin also constitute a considerable part of the GDR's income in hard currency.

The GDR has not been able to achieve such major goals as full recognition of its sovereignty (especially by the FRG), complete freedom of action within the framework of the Soviet bloc, and absolute control over the whole of Berlin. It has nevertheless decided to go along with the modus vivendi worked out under the aegis of the four Powers, evidently in the hope that it can use this breathing space for its own purposes and in the expectation that, ultimately, time is on its side.

In its relations with the GDR, West Berlin faces dilemmas of major proportions. First, while it wants improvement in its situation that only negotiations with the GDR can bring about, it is reluctant to conduct such negotiations directly. West Berlin officials fear, quite rightly as it turns out, that bypassing a formal role for the FRG provides the GDR with confirmation of its thesis that the Quadripartite Agreement makes West Berlin totally independent of West Germany. When formal discussions do take place, both sides couch them in language that protects their legal positions (with West Berlin officials, for instance, acting as "agents" of the Western allies). It is also true, however, that the GDR, when it wants something badly enough, will negotiate directly with the FRG on matters pertaining to West Berlin.[19]

Second, while West Berlin would profit from increased trade and other forms of interaction with the GDR and other Soviet bloc countries, it is reluctant to go too far in facilitating it. For one thing, significant political concessions might be the price. The main barrier to more extensive interaction, from the East's perspective, is West Berlin's unwillingness to act independently of the FRG. A result is that, despite the fact that the FRG routes its trade with the GDR through the Inter-German Trading Commission, located in West Berlin, the city itself does not share much in this trade.[20] For another thing, dependency on the East might be the result. From the time of the blockade, when almost total reliance on electricity produced in East Berlin gave Soviet military authorities a powerful weapon to use against West Berliners, until the present day, the city and its citizens have learned not to count on the East's commitments should the latter see a political advantage in breaking them.[21] West Berlin thus views the dangers of intensified interaction as outweighing by far the advantages.

The broader environment

Warsaw Pact states The situation of Berlin does not play a significant role in the politics of other Soviet bloc states. A concentrated effort in the late 1960s by the FRG's Grand Coalition to gain the support of these countries for a wide range of West German policies, including, in effect, the isolation of East Germany, failed in 1968 when Ulbricht persuaded the Soviet Union to insist that any pact between a Soviet bloc state and the FRG have as a precondition the latter's full-fledged recognition of the GDR. Only Romania, which had already agreed to a treaty with the FRG, was able to escape this demand.

The Quadripartite Agreement raised new dimensions of East Germany's dilemma. Ambiguities in wording led to differing interpretations in the East and West about the nature of West Berlin's permissible links with the Federal Republic. The GDR took the position, supported by the Soviet Union in their mutual assistance treaty of 1975, that West Berlin was not a part of the FRG—in contradistinction to the Quadripartite Agreement's wording that the former was not a *constituent* part of the latter—and that the FRG had no right to fulfill certain functions on behalf of West Berlin or to install its offices in the city. Other Soviet bloc states, again save Romania, had little choice but to accept this interpretation and act accordingly. Even Romania accepted the Soviet injunction against dealing with FRG offices in West Berlin. West Berliners' hopes that their city could act as the pivot between East and West have not been fully realized because of the East's firm stance.

European Community On the other side of Europe, the FRG's partners in the European Community, albeit not under pressure from a Superpower, have been just as forthcoming in supporting its position. Indeed, integrating West Berlin as fully into EC institutions as it is in those of the FRG has been a cause of sustained East–West dispute. Soviet and East German leaders have seen such steps, particularly the decision to permit West Berlin in 1981 to send delegates to the directly-elected European Parliament, as a breach of the Four-power agreement that kept the city distinct from the Federal Republic. (It was surely not coincidental that, shortly thereafter, the Soviet Union permitted the GDR to take a significant step toward integrating East Berlin fully into its legal system: allowing East Berliners directly to elect members of the People's Chamber [*Volkskammer*].)

Several mutual advantages stem from West Berlin's link through the FRG to the European Community. On the German side, it strengthens the visibility of the city's structural integration into the Federal Republic, a fact of some psychological importance. Insofar as the EC connection enhances the overall West German economy, and especially the FRG–GDR trade that flows through West Berlin, it improves the city's economic situation as well. The ten full members of the EC also accounted in 1983 for 45 percent of West Berlin's non-German trade (that is, with countries other than the FRG and GDR). On the side of the EC members, in addition to whatever political credit they earn by acceding to one of the FRG's most vital interests, they are able to take advantage of the latter's tax credits, subsidies, and other forms of preferential treatment accorded firms with productive facilities in the island-city.

Third World states   Countries outside the European framework are affected by Berlin's situation to the extent that they choose, for whatever reason, to align themselves with positions and interpretations espoused by East and West. This is especially true of states in the Third World that rely on trade, assistance, and credits from one or the other of the two Germanys. Thus the GDR has successfully persuaded some of its client states to boycott federal institutions housed in West Berlin, and West Berliners register a triumph with every foreign head of state who visits West Germany and makes an official sidetrip to their city. By and large, however, the side-taking on the part of Third World states has not assumed such importance that, like the question of Israel, it leads to open international dispute in a forum such as the United Nations.

The Future of West Berlin

The wall as a fact of political life is but one in a complex web of factors that will determine West Berlin's future. Others include economic, demographic, and political changes in West Berlin itself; relationships between West Berlin and the FRG on the one hand and, on the other, between East Berlin and the GDR; shifts in a dynamic international system, especially in relations between the United States and the Soviet Union, the FRG and its European Community neighbors, and the GDR and its Warsaw Pact associates; and, perhaps most significantly, the attitudes and behavior of Berliners and Germans alike. Past changes and current trends with respect to such factors suggest a number of possible scenarios for the city's future.

One scenario, at this point highly improbable although certainly possible, would result from the failure by any party to implement its treaty obligations in good faith. In such an eventuality, Berlin might revert to the hotbox that it was for more than two decades—but with a difference. The frustration of unfulfilled hopes might well enhance the brittleness of the renewed cold war, thereby increasing the danger that the city would pose to itself and the outside world.

Another possible although equally improbable development is West Berlin's atrophy. Should economic activity resume its decline of recent years, young people leave in growing numbers, and the budget become ever more dependent on assistance from the FRG, the city might well gain an image among West Germans as an albatross around their necks. In this case we might expect any of a number of consequences. West Germany might increasingly neglect West Berlin, thereby contributing to a dreary downward spiral that would turn the city into a depopulated shell of its former self, sustained mainly by tourism and subsidies from Bonn. Alternatively, especially should East Berlin prosper because of economic growth in the GDR, the remaining West Berliners might begin considering some form of municipal reunification under the GDR's aegis. Still another possibility might be the decision by the FRG to exchange the island city to the GDR for something it considers important, such as improved living conditions in East Germany and greater access for West Germans.

A scenario that is somewhat more probable, although barely so in the foreseeable future, envisions sufficient rapprochement between East and West Germany that the latter is willing to seek a change in West Berlin's status quo. An analogue might be Hong Kong, which, according to a joint declaration signed in September 1984 by Britain and the People's Republic of China, will become in 1997 for the next fifty years a semi-autonomous unit under the PRC's protection (with the latter also responsible for Hong Kong's foreign policy). Any such design, of course, would require approval by the four Powers—and it is difficult at present to imagine that, for a very long time, any of them is likely to go along with such a degree of rapprochement.

The most probable scenario projects less extreme developments than the renewal of cold war tensions or the "disappearance" of West Berlin. It rests on a general acceptance and implementation of the Berlin accords and expansion of détente in the heart of Europe. It also rests on the assumption that the Federal Republic is sufficiently desirous of maintaining its ties to West Berlin that it will continue its economic and political support. Finally, it assumes that West Berliners themselves treat the existing status quo as a platform on which to build rather than a cause for despair. Given the previous behavior and pronouncements of the interested parties, each of these assumptions is reasonable. But what are their consequences? At the very least they provide leaders in East and West Berlin with opportunities to explore cooperative steps that do not create dependencies, to dismantle some of the psychological barriers to fruitful interaction, and to initiate a greater measure of coordinated policy on such matters as environmental protection. The long-range result might be an improved quality of life and even greater security in both parts of Berlin.

To the extent that such steps prove successful, they may tie East and West Berlin together much as sister cities facing each other across more "normal" political borders or such natural barriers as rivers. To the extent that policy planners want détente in the Berlin area, it behooves them to search out not the grandiose schemes for reunification, but rather these areas of limited, low-risk, but cumulative cooperation between autonomous entities.

In the meantime, a certain ambivalence about the wall will continue to characterize the situation. West Berlin has proved that, with support from the FRG, it can live with the wall, and West Berliners are making the adjustments that life in its shadow requires. To some measure they may even shut the wall's existence out of their minds—almost as if in the belief that, by ignoring it, the wall will disappear. But, in the words of poet Federico García Lorca:

> I have shut my balcony
> because I do not want to hear the weeping,
> but from behind the gray walls
> nothing else is heard but the weeping.[22]

Behind the Berlin wall West Berliners too hear the muffled sounds of weeping, and that weeping ensures that the division of the city will remain an open wound. In its presence, the Quadripartite and subsequent inter-German agreements may provide medium-term stability, but they are no guarantee of stability in the long run. Neither the complex of accords nor the wall itself has killed the dream of German reunification—a dream that has produced powerful political action in the past and expectations of change at a future time when the East–West confrontation in Europe is more fluid than is now the case. Until then, Berliners must, however heavy be their hearts, continue to live with the wall.

Notes

1 A Transformed Crisis: The Berlin Wall

This chapter was prepared with financial assistance from the Social Science Research Council (1960–61) and the Stimson Fund of Yale University (1966–67) and written while the author was Fulbright Research Professor at the Otto Suhr Institute of the Free University of Berlin. The chapter, which originally appeared in *Modern European Governments: Cases in Comparative Policy Making,* ed. Roy C. Macridis (Englewood Cliffs, N.J.: Prentice-Hall, Inc., 1968), pp. 140–73, has been extensively updated for this volume.

1 Otto M. von der Gablentz, ed., *Documents on the Status of Berlin, 1944–1959* (München: R. Oldenbourg KG, 1959), p. 18; italics added.
2 Data from Bundesministerium für gesamtdeutsche Fragen, *Die Flucht aus der Sowjetzone und die Sperrmassnahmen des kommunistischen Regimes vom 13. August 1961 in Berlin* (Bonn and Berlin: Bundesministerium für gesamtdeutsche Fragen, 1961), pp. 15–18.
3 The discussion in this section on activity among the Warsaw Pact states rests heavily on Hermann Zolling and Uwe Bahnsen, *Kalter Winter im August: Die Berlin-Krise 1961/63* (Oldenburg: Gerhard Stalling Verlag, 1967), which in turn relied primarily on the report of a Czech defector, Jan Séjna, who, as Deputy Defense Minister, was present at the meetings. For additional details, see Honoré Marc Catudal, Jr., *Kennedy and the Berlin Wall Crisis: A Case Study in U.S. Decision Making* (Berlin: Berlin Verlag, 1980), pp. 49–51, 208–12.
4 Catudal, *Kennedy and the Berlin Wall Crisis,* p. 118, reports the view of an "insider" that Kennedy's statement to the effect that the "United States could not and would not interfere with decisions taken by the Soviet Union in its own sphere of influence" was a signal to Khrushchev, "the confirming indicator that we would acquiesce" to the closure of the Berlin border.
5 The best description of the extensive planning conducted by the Kennedy administration is in Catudal, *Kennedy and the Berlin Wall Crisis.*
6 *The New York Times,* July 26, 1961, p. 1.
7 Robert M. Slusser, *The Berlin Crisis of 1961: Soviet-American Relations and*

the Struggle for Power in the Kremlin, June–November 1961 (Baltimore and London: The Johns Hopkins University Press, 1973), pp. 90–95, infers that Khrushchev made up his mind on July 26 or 27 (after reading Kennedy's speech but before meeting with John J. McCloy) and on August 2 obtained the approval of the Presidium of the Communist party of the Soviet Union. On Ulbricht's influence, see Anita Dasbach Mallinckrodt, *Propaganda hinter der Mauer: Die Propaganda der Sowjetunion und der DDR als Werkzeug der Aussenpolitik im Jahre 1961* (Stuttgart: Verlag W. Kohlhammer, 1971).

8 *Neues Deutschland,* June 16, 1961, p. 4. Neither the West Berlin nor the New York press took notice of this point at the time, but concentrated instead on Ulbricht's apparent threat to air corridors.

9 "The enemy must not be given an inch," he added. The speech, delivered in a small town near Leipzig on July 23, was not reported until three days later in *Neues Deutschland,* July 26, 1961, p. 1.

10 *The New York Times,* August 3, 1961, p. 2.

11 Jack M. Schick, *The Berlin Crisis, 1958–1962* (Philadelphia: University of Pennsylvania Press, 1971), p. 170, states: "Perhaps it is too sinister to suggest"—but he does so, anyway—"that Pankow took advantage of the economic disorder in the GDR to settle outstanding legal and political issues pertaining to the status of East Berlin."

12 This may have worked to the GDR's ultimate disadvantage because the other Warsaw Pact allies grew warier of their wily colleague in East Berlin. For a strong statement emphasizing Khrushchev's rational motives, see Hannes Adomeit, *Soviet Risk-Taking and Crisis Behavior: A Theoretical and Empirical Analysis* (London: George Allen & Unwin, 1982), pp. 220–74, 292–94.

13 *Neues Deutschland,* August 13, 1961, pp. 1–3. The decisions of the Warsaw Pact Council and GDR Council of Ministers appear in *The New York Times,* August 14, 1961, p. 6. The chronology reported in ensuing paragraphs rests upon "Der 13. August 1961," a special supplement to the *Berliner Morgenpost,* August 12–13, 1962; Kurt L. Shell, *Bedrohung und Bewährung: Führung und Bevölkerung in der Berlin-Krise* (Köln and Opladen: Westdeutscher Verlag, 1965); and Zolling and Bahnsen, *Kalter Winter im August.*

14 Their inactivity later gave rise to rumors (apparently spawned by a Soviet agent; see footnote 41 below) that the Allies had known all along what the Soviet Union and the GDR planned. Khrushchev evidently told John J. McCloy in late July that action would have to be taken. A State Department message of July 22 to Ambassador Dowling postulated that the GDR "might take measures to control" the tide of refugees: "They could do this either by tightening controls over travel from the Soviet zone to East Berlin or by severely restricting travel from East to West Berlin." In the latter event, countermeasures aimed at East German functionaries traveling in the West as well as, perhaps, economic action were envisioned. (See Catudal, *Kennedy and the Berlin Wall Crisis,* pp. 187–88.) Further, at a reception he gave in Potsdam on August 10 for the Western commandants, Marshal Konev explained that, whatever might happen in the foreseeable future, Western rights and West Berlin itself would remain untouched. (See Zolling and Bahnsen, *Kalter Winter im August,* p. 120.)

Although bits and pieces of evidence were available that *could* have led

Western intelligence to predict the building of a wall—see particularly the views of Colonel Ernst von Pawel, chief of the U.S. Military Liaison Mission to the commander-in-chief of Soviet forces in the GDR, as reported in Catudal, *Kennedy and the Berlin Crisis* pp. 234–37—the form and content of what actually did happen came as a surprise which caught the Allies badly off guard. Theodore S. Sorensen comments: "Our contingency plans had been prepared for interference with our access to West Berlin, not emigration from the East." Sorensen, *Kennedy* (New York: Harper & Row, 1965), p. 594. The British Minister in Berlin, Geoffrey McDermott, recalled dryly, "Looking back with hindsight it is now clear that our intelligence was not too good." Geoffrey McDermott, *Berlin: Success of a Mission?* (New York: Harper & Row, 1963), p. 31.

15 Sorensen writes: "Not one responsible official—in this country, in West Berlin, West Germany or Western Europe—suggested that Allied forces should march into East German territory and tear the wall down. For the Communists, as General Lucius Clay later pointed out, could have built another, ten or twenty or five hundred yards back, and then another, unless the West was prepared to fight a war over extending its area of vital interest into East Berlin. Nor did any ally or adviser want an excited Western response that might trigger an uprising among the desperate East Berliners—that would only produce another Budapest massacre." Sorensen, *Kennedy*, p. 594. Adomeit, *Soviet Risk-Taking and Crisis Behavior*, p. 304, terms the view I have taken in this and the following paragraphs as "positivistic," as "an awkwardly argued rationalization of an unambiguous Western retreat." The point is rather that there was little the West could or, better, was prepared to do, and that those representing the West might just as well try to look for bright spots in an otherwise dismal situation. Today most Western policy makers and analysts (see the subsequent chapters and discussions in this volume), however unhappy they may be about the wall itself, seem to recognize its contribution to at least intermediate-range stability in the area.

16 Zolling and Bahnsen, *Kalter Winter im August*, p. 126.

17 John C. Ausland, the duty officer for the Berlin Task Force that weekend, reported that the duty officer of the State Department's Operations Center telephoned him shortly after midnight to pass on a report from a news agency, and then again around 4:00 a.m. EDT—that is, 9:00 a.m. in Berlin, almost eight hours after the action began—with official news from the CIA in Berlin. See Catudal, *Kennedy and the Berlin Wall Crisis*, pp. 22–23.

18 Max Frankel, writing for "The News of the Week in Review" supplement of *The New York Times*, August 20, 1961, p. 3, notes that late Saturday night (August 12 in Washington but almost daybreak in Berlin) "Officials who had lived with expectations of a Berlin 'crisis' for three years were rooted from bed." A West German reporter in Washington, however, found German experts in the State Department to be virtually uninformed of the events as late as 7 a.m. Sunday. See Zolling and Bahnsen, *Kalter Winter im August*, pp. 127–28.

19 *The New York Times*, August 14, 1961, p. 1.

20 *The Times* (London), August 14, 1961, p. 8.

21 Walther Stützle, *Kennedy und Adenauer in der Berlin-Krise 1961–1962* (Bonn-

Bad Godesberg: Verlag Neue Gesellschaft GmbH, 1973), argues that Chancellor Adenauer feared that Kennedy would expose the contradictions in the FRG's policies on Germany as soon as he had had a chance to discuss the Berlin issue with Khrushchev. This fear lay behind Adenauer's rather clumsy efforts to support the candidacy of Richard M. Nixon in the presidential election of 1960.

22 Adenauer made his only public statement of the day late in the afternoon. Together with the Allies, said the chancellor, the appropriate countermeasures would be undertaken; the German people should have confidence in these steps. *Die Welt* (Berlin edition), August 14, 1961, p. 1.

23. For Willy Brandt's own description of his impressions and actions, see his *People and Politics: The Years 1960–1975*, tr. J. Maxwell Brownjohn (Boston: Little, Brown and Company, 1978), pp. 13–41.

24 Zolling and Bahnsen, *Kalter Winter im August*, p. 15.

25 McDermott, *Berlin*, p. 32.

26 Zolling and Bahnsen, *Kalter Winter im August*, p. 17. In his subsequent comment on the serialized version of this book, Heinrich Albertz, Brandt's successor as Berlin's governing mayor and a participant in the Kommandatura meeting, did not mention this aspect of the report; see his "War die Mauer zu verhindern?," in *Der Spiegel*, 20:44 (October 24, 1966), pp. 72–85, particularly p. 78. See also Brandt, *People and Politics*, pp. 14–15; and Curtis Cate, *The Ides of August: The Berlin Wall Crisis, 1961* (New York: M. Evans and Company, Inc., 1978), pp. 300–304.

27 *Berliner Morgenpost*, Sonderausgabe, August 13, 1961, p. 1.

28 Abgeordnetenhaus von Berlin, *Stenographischer Bericht, III. Wahlperiode; 66. Sitzung*, 3:15 (August 13, 1961), pp. 251–54.

29 Excerpts from the police calendar for the day (including the estimated size of crowds) appear in "Der 13. August 1961," a special supplement to the *Berliner Morgenpost* August 12–13, 1962. Sidney Gruson, *The New York Times* August 14, 1961, p. 6, estimated the number of persons at 4,000. As an eyewitness to some of these events, my own feeling is that the police estimates are exaggerated, that Gruson's figure is closer to the truth.

30 The headlines in the August 9, 1961, edition of the respectable *Tagesspiegel*, for instance, reported, "Fear of Closure of Escape Routes Increases."

31 Why Bahr did not deliver the message is not quite clear. Zolling and Bahnsen report the impression of the man asked to relay the message that Bahr viewed the Clay mission as "an *idée fixe* of the Springer press." Zolling and Bahnsen, *Kalter Winter im August*, p. 133. Cate's impression, recorded in *The Ides of August*, pp. 349–52, is that the lateness of the hour (3:00 a.m., after a day that had begun almost 24 hours earlier) together with, perhaps, the vagueness of the decision's direct linkage to Kennedy led Bahr to forget all about it as soon as he put down the telephone receiver. See also Antoinette May, *Witness to War: A Biography of Marguerite Higgins* (New York and Toronto: Beaufort Books, 1983), pp. 226–27.

32 Adenauer evidently understood the Western position well. Indeed, late that very evening Bonn received word from its ambassador in the United States, Wilhelm von Grewe, that he had been unable to persuade either Secretary of State Rusk or the Berlin Committee of the Ambassadorial Group, com-

prising representatives of the three Western occupying powers, to take vigorous countermeasures. See Cate, *The Ides of August,* pp. 376–77.
33 *Der Spiegel,* 15:35 (August 23, 1961), p. 17.
34 Shell, *Bedrohung und Bewährung,* p. 41.
35 *Die Welt* (Berlin), August 15, 1961, pp. 1 and 4. The prohibition stemmed from the times when unemployment was extremely high in Berlin.
36 Courts later ruled that workers fired because of their membership in the SED had to be reinstated and receive just compensation for the period during which they were laid off.
37 Zolling and Bahnsen, *Kalter Winter im August,* pp. 130–40.
38 *B.Z.,* August 16, 1961, p. 2.
39 Willy Brandt, *Begegnungen mit Kennedy* (München: Kindler Verlag, 1964), p. 72. Through an indiscretion in Bonn, the full text of Brandt's letter appeared in *Frankfurter Allgemeine Zeitung,* August 19, 1961, p. 1.
40 Zolling and Bahnsen, *Kalter Winter im August,* p. 142.
41 See footnote 14. Cate, *The Ides of August,* p. 389, citing Western intelligence sources, states that the story "had been deliberately leaked to the West Berlin newspapers by a Soviet agent." Allied denials of the rumor were reported in a small article in *Der Kurier,* August 17, 1981, p. 2. Brandt, in his *Begegnungen mit Kennedy,* pp. 76–77, reports his conviction that the Allies had no prior warning of details.
42 Four-power agreements left control of the elevated railway as well as the Reichsbahn of which it is a part in the hands of authorities in the Soviet sector of Berlin. Until the 1980s the Western allies refused to alter this arrangement. As a private effort to undermine the economic basis of the elevated railway, the boycott received informal support from the municipal government and formal support insofar as the Berlin Transit Authority (BVG) set up parallel bus lines to carry passengers wanting to avoid the elevated railway (prices on which, incidentally, were about half those of the buses and subways). Although the boycott received widespread popular support, most West Berliners (66 percent) expressed an understanding for those who did not support it, according to a survey conducted in the spring of 1962; Shell, *Bedrohung und Bewährung,* p. 203.
43 Albertz, "War die Mauer zu verhindern?" p. 78.
44 Brandt, *Begegnungen mit Kennedy,* p. 69.
45 The speeches by Amrehn and Brandt appear in *Der Tagesspiegel,* August 17, 1961, p. 3.
46 Albertz, "War die Mauer zu verhindern?" p. 75. This article, signed by Brandt's successor as governing mayor but reportedly written by Egon Bahr, attributes the phrase to Bahr.
47 In subsequent years West Berlin bargained hard to gain what East Berlin was apparently offering it in August, 1961, and what Western authorities rejected at the time. From 1966 to 1971 entry permits were granted only to West Berliners with pressing family problems. Good discussions of the *Passierschein* question are in Shell, *Bedrohung und Bewährung,* pp. 304–15; and Kai Hermann, "Die Mauer bleibt zu," *Die Zeit,* December 23, 1966, p. 3.
48 *Der Spiegel,* 15:35 (August 23, 1961), p. 19.
49 Survey data from Shell, *Bedrohung und Bewährung,* p. 143. See "Inspektor

sagt: Schluss mit der Schlafmützigkeit!" *B.Z.*, August 15, 1961, p. 2. In their conversation with Murrow, however, Springer and his Berlin editors were unanimous in suggesting that the United States should remove the barriers; see Zolling and Bahnsen, *Kalter Winter im August*, p. 139.

50 After Sunday morning's meeting of the Kommandatura with Brandt, the three political advisers of the Western missions in Berlin met to draft a joint protest. Secretary of State Rusk nonetheless vetoed it and instructed the U.S. Mission to make no statement whatever. See Cate, *The Ides of August*, pp. 320–21.

51 Ibid., p. 147; see also *Frankfurter Allgemeine Zeitung*, August 19, 1961, p. 1, for general reaction.

52 Loc. cit.

53 Albertz, "War die Mauer zu verhindern?," pp. 80, 82. Parts of the letter appear in Brandt, *Begegnungen mit Kennedy*, pp. 86–87.

54 Zolling and Bahnsen, *Kalter Winter im August*, p. 154. Upon receiving word of Kennedy's response, Brandt exclaimed, "What a great guy!"

55 Willy Brandt summarizes and paraphrases Kennedy's letter in his *People and Politics*, p. 32.

56 The *Bild Zeitung* of August 19, 1961, p. 8, in an article entitled "Bitter—aber wahr," nonetheless expressed its regret that partisan electoral politics kept the three parties from drafting a common statement of support.

57 Zolling and Bahnsen, *Kalter Winter im August*, p. 152.

58 *The New York Times*, August 20, 1961, p. 4.

59 Albertz, "War die Mauer zu verhindern?" p. 82. In his report to Secretary of State Rusk, Bohlen termed the visit a "complete and unqualified success" and went on to recommend that the United States "be prepared to react swiftly and decisively and, indeed, to overreact, if necessary, to any clear signs of harassment or any attempts by the Communists to erode our rights, and especially in regard to access (which includes the communications between West Berlin and the Federal Republic.)" Any hesitancy or delay in doing so, he added, "would rapidly cast the morale of the West Berliners back to the depths where it was immediately after August 13, and prior to the Vice President's visit." See Charles E. Bohlen, *Witness to History, 1929–1969* (New York: W. W. Norton & Company, Inc., 1973), pp. 485–86.

60 *The New York Times*, August 21, 1961, p. 2.

61 The FRG's ambassador in Moscow, Hans Kroll, reports that Khrushchev was intent on preventing any incident that could lead to war, and even ordered that Soviet tanks withdraw first from the confrontation at Checkpoint Charlie so as to avoid an escalation of the conflict. See his *Lebenserinnerungen eines Botschafters* (Köln and Berlin: Verlag Kiepenheuer & Witsch, 1967), pp. 511, 514.

2 The Wall and West Berlin's Development

1 The term "morale" has posed some problems. The German word *Moral*, pronounced in roughly the same way, refers to morals, ethics, and moral philosophy (or the lesson to be learned from one of Aesop's fables). Eventually, however, Germans learned to use the term "morale" as a substitute for the concept of *Standhaftigkeit der geistlichen Haltung*.

2   This led to an amusing incident after Johnson's arrival in the city. Seeing a pair of shoes he liked, he asked for a pair just like them, but was told that it would be impossible to obtain them since the shops had already closed for the weekend. His response was, "Go over to this man, Willy Brandt, and tell him that I want action, not words." He got his shoes!

3   After becoming a member of the Berlin Senate in December 1961, I recall we met every Tuesday morning to review a special file, stamped "secret," that contained the latest statistics on emigration from and immigration to the city; these alarming data were underscored by the sight, which was there for all to see, of columns of furniture vans leaving the city.

4   The SPD formally dissolved these units after access was restricted, in part because they could no longer be effective and also in part because the party feared their takeover by East Berlin communists.

3   Puzzling About the Wall

1   Honoré Marc Catudal, Jr., *Kennedy and the Berlin Wall Crisis: A Case Study in U.S. Decision Making* (Berlin: Berlin Verlag, 1980), pp. 229–50.

2   See, for example, Robert M. Slusser, *The Berlin Crisis of 1961: Soviet-American Relations and the Struggle for Power in the Kremlin, June–November 1961* (Baltimore, and London: The Johns Hopkins University Press, 1973), pp. x–xi, 17 passim. Hannes Adomeit, *Soviet Risk-Taking and Crisis Behavior: A Theoretical and Empirical Analysis* (London: George Allen & Unwin, 1982), pp. 256–71, rejects domestic factionalism as a major factor changing Soviet policies.

3   For evidence of Dulles's flexibility, aimed at getting negotiations started, see Jack M. Schick, *The Berlin Crisis, 1948–1962* (Philadelphia: University of Pennsylvania Press, 1971), pp. 29–68, esp. pp. 40–49.

4   *Khrushchev Remembers,* with an introduction, commentary, and notes by Edward Crankshaw, Jr. and Strobe Talbot (Boston and Toronto: Little, Brown and Company, 1970), p. 458.

5   Walther Stützle, *Kennedy and Adenauer in der Berlin-Krise 1961-1962* (Bonn-Bad Godesberg: Verlag Neue Gesellschaft GmbH, 1973).

6   Richard J. Walton, *Cold War and Counter-Revolution: The Foreign Policy of John F. Kennedy* (Baltimore, Md.: Penguin Books, 1973).

7   The U.S. Commandant in West Berlin, Major General Albert Watson II, expressed such a view in a letter to Catudal; see Catudal, *Kennedy and the Berlin Wall Crisis,* pp. 192–93.

8   The Western allies, of course, had had very little to say about what went on in East Berlin since 1948, when the Soviets walked out of the Four-power Komandatura in March and split the city's government in September. The point here is that, by stressing *West* Berlin, Kennedy was granting symbolic legitimacy to the situation that had existed de facto for more than a dozen years. This represented a significant shift in U.S. policy toward Berlin.

9   When Khrushchev learned that Marshal Konev had brought up tanks to face the American ones at Checkpoint Charlie in late October 1961, for example, he ordered their withdrawal. "Because of prestige the Americans cannot be the first to pull back," he told the West German ambassador to the Soviet Union; "therefore we want to make the beginning." See Hans Kroll, *Lebens-*

erinnerungen eines Botschafters (Cologne and Berlin: Verlag Kiepenheuer & Witsch, 1967), p. 514.

10   Kennedy made a hobby of studying the Berlin issue. Martin J. Hillenbrand, director of the State Department's Office of German Affairs, lamented, however, that the president had "some surprising gaps in his knowledge," and John C. Ausland, the duty officer for the Berlin Task Force on the weekend of August 12–13, 1961, commented that the "difficulty was that [Kennedy] couldn't devote full time" to the task of being "the Berlin Desk Officer." See Catudal, *Kennedy and the Berlin Wall Crisis,* pp. 151–52.

11   Ibid., p. 250.

12   Two West German correspondents, Hermann Zolling and Uwe Bahnsen, in their book *Kalter Winter im August: Die Berlin Krise 1961/63* (Oldenburg: Gerhard Stalling Verlag, 1967), p. 133, report that Kennedy's message, relayed by the journalist James O'Donnell to a colleague in West Berlin for further transmission to the city's government, fell on deaf ears. For more details see footnote 31 in my earlier chapter, "A Transformed Crisis: The Berlin Wall."

13   The high spirits raised in West Berlin during the visit by Johnson and Clay also made some people in both East and West a bit nervous. The brave words spoken on that occasion seemed to promise more than they could deliver. West Berliners needed only to go to the sectoral boundary to see that East German soldiers and workmen were in fact strengthening the barriers, and before another week would pass the GDR had in effect barred West Berliners from entering East Berlin. Moreover, Clay's remark on August 19 that "Berlin will still be free," did not accord well with Kennedy's earlier statements, which had carefully distinguished between Berlin as a whole and West Berlin.

14   I recall that, after Khrushchev's ultimatum in 1958, President Eisenhower's defense liaison officer and staff secretary, General Andrew J. Goodpaster, presented him with a memorandum from the Joint Chiefs proposing a very substantial increase in appropriations to deal with the Soviet threat. Eisenhower responded, in effect, that the Soviet threat had been around for decades and was going to be around for decades longer, that the Soviet threat to Berlin was essentially a political problem. You worry about the state of our defenses, Eisenhower said, and I will worry about the politics. Let us not get discombobulated by Khrushchev's remarks. I showed this exchange to McGeorge Bundy, who said it was too bad that JFK did not learn this earlier.

15   This Kennedy "doctrine" appears clearly in his speech at American University before his trip to Berlin in 1963 and then again in his speech at the Free University of Berlin.

16   *David Klein:* As early as 1960, according to his personal papers, President Eisenhower concluded that the GDR would soon have to do something to stop the manpower drain.

17   The role of Higgins and O'Donnell, as described by Zolling and Bahnsen in *Kalter Winter im August,* p. 133, is surely exaggerated; such people did not convey instructions to other governments.

18   Eleanor Dulles (in 1958 the Berlin desk officer in the State Department) once told me how she had protested vehemently to her brother his remarks. "Look," she said, "you mustn't say that kind of thing about Germany, for it will demoralize the Germans."

19 Although it is inaccurate in some other respects, the book by Catudal, *Kennedy and the Berlin Wall Crisis*, is a fairly reliable account of the thinking of the Kennedy administration, its actual consideration of alternatives, and the reason why they were not implemented.
20 I recall that the White House expected but did not in fact receive a noisy response from the West Germans to this speech.
21 For precisely this reason I do not place any credence in the report by Zolling and Bahnsen that Egon Bahr ignored a message to this effect that Peter Boenisch is said to have delivered (see footnote 12 above). In fact, having Clay come to Berlin was much more important than, with all due respect to the vice president, receiving Johnson. In the municipal elections of 1963 we even put up a poster with the slogan, "Clay says Yes to Brandt." Such was his prestige in the city.
22 Hannes Adomeit, in a book published a year after the conference reported here took place, *Soviet Risk-Taking and Crisis Behavior: A Theoretical and Empirical Analysis* (London: George Allen & Unwin, 1982), provides an insightful account of Soviet motives—an account flawed, however, by an excessively anti-Soviet stance.
23 *Renata Fritsch-Bournazel:* It is striking that all French accounts of the crisis stress the fact that it occurred on a weekend—in fact, since Assumption Day fell on Tuesday, August 15, France's longest weekend of the year—and some suggest that the Soviets timed the démarche to take advantage of the French holidays.
24 Geoffrey McDermott, *Berlin: Success of a Mission?* (New York: Harper & Row Publishers, 1963), p. 31.

Part 2 Introduction

1 Press and Information Office of the Government of the Federal Republic of Germany, *Bulletin*, 19:30 (September 4, 1971), 225–32.
2 Press and Information Office of the Government of the Federal Republic of Germany, *Bulletin*, 20:38 (November 14, 1972), 293–304.

4 The Quadripartite Agreement on Berlin

1 The memoirs of Henry Kissinger, *White House Years* (Boston and Toronto: Little, Brown and Company, 1979), esp. pp. 823–33, provide an interesting but not particularly reliable account of the Four-power negotiations.
2 *Europa Archiv*, October 25, 1976, pp. 647–56.

5 Long-Range Effects of the Quadripartite Agreement

1 Peter Bender, "Die Absurdität Berlin," *Der Spiegel*, 35:20 (May 11, 1981), pp. 40–41.
2 See Nina Grunenberg, "Ist Berlin noch seine Prämie wert?" *Die Zeit*, 35:49 (November 28, 1980), pp. 9–10.

6 Twenty Years of Berlin History

1. For a description of the critical five years, see Martin J. Hillenbrand, editor, *The Future of Berlin* (Montclair, N.J.: Allanheld, Osmun & Co., Publishers, 1980), pp. 13ff.; also Barry M. Blechman and Stephen S. Kaplan, editors, *Force Without War* (Washington, D.C.: Brookings Institution, 1978), pp. 349ff.
2. See Honoré Marc Catudal, Jr., *Kennedy and the Berlin Wall Crisis: A Case Study in U.S. Decision Making* (Berlin: Berlin Verlag, 1980), pp. 230–50; also Hillenbrand, *The Future of Berlin*, pp. 17–18.
3. Hillenbrand, *The Future of Berlin*, p. 20.
4. Ibid., pp. 95–104.
5. For a description of the complicated relationship between NATO and the three western sectors of the city, see ibid., pp. 20–25.
6. See the account in Henry Kissinger, *The White House Years* (Boston: Little, Brown, 1979), pp. 408ff.
7. Such an account may be found in my chapter on "The Legal Background of the Berlin Situation," in Hillenbrand, *The Future of Berlin*, pp. 41–80.
8. Texts of the relevant military governors' letter and Berlin commandants' statement are in United States Senate, Committee on Foreign Relations, *Documents on Germany, 1944–1970* (Washington, D.C.: U.S. Government Printing Office, 1971), pp. 156–60.
9. See Hillenbrand, *The Future of Berlin*, p. 65.
10. Kissinger, *The White House Years*, pp. 823–33.
11. In an as yet unpublished study by James S. Sutterlin and David Klein, this whole question is examined at some length with negative conclusions as to the necessity for back-channel diplomacy. Sutterlin was director of German Affairs in the State Department during the negotiations, and Klein head of the U.S. Mission in Berlin.
12. The full text of the agreement is in U.S. Department of State, *Quadripartite Agreement on Berlin, Final Quadripartite Protocol*, Department of State Treaties and Other International Acts Series 7551 (Washington, D.C.: U.S. Government Printing Office, undated).
13. See Hillenbrand, *The Future of Berlin*, pp. 121–22.
14. Ibid., pp. 129–38.
15. Ministerium für Auswärtige Angelegenheiten der DDR and Ministerium für Auswärtige Angelegenheiten der UdSSR, *Das Vierseitige Abdommen über Westberlin und seine Realisierung, Dokumente 1971–1977* (Berlin: Staatsverlag der Deutschen Demokratischen Republik, 1977).
16. Hillenbrand, *The Future of Berlin*, p. 68.
17. See Günther van Well, "Die Teilnahme Berlins am internationalen Geschehen: ein dringender Punkt auf der Ost-West Tagesordnung," *Europa Archiv*, October 25, 1976, pp. 647–56.
18. Text released by NATO Press Service, Brussels, May 31, 1978.
19. See the chapter by Gerhard Mensch, "Economic Perspectives for Berlin," in Hillenbrand, *The Future of Berlin*, pp. 153–228.

7 The West Berlin Economy

1 Gerhard Mensch cited data for 1977 indicating that 46.6 percent of West Berlin's gross product came from goods-producing firms, in contrast to 53.4 percent from the state sector (19.0 percent) and trade, transport, and services (34.4 percent). See his "Economic Perspectives for Berlin," in *The Future of Berlin,* ed. Martin J. Hillenbrand, pp. 153–228 (Montclair, N.J.: Allanheld, Osmun & Company, 1980).
2 See Mensch, "Economic Perspectives for Berlin," pp. 162ff.

8 Berlin between East and West

Chapter 8 was translated from German by Alison Donaldson.
1 Peter Bender, *Das Ende des ideologischen Zeitalters: Die Europäisierung Europas* (Berlin: Severin & Siedler, Quadriga GmbH, 1981).
2 John Henry Mackay, *Der Freiheitsucher: Psychologie einer Entwicklung* (Berlin-Charlottenburg: privately printed manuscript, 1921; reprinted in Freiburg-im-Breisgau: Mackay Gesellschaft, 1975); excerpts are in Karl Schwedhelm, editor, *John Henry Mackay: Eine Auswahl aus seinem Werk* (Wiesbaden: Franz Steiner Verlag GmbH, "Verschollene und Vergessene" series, 1980), pp. 133–46.
3 Ingrid Mittenzwei, *Friedrich II. von Preussen: eine Biographie* (Berlin [East]: VEB Deutscher Verlag der Wissenschaften, 1979; Köln: Pahl-Rügenstein Verlag, 1980).

9 Interpersonal Transactions across the Wall

1 The first two sections of this paper are taken from my article, "Political Disintegration in Postwar Berlin," in *From National Development to Global Community: Essays in Honor of Karl W. Deutsch,* ed. Richard L. Merritt and Bruce M. Russett (London: George Allen & Unwin Ltd., 1981), pp. 206–30.
2 Disintegration is thus different from both *decay,* which implies a loss in the unit's capabilities, abilities to frame goals commensurate with its capabilities, and combinatorial resourcefulness or ability to develop strategies to use available resources in a reasonably efficient manner to obtain realistic goals, and mere *disaggregation,* the division of the unit into its component parts. For further elaboration, see Richard L. Merritt, "Decay in Social Systems," in *Systems in Society,* ed. Milton D. Rubin (Washington, D.C.: Society for General Systems Research, 1973), pp. 71–103.
3 See W. Phillips Davison, *The Berlin Blockade: A Study in Cold War Politics* (Princeton, N.J.: Princeton University Press, 1958); G. Keiderling and Percy Stulz, *Berlin 1945–1968: Zur Geschichte der Hauptstadt der DDR und der selbständigen politischen Einheit Westberlin* (Berlin [East]: Dietz Verlag, 1970); and Hans Herzfeld, *Berlin in der Weltpolitik 1945–1970* (Berlin and New York: Walter de Gruyter Verlag, 1973).
4 For data and some interpretations on the larger question of Germany as a

whole, see Gebhard Schweigler, *National Consciousness in Divided Germany* (Beverly Hills, Calif., and London: Sage Publications, Inc., 1972).
5 See, for example, Richard L. Merritt, *Symbols of American Community, 1735–1775* (New Haven, Conn., and London: Yale University Press, 1966); and Donald J. Puchala, "The Pattern of Contemporary Regional Integration," *International Studies Quarterly*, 12:1 (March 1968), pp. 38–64.
6 The elevated railway (*S-Bahn*) system throughout Berlin and its pre-1945 suburbs was owned by the Reichsbahn, which, according to early Quadripartite agreements, was given over to the Soviet occupation authorities. At the end of 1983, after ten years of discussion and negotiation, West Berlin bought the elevated railroad and set about renovating it.
7 Data on mail flows were provided by the Landespostdirektion Berlin.
8 Data from "Mitteilung zur Kenntnisnahme über Durchführung des Viermächte-Abkommens und der ergänzenden Vereinbarungen zwischen dem 1. June 1983 und dem 31. Mai 1984," Abgeordnetenhaus von Berlin, 9. Wahlperiode, Drucksache 9/1943, May 7, 1984, pp. 5, 9.
9 Contrast this figure of 0.9 visits per West Berlin citizen in 1983–84 with the 13.7 trips per West Berlin citizen between the Federal Republic and West Berlin (up from 2.2 such trips in 1957) for an idea of the relative importance for West Berliners of the East as opposed to West Germany. Ibid., p. 10.
10 Various "Berichte [Mitteilungen] über die Durchführung . . . ," 1972–73 to 1981–82. In the latter year, there were 412 lines from West Berlin into East Berlin and 113 into the GDR, as well as 60 lines into West Berlin from East Berlin and 24 from the GDR.
11 In June 1980 the current number of telephone calls into East Berlin was reported to average 30,000 per day (although later statistics for the entire year indicated an average for 1980 of 25,787 calls per day); the figure for 1981 was 20.5 (7.5) percent lower. It is difficult to assess the efficiency of the telephone service because of both the increased number of lines and marked improvements in the type of equipment used. In 1972–73, when less than a tenth of the calls were directly dialed, each line from West Berlin into the East accounted for an average of 50.7 calls per day; in 1981, roughly 19 in 20 of the lines were fully automatic, and the average load was 55.9 calls per day.
12 The statement prepared by West Berlin's Alternative movement, which declined to send a representative to the conference, begins by terming the division of Germany an unsolved problem: "The continuing military occupation of Berlin demonstrates that the system of military blocs in Europe, led by the USA and the Soviet Union, and the division of Germany contain in themselves several unsolved problems. Berlin can find a perspective for the future only through solution of the German problem and dissolution of the confrontation between blocs in Europe. This is why politicians in Berlin must also seek to come to terms with the possible perspectives for the life of the city."

The statement goes on to outline the need for addressing directly the question of German unity, for both German states to withdraw from military confrontation, and for one of the two Germanies to start the ball rolling by making an offer of neutrality. It suggests a number of specific policies aimed at reducing the Allies' military presence in Berlin and enhancing contacts among persons in East and West. It concludes: "We wish to use the untenable legal, economic and political situation of Berlin as a chance to construct a policy whose long-term goal is German nonalignment as a contribution to peace in Europe."

10 Living with the Wall

1 I am using the term "myth" in the Platonic sense as brought up to date by Robert M. MacIver: "Social myth at every level enjoins some kind of order among men, and enshrines that order in a context of value-impregnated lore and legend, in tradition and in philosophy." See his *The Web of Government* (New York: The Macmillan Company, 1957), p. 42.
2 For a fuller discussion of this point, see Richard L. Merritt, "The Lost Center: Dispersing Berlin's Capital City Functions, 1945–78," in *Western European Cities in Crisis,* ed. Michael C. Romanos, pp. 185–202 (Lexington, Mass.: D. C. Heath, Lexington Books, 1979).
3 In 1953 and 1978, respectively, about half of representative samples of the West German population denied that the FRG was unnecessarily pumping too much money into West Berlin and agreed with the proposition, "The more serious the situation is, the more help we must send to West Berliners"; about a fifth responded in the opposite direction. In summer 1984 only 13 percent of a West German sample argued that the financial assistance to Berlin should be cut, 50 percent that it should stay at its current level, and 24 percent that it should be increased. See Elisabeth Noelle-Neumann, "Berlin bleibt auch weiterhin eine 'Hauptstadt aus eigenem Rang," pp. B2 and B10 of a special supplement, "Berlin—die Stadt mit Zukunft," of *Das Handelsblatt,* November 2–3, 1984.
4 For a conservative critique of earlier policies, see Herbert Krafft, *Marktwirtschaft auf dem Prüfstand: 45 Jahre Berliner Wirtschaft* (Berlin and Offenbach: VDE-Verlag GmbH, 1984); see also the analyses by CDU and SPD leaders of economic growth patterns since 1981, in the special supplement, "Berlin—die Stadt mit Zukunft," of *Das Handelsblatt,* November 2–3, 1984, pp. B1–20.
5 Unless otherwise indicated, data in this chapter are from Statistisches Landesamt Berlin, *Statistisches Jahrbuch* (Berlin: Kulturbuch-Verlag), various editions, and the monthly *Berliner Statistik.*
6 Eberhard Diepgen, "Innovationsgesellschaften sind die Magnete für andere Unternehmen," p. B3 of the special supplement, "Berlin—die Stadt mit Zukunft," *Das Handelsblatt,* November 2–3, 1984.
7 I have written extensively on this in "The Student Protest Movement in West Berlin," *Comparative Politics,* 1:4 (July 1969), 516–33.
8 See, for example, R. Schmidt, "Schlechte Noten für rote Unis," *Manager-Magazin,* April 1978, pp. 146–52.
9 That the potential for protest, with its attendant ambivalence on the part of left-leaning intellectuals and politicians, continues to exist is indicated by a demonstration on November 5, 1984, that is, on the eve of the American presidential election, to denounce President Reagan's policies on arms control and Central America. The SPD's leadership (and others) publicly regretted the

10   When the squatting crisis began, as many as 10,000 empty apartments were awaiting either demolition or refurbishing into more luxurious apartments; see "Für das letzte besetzte Haus wurde der Pachtvertrag endgültig besiegelt," *Der Tagesspiegel,* November 9, 1984, p. 16.

11   For data, see Noelle-Neumann, "Berlin bleibt . . ." pp. B2, B10.

12   The city's statisticians informally add to this number 102,000 persons, who are officially counted as West Germans since they maintain a second home there; see Statistisches Landesamt Berlin, *Statistisches Jahrbuch 1983,* p. 40, n. 2.

13   In summer 1984 almost three in five (57 percent) of a sample of West Berliners agreed with the statement that "Berlin is a young city," that it is attractive to and filled with young people and new ideas; see Noelle-Neumann, "Berlin bleibt . . ." p. B10.

14   Statement made in the course of a debate with the Hessian minister of the interior, Horst Winterstein (SPD), as reported in *Der Spiegel,* 38:42 (October 15, 1984), 45–94, esp. p. 90. The proposal to deny entry to children over six years of age was vetoed at the federal level in favor of a measure letting in children under the age of sixteen (although some states, such as Hessia, have extended that limit to eighteen).

15   The data in this paragraph are from *Der Tagesspiegel,* October 26, 1984, p. 12, and November 8, 1984, p. 17; the acceptance rate for asylants from Ghana was 0.2 percent in 1984.

16   In October 1984 the Federal Administrative Court ruled that Tamils are not ipso facto entitled to political asylum since, isolated instances notwithstanding, there was no evidence of systematic pogroms against them in Sri Lanka (BVerwG 9 C 24.84).

17   Environmental protection is an especially thorny issue for West Berlin because much of the damage currently being done derives from industrial pollution in the GDR—a country that is putting industrial growth far above environmental protection in its own list of political priorities. Among other things, SPD leaders in West Berlin have called for the FRG to make available to the GDR low-interest loans and transfers of whatever technologies are necessary to stop this pollution; see "Berliner SPD-Fraktion berichtete über Besuch des Kohlekraftwerkes Cottbus," *Der Tagesspiegel,* October 25, 1984, p. 2.

18   Especially West Berlin's elevated railway system, bought from the GDR in 1983 after several decades of deterioration; the Berlin Transit Authority (BVG) is now refurbishing the stations, rolling stock, and tracks, with the aim of integrating the system fully with its subway and bus networks.

19   A recent example was the agreement in 1983 whereby, in exchange for credits from the FRG, the East Germans exempted children under the age of fourteen from the minimum currency exchange required for visits to the East; the FRG did not fully consult West Berlin officials until the deal was struck. The city's governing mayor, Eberhard Diepgen, in responding to an interviewer's question about such episodes, commented laconically, "The flow of information between the Berlin government and Bonn can surely be organized better."

See "Berlin ist schon lange kein Schlusslicht mehr," *Quick,* no. 44 (October 25, 1984), 44.
20 Only 3.5 percent of West Berlin's total trade in 1983 was with the GDR (in contrast to 78 percent with the Federal Republic, 1.3 percent with other Soviet bloc states, and 17.2 percent with the rest of the world), 6 percent imports (mostly mineral oils, clothing, and foodstuffs) and 1.1 percent exports.
21 On the imperative of independence in vital matters, see Richard L. Merritt, "Political Division and Municipal Services in Postwar Berlin," pp. 165–98 in *Public Policy 17,* ed. John D. Montgomery and Albert O. Hirschmann (Cambridge, Mass.: Harvard University Press, 1968). Even today, when Soviet delegations agree to participate in a film festival or other event, West Berlin organizers know not to count on their presence until they actually appear.
22 The first four lines of García Lorca's "Casida del llanto" (Casida of the Lament), which appears in his *Diván del Tamarit* (1936), run:

>   He cerrado mi balcón
>   porque no quiero oír el llanto,
>   pero por detrás de los grises muros
>   no se oye otra cosa que el llanto.

The poem and English translation (by Stephen Spender and J. L. Gili) are reprinted in *The Selected Poems of Federico García Lorca,* ed. Francisco García Lorca and Donald M. Allen (Norfolk, Conn: New Directions Books, The New Classics Series, 1955), pp. 170–73.

Index

Acheson, Dean: June memorandum on Berlin, 54
Adenauer, Konrad: actions on August 13, 14; reference to Brandt's illegitimate birth, 14, 21, 24; actions during first week of wall, 20–21; Berlin Senate reaction to speech, 24; not permitted to accompany Johnson, 65; mistrust for Berlin, 150; support for Nixon's candidacy, 222
Adomeit, Hannes, 220, 221, 225, 227
Agnew, Spiro, 115
Agriculture: collectivization in GDR after wall, 63
Albertz, Heinrich, 222, 223, 224
Alternative movement, 158–60, 185, 186, 199–200, 230
Anderson, David, 141–42
Ausland, John C., 221, 226

Bahnsen, Uwe, 219, 220, 221, 222, 223, 224, 226, 227
Bahr, Egon, 222, 223, 227; philosophy on East-West relations, 68, 115
Basic Law: reunification as part of, 38; Articles 23 and 144, 124
Bauer, Leo, 115
Bay of Pigs, 43, 54. *See also* Cuba
Bender, Peter, 68, 108, 152, 227, 229
Berlin: divided before wall, 62; shared responsibility for, 79; reluctance of West to discuss, 80; as leverage in early East-West talks, 81; East's policy on not changed, 103; effect of agreement on, 105; role of in détente, 107–8; since 1972, 129–33; and German identity, 150–51; wartime disruptions, 167. *See also* East Berlin *and* West Berlin
Berlin talks: three themes, 83; change in Western goals, 87–88; importance of other events for success of, 89–90, 94–95; U.S.-China relations and, 89–90; and GDR obstructionism, 90–91; Bonn government planning for, 93–94, 107, 111; Soviet goals, 100–101; start of, 124. *See also* Quadripartite Agreement
Blockade: contingency plan for, 140, 141
Bohlen, Charles, 224
Brandt, Willy, 105, 121, 222, 223; return to Berlin on August 13, 15–16; letter to Kennedy, 25–26, 32–33, 50–51; speech on August 16, 26–28; effect of wall on campaign for chancellorship, 68–69; détente policy, 75; early interest in Berlin talks, 80; pushes *Ostpolitik*, 123–24
Bräutigam, Hans Otto, 57–58, 66, 91–92, 96, 110–11, 141, 185
Bundestag: West Berlin delegates to, 5

Carter, Jimmy: visit to Berlin, 131
Cate, Curtis, 222, 223, 224
Catudal, Honoré Marc, Jr., 219, 220, 221, 225, 226, 227, 228
Checkpoint Charlie: confrontation of U.S. and Soviet tanks at, 36, 46, 51, 52, 55, 56, 62, 224, 225
China: U.S. relations with and Berlin talks, 89–90
Church: as medium for East-West interaction, 176–78
Civil service: extent of in West Berlin, 145
Clarke, Bruce C., 11, 12, 26
Clay, Lucius D., 39, 61–62; Berlin visit in August 1961, 20, 25, 33, 34–35, 51; return to Berlin in fall 1961, appointment regretted, 55, 56
Conference on Security and Cooperation in Europe, 80, 87, 88, 94, 125, 126
Cooney, James, 67
CSCE. *See* Conference on Security and Cooperation in Europe
Cuba: link to wall in Soviet strategy, 59, 60; and Berlin crises, 114, 147–48; missile crisis and Berlin, 120. *See also* Bay of Pigs
Czechoslovakia: 1968 Soviet invasion, 80, 81

Davison, W. Phillips, 229
Dean, Jonathan, 85–86, 88, 90, 91, 95, 97, 105–6, 112–13
Détente, 75–78; and Berlin talks, 99–101; importance to FRG and GDR, 210
Deutsch, Karl W., 147–48
Diepgen, Eberhard, 231
Duisberg, Claus, 61
Dulles, Eleanor Lansing, 49, 226
Dulles, John Foster, 226; role in Berlin policy, 49, 56–57

East Berlin: status of, 103–4; acceptance as capital city, 106; status of in GDR, 113–14

East-West relations: as test of willpower, 53; changing pattern of, 170–83
East-West talks: role of Berlin in, 81–82. *See also* Berlin talks
Economy: of West Berlin, 136–48, 194–96
Eitel, Antonius, 87–88, 95, 111–12
Election, 1961, in FRG, 13, 14, 21, 24, 68–69. *See also* Adenauer *and* Brandt
Electricity: need for in West Berlin, 140–41, 144
Elevated railway, 223, 230, 232
Engert, Jürgen, 113–14, 184–85, 186
Erhard, Ludwig, 114
European Community: and West Berlin, 214–15

France: culture of compared to Germany, 149; interest in Berlin, 208–9
Francisco, Ronald, 63, 142–43
Frankel, Max, 221
Free University of Berlin, 122
FRG: 1961 election campaign, 13, 14, 21, 24, 68–69; relationship to West Berlin, 78, 102–3; 124–25, 128, 130, 134, 138–39, 210, 211; and Berlin talks, 93–94, 107, 111, 116, 125–26; external representation of West Berlin, 131; improved relations with GDR, 135; reunification as ultimate goal, 38, 209, 210–12; and détente, 210–11; as hostage of Berlin situation, 211–12
Fritsch-Bournazel, Renata, 60–61, 88–89, 108–9, 140, 227
Fulbright, William J.: July 1961 television interview, 9, 59–60

Gablentz, Otto M. von der, 219
García Lorca, Federico, 233
GDR: refugees from, 3, 6, 7, 9, 44–45; destabilizing effect of West Berlin on, 60–61; morale in after wall, 61; reaction to Quadripartite Agreement, 77; obstructionism on Berlin talks, 90–91; leadership of and Soviet bloc policy, 95; effect of wall, 98–99;

goals in Berlin talks, 100–101; unchanged status of, 105; improved relations with FRG, 135; interest in separation of Germanies, 209–10, 212–14
Gradl, Johann Baptist, 58–59, 65, 69, 114–15
Great Britain: interest in Berlin, 208–9
Greens. *See* Alternative movement
Grunenberg, Nina, 227
Gruson, Sidney, 222
Guest workers, 142, 202–3. *See also* Turks

Haftendorn, Helga, 67–68, 88, 145, 184
Hallstein Doctrine, 125; and *Ostpolitik*, 93
Heinemann, Gustav, 78
Hermann, Kai, 223
Herzfeld, Hans, 229
Hillenbrand, Martin J., 54–55, 56, 65, 70–71, 86–87, 92–93, 96, 115–16, 143–45, 148, 228, 229
History: need for awareness of, 163–65
Honecker, Erich: visit to Japan, 63–64; replaces Ulbricht, 90

Ideology: end of, 152–53
India: recognizes DDR, 93
Intelligence: failure of before wall, 70, 220, 221
Inter-German agreement, 77, 94; significance of negotiating partners, 103
Israel: comparison with West Berlin, 185–86

Japan: visit by Honecker, 63–64
Johns, Grover S.: reception in West Berlin, 35
Johnson, Lyndon B.: Berlin visit, 33–35, 39, 51, 225, 226

Keiderling, G., 229
Kennedy, John F.: Vienna meeting with Khrushchev, 7–8, 43–44, 54; speech on the "three essentials," 8, 28, 47, 193; reaction to Brandt's letter, 32–33; "Ich bin ein Berliner" speech, 39, 156; goals of Berlin policy, 46–49; and views of military, 53; "doctrine," 226
Khrushchev, Nikita: proposal for "free city," 6–7; Vienna meeting with Kennedy, 7–8, 43–44, 54; reasons for wanting wall, 43–46; reasons for inaction in early 1961, 54, 59–60 (*see also* Warsaw Pact); reaction to Dulles statements, 56–57; domestic difficulties, 60; relationship to Ulbricht, 69; 1958 ultimatum, 119
Kiesinger, Kurt Georg, 114, 121
Kissinger, Henry, 227; on *Ostpolitik*, 86; discussions with Soviets, 126
Klein, David, 53–54, 55, 56, 62, 66, 67, 89–90, 96, 97, 109, 110, 148, 226, 228
Kommandatura, 4, 5, 78; meeting on August 13, 12, 15
Kornblum, John, 66–67, 94–95, 112, 184, 186–87
Krafft, Herbert, 231
Kroll, Hans, 224, 225

Lightner, E. Allan, 23, 25, 32
London Protocol, 4

McDermott, Geoffrey, 15, 221, 222, 227
Mac Ginnis, Francis, 53, 64, 71, 94–95, 111
MacIver, Robert M., 231
Mackay, John Henry, 159, 229
Mahncke, Dieter, 55, 56, 71, 107, 112
Mallinckrodt, Anita Dasbach, 220
May, Antoinette, 222
Mensch, Gerhard, 228, 229
Merritt, Richard L., 68, 69–70, 71, 86, 105, 109–10, 140, 186, 187, 229, 230, 231, 233
Mittenzwei, Ingrid, 164, 229
Morgan, Roger, 56–57, 90, 147
Moscow treaty, 125
Murrow, Edward R., 23, 25, 32
Mushaben, Joyce, 97, 146
Mutual and Balanced Force Reductions, 125, 126

NATO: and security of West Berlin, 123; 1978 communiqué, 132
Neustadt, Richard, 53
Nixon: policy toward East, 86–87; candidacy supported by Adenauer, 222
Noelle-Neumann, Elisazeth, 232
Norstad, Lauris, 56

Osgood, Charles E., 48
Ostpolitik: and reality, 67; Kissinger on, 86; significance of, 87; and Hallstein Doctrine, 93; initial Western reaction to, 93, 123–24; philosophy behind, 115–16; wall as justification for, 152

Paris summit conference (1960), 7
Prussia: renewed interest in, 163–65
Puchala, Donald J., 230

Quadripartite Agreement, 83–85; contents, 76–77, 127–29; and access agreement, 77; equivalent of peace treaty, 89, 94; strength of, 91, 96–97; Article 4 of protocol attached to, 92; provision for violations, 95, 96, 131; as concrete result of détente, 102–3; difficulties of implementing, 130; effect on East-West interaction, 178–81. See also Berlin talks

Reagan, Ronald, 148
Reunification: as ultimate FRG goal, 38, 209, 210–12; effect of wall on, 99; increasing difficulty of implementing, 182–83
Reuter, Ernst, 17
Rostow, Walter W., 50
Rush, Kenneth, 126
Rusk, Dean, 12–13

Schick, Jack M., 220, 225
Schlicht, Uwe, 65–66
Schmidt, R., 231
Schroeder, Gerhard, 68
Schütz, Klaus, 61–62, 64–65, 67, 68–69, 71, 87, 91, 93–94, 96, 106–8, 185–86
Schwedhelm, Karl, 229

Schweigler, Gebhard, 230
Shell, Kurt L., 220, 223
Signals: importance of, 60
Slusser, Robert M., 219, 225
Sodaro, Michael, 59–60, 90, 146
Sorensen, Theodore S., 221
Soviet Union. See USSR
Springer, Axel Caesar, 224; reaction to wall in newspapers owned by, 22–23, 26, 30; opposition to Quadripartite Agreement, 76–77
Steinstücken: Clay's visit to, 51; in Quadripartite Agreement, 128
Stobbe, Dietrich, 109
Stone, Shepard, 53, 59, 63–64, 65, 69, 70, 71, 85, 93, 94, 95, 97, 111, 139, 141, 143, 146, 184, 187
Student unrest, 122, 155, 157–58, 196–200
Stulz, Percy, 229
Stützle, Walther, 221, 225
Sutterlin, James S., 228

Telephone: between East and West Berlin, 230
Television: role of in East-West contacts, 184
Third world: asylants from, 204–5, 232; interest in Berlin, 215
Tradition: lack of in Berlin, 160–62
Turks: in West Berlin, 129–30, 135, 138, 141–42, 202, 203. See also Guest workers

Ulbricht, Walter: "No one intends to build a wall," 9; wall not a victory for, 60; relationship to Khrushchev, 69; replaced by Honecker, 90
U.S.: attitude toward in West Berlin, 99, 107, 122–23; interest in Berlin, 206–7
USSR: wall as turning point in policy toward West, 57; interest in Berlin, 85, 88–89, 109, 120, 132–33, 207–8; economic cooperation with, 140

Wall: stabilizing effect of, 62, 65–67; possible alternative responses to, 64–

65; reasons for responses to, 65; timing, 70, 227; effects on East and West, 98–99, 121, 173–78
Walton, Richard J., 225
Warsaw Pact: refusal to seal boundaries (March 1961), 7; agreement to seal boundaries (August 1961), 9; interest in Berlin, 214
Warsaw treaty, 125
Watter, Wolfgang, 140–41, 142, 143, 145, 146–47
Weizsäcker, Richard von, 133, 134
Well, Günther van, 228
West Berlin: government, 4–5; links to FRG, 5, 78, 102–3, 106, 109–13, 114–15, 124–25, 128, 130, 138, 210, 231; popular demonstrations in 1948 and 1956, 17; public reaction on August 13, 18–19; concern over city's security, 38, 39; viability of, 38–39; morale, 39–40; destabilizing effect on GDR, 60–61; different East-West goals toward, 100–101; absence of long-term policy on, 104–5; function of, 106, 108, 109, 110–12, 120, 153–55, 192; Soviet policy toward, 109, 120, 132–33; external representation of, 112–13, 131; subsidy mentality, 122, 134, 146–47, 157, 161; passive role during talks, 127; political situation in 1981, 133–34; demographics, 136, 137, 138, 200–205; competition with other cities for industry, 139, 140, 146; need to look for high-tech industries, 142–43; trade with East, 146, 233; cultural center before wall, 151; opportunity for pan-European identity, 153; special mentality of citizens, 156–57; response to postwar division, 170–83

Youth: search for identity, 157–58, 184. *See also* Student unrest

Zolling, Hermann, 219, 220, 221, 222, 223, 224, 226, 227

About the Contributors

David Anderson was director of Central European Affairs, U.S. Department of State, and U.S. minister in Berlin (1978–81) before assuming his current post as ambassador to Yugoslavia.

Hans Otto Bräutigam is currently the permanent representative of the Federal Republic of Germany in the German Democratic Republic, with the rank of state secretary.

James A. Cooney, formerly assistant director of the Aspen Institute Berlin, now directs the John J. McCloy Program at the John F. Kennedy School of Government, Harvard University.

Jonathan Dean served as deputy U.S. negotiator for the Quadripartite Agreement on Berlin (1971), subsequently as deputy representative and then representative (with the rank of ambassador) to the NATO–Warsaw Pact force reduction (MBFR) negotiations in Vienna (1973–81), and is now arms control adviser to the Union of Concerned Scientists.

Karl W. Deutsch, Stanfield professor emeritus of international peace, Harvard University, and director of the International Institute for Comparative Social Research, Science Center Berlin, has written extensively on German and international politics.

Claus Duisberg holds the rank of legation councillor (1st class) in the Foreign Office of the Federal Republic of Germany.

Antonius Eitel is the ambassador of the Federal Republic of Germany to Lebanon.

Jürgen Engert directs the Division of Politics and Current Affairs and is deputy editor-in-chief for television, Sender Freies Berlin (SFB).

Ronald A. Francisco, associate professor of political science, University of Kansas, has coedited *Agricultural Policies in the USSR and Eastern Europe* (1980).

Renata Fritsch-Bournazel, professor at the Fondation Nationales des Sciences Politiques, Paris, has written *L'Union Soviétique et les Allemagnes* (1979) and coauthored *Les Allemands au coeur de l'Europe* (1983).

Johann Baptist Gradl, retired Federal Minister for Expellees, Refugees, and War Victims, published two West Berlin newspapers, *Der Tag* and *Der Kurier* (1948–

65), was a member of the national committee of the Christian Democratic Union (1953–71), and served as West Berlin's representative to the Bundestag (1957–80).

Helga Haftendorn is professor of international relations at the Free University of Berlin, whose latest book on West German foreign policy is *Sicherheit und Entspannung* (1983).

Martin J. Hillenbrand directed the U.S. Department of State's Office of German Affairs (1958–62), was Assistant Secretary of State for European Affairs (1969–72), served as ambassador to the Federal Republic of Germany (1972–76), and is now Dean Rusk professor of international relations, University of Georgia.

David Klein served as first secretary, U.S. Embassy in Bonn (1957–60), and as political adviser (1968–70) and U.S. Minister in Berlin (1970–74), before becoming director of the American Council in Germany.

John Kornblum, formerly director of Central European Affairs, U.S. Department of State, is now U.S. Minister in Berlin.

Francis Mac Ginnis, now retired from Her Majesty's Diplomatic Service, was Minister and Deputy Commandant of the British Military Government in Berlin (1977–83).

Dieter Mahncke is ministerial director in the President's Office, Federal Republic of Germany, and has authored inter alia *Berlin im geteilten Deutschland* (1973).

Anna J. Merritt, staff associate and editor, Institute of Government and Public Affairs, University of Illinois at Urbana-Champaign, has coauthored and coedited (with Richard L. Merritt) several books on German politics.

Richard L. Merritt is professor of political science and research professor in communications, University of Illinois at Urbana-Champaign.

Roger Morgan, head of the European Center for Political Studies, Policy Institute, London, has written several books on Germany, including *The United States and West Germany, 1945–1973* (1974), and is currently completing a book on West Berlin and the European Economic Community.

Joyce Marie Mushaben is assistant professor of political science, University of Missouri–St. Louis.

Uwe Schlicht, reporter with *Der Tagesspiegel* since 1962, focuses on research and higher education.

Klaus Schütz, currently general director of the Deutsche Welle, served as West Berlin's Senator for Federal Affairs (1961–66), state secretary in the Foreign Office of the Federal Republic of Germany (1966–67), governing mayor of West Berlin (1967–77), and the Federal Republic's ambassador to Israel (1977–81).

Michael Sodaro, associate professor of international affairs and political science, Institute for Sino-Soviet Studies, George Washington University, coedited *Foreign and Domestic Policy in Eastern Europe in the 1980s* (1983).

Shepard Stone, director of the Aspen Institute Berlin, served as political adviser to U.S. High Commissioner John J. McCloy, director of the Ford Foundation (1954–68), and president of the International Association for Cultural Freedom, Paris (1968–73).

Wolfgang Watter is senate director in the Office of the Senator for Economics and Labor, West Berlin.